Women in Baseball

Women in Baseball

THE FORGOTTEN HISTORY

Gai Ingham Berlage

PRAEGER

Westport, Connecticut
London

Library of Congress Cataloging-in-Publication Data

Berlage, Gai.
    Women in baseball : the forgotten history / Gai Ingham Berlage.
        p.   cm.
    Includes bibliographical references and index.
    ISBN 0–275–94735–1 (alk. paper)
    1. Women baseball players—United States.   2. Baseball—United
States—History.   I. Title.
    GV880.7.B47   1994
    796.357′0973—dc20   93–25049

British Library Cataloguing in Publication Data is available.

Copyright © 1994 by Greenwood Publishing Group, Inc.

Library of Congress Catalog Card Number: 93–25049
ISBN: 0–275–94735–1

First published in 1994

Praeger Publishers, 88 Post Road West, Westport, CT 06881
An imprint of Greenwood Publishing Group, Inc.

Printed in the United States of America

∞™

The paper used in this book complies with the
Permanent Paper Standard issued by the National
Information Standards Organization (Z39.48–1984).

10 9 8 7 6 5 4 3 2 1

To my daughter, Cari Coxe Berlage,
and my son, Jan Ingham Berlage,
two ex–Little Leaguers

Contents

Acknowledgments

I am extremely thankful to all the people who helped to make this book possible. Although only some of the names can be listed here, there were many others who assisted in many ways. Special thanks are given to William T. Spencer, Jr., Curator of the National Baseball Hall of Fame and Museum; Thomas R. Heitz and Bill Deane, National Baseball Hall of Fame Library; and Diane Barts, Northern Indiana Historical Society; library archivists: Maida Goodwin, Smith College; Patricia Albright, Mount Holyoke College; Jane S. Knowles, Radcliffe College; Carla Stewart, Wellesley College; Caroline Rittenhouse, Bryn Mawr College; Nancy MacKechnie, Vassar College; Diane Stalker, Barnard College; Karen Lamoree, Brown University; Eda Regan, Mills College; Anne Pearson, Oberlin College; Zephorene Steckney, Wheaton College; Elizabeth Foye, Skidmore College; and Lynn Beideck-Porn, University of Nebraska Lincoln; former baseball players Billie Taylor Rota, Margaret Gisolo, Julie Croteau, Ruby Heafner, Dottie Green, Joan Berger Knebl, Dolores Lee Dries, Ruth Richard, Dr. Lois Youngen, Jean Geissinger Harding, Maxine Kline Randall, Katie Horstman, Dr. Lois Youngen, Doris Sams, Jeneane Lesko, Gertie Dunn, Noella LeDuc Alverson, Lex McCutchan, Shirley Jameson, Madeline English, Bonnie Baker, Dottie Schroeder, Eunice Taylor, Helen Campbell, Thelma "Tiby" Eisen, Barbara Liebrich, Erma Bergman, Joanne, Betty and Jean Weaver, Beth Johnson, Anastasis Batikis, Ysara Castillo Kinney, Earlene "Beans" Risinger, Elizabeth Mahon, Pat Scott and Alma Pucci Korneski; and the family and friends of players: Dr. Douglas Noble, Ray Hisrich, Don Allan, Lulu Gourley, and Maxine Eberle.

I also want to especially thank my support group: Iona College for granting me a sabbatical; Adrienne Franco, interlibrary loan; everyone in secretarial services—Mary Bruno, Patti Besen, Terry Martin, Philomena

Cohen and especially Nancy Girardi; my colleague, William Egelman; my husband, Jan, and children, J. B. and Cari.

And of course special thanks goes to the people at Greenwood Publishing Group who made this book a reality: Dr. James Sabin, Executive Vice President; Margaret Maybury, Managing Editor; Andrew Schub, Production Editor; and Brennan McCarthy, Marketing.

Introduction

When you first glanced at the title of this book—*Women in Baseball: The Forgotten History*—you may have done a double-take. You may have asked yourself, "Were there women in baseball, or is this another book about fans or groupies?" Most people think of hardball as a man's game. Very few people are aware that women were playing baseball in the United States as early as 1866. In fact, to compare women's participation in baseball today with the 1890s and early 1900s is to experience *déjà vu*. At the turn of the century, there were women professional players, umpires, owners, and sportswriters. In light of women's historical participation, today's issues should be non-issues.

The press treats issues such as whether or not Pam Postema should have been a major league umpire as new occurrences, as products of the women's liberation movement of the 1960s. Yet Lizzie Arlington was a pitcher in 1898; Alta Weiss, a pitcher from 1907 to 1922; Lizzie Murphy, a first basewoman from 1918 to 1935; Amanda Clement, an umpire from 1905 to 1911; and Helene Britton, the owner of the St. Louis Cardinals from 1908 through 1917. In the late 1800s and early 1900s sportswriters such as Ella Black wrote for the *Sporting Life*, Ina Eloise Young wrote for the *Chronicle-News* of Trinidad, Colorado, and Sallie Van Pelt was the baseball editor of the Dubuque, Iowa, *Times*. Based on this, it seems hard to believe that questions of whether or not women should umpire or play in the major leagues or be baseball sportswriters and sportscasters are controversial ones.

It is not only professional baseball that is seen as a male domain. It took a court order in 1974 to permit young girls to play Little League baseball. The Supreme Court ruled that barring girls from participation in Little League was a form of sexual discrimination. Little League was forced to change its charter to allow girls to play. This legal victory was signaled by the press as a significant one for the feminist movement. Allowing girls to play on boys' teams was heralded as a first for girls. But this was not the first time that girls had been allowed to play in boys' baseball leagues. In 1928 Margaret Gisolo played American Legion Junior Baseball in Indiana. She played on the team that won the state championship and went on to the national tournament.

One has to wonder what happened to the early history of women in baseball? Why has their participation been forgotten and ignored?

One of the most heated controversies today involves what role, if any, women should have in professional baseball. The issue focuses not only on whether or not women should play major league baseball but also on whether or not they should even be allowed to occupy administrative positions. Yet in the early years of baseball women were in these roles. In fact, not until 1952 was there a rule barring women from being professional players.

Professional baseball today is a male bastion, with the philosophy that women need not apply unless they want to hold such traditional female jobs as secretary, usherette, or, more recently, ball girl. Women players are prohibited by the rules. And the rules probably won't change in the near future. Women owners, however, have been the exception to the rule, tolerated because of the power of wealth.

Although the possibility of a woman playing in the major leagues surfaces periodically, it is usually in a fictional story. When journalists ask managers, coaches, and players if they think a woman could play professional ball, they are usually greeted with a "no." Some who are more sensitive to the feminist issue and who wish to avoid controversy will state that although it's very unlikely, it might occur in the distant future. It appears that very few in the baseball world know the history of their game and therefore understand the irony of such a statement.

Women were playing baseball at Vassar College as early as 1866. This is only a few years after the first intercollegiate baseball game was played between Amherst and Williams College in 1859. At the Baseball Hall of Fame Museum at Cooperstown, one can buy a postcard of the Young Ladies Baseball Club Number 1 of 1890. The Cincinnati *Enquirer* in 1899 had numerous articles on the Chicago Bloomer Girls' professional baseball team that competed against men's teams throughout the Midwest. There were also Bloomer Girls' teams in Massachusetts, Texas, and other states that barnstormed from state to state playing men's teams. So based on the establishment of the first professional club, the Cincinnati Red Stockings, in 1869, women could rightfully be called pioneers of the game.

In the late 1800s and early 1900s, women played in their own leagues, in competition with men's and women's leagues, and even as women on men's teams. Yet who has read about women baseball players of the Victorian period? Even if one examines books on the history of baseball, rarely is any mention made of women. If any mention is made, it is usually about the first "Ladies' Days" at the ball parks. Women are perceived of as fans or "groupies," not as players. Even as fans, they are assumed to have more interest in the players than the game.

Recently the All American Girls' Professional Baseball League of 1943–1954 has received publicity. The Baseball Hall of Fame Museum in Cooperstown in the spring of 1989 added an exhibit on women in baseball. Some baseball books have added a paragraph or so on the All American Girls' Professional Baseball League. But most books omit this. Women are notably absent. With the Columbia Pictures release of the film *A League of Their Own*, a fictionalized version of the All American Girls' Professional Baseball League, the public has become aware of the fact that women played baseball during World War II. But most are still unaware of any playing prior to that.

In conducting research for this book and writing for information on women's baseball to the archive librarians and heads of physical education departments at some of the early women's colleges where baseball was played, I often received responses stating that as far as they knew, women did not play baseball at these colleges. A letter to the Chicago Historical Society resulted in the reply that it had no information on the Chicago Bloomer Girls' baseball team of the 1890s. It is as if women in baseball were such an anomaly that they ceased to exist and were lost from public view.

Perhaps this early history has largely been forgotten because of the long-lasting Victorian influence on American ideals of womanhood. The image of Victorian women playing baseball seems an aberration, an impossibility. History tells us that women of the Victorian period were frail, delicate ladies whom men placed on pedestals in order to protect them from the harsh realities of life. Certainly the frail constitution of upper-class women would never have permitted them to do strenuous exercise. Even if women could have worked thus, no fathers or husbands would have permitted their daughters or wives to be so unladylike as to play baseball. The image of the swooning damsel with her smelling salts stands in stark contrast to the reality of healthy, robust, active upper-class women playing baseball at the Eastern women's colleges or of women from the lower and middle classes playing on professional women's teams.

The history of women in baseball is very important because it parallels the rise and fall of the women's liberation movement throughout the history of the United States. Women's participation in baseball is a result of social, political, and economic factors. This book examines the history of women in baseball from a socio-cultural perspective. It analyzes the social forces that provided women opportunities to step outside of traditional roles and to participate in baseball.

Although women have participated in baseball in various capacities from the late 1800s to the present, two major periods dominate: the Victorian period and the World War II period. Both offered women unprecedented opportunities for participation. Both eras, however, were short-lived. Baseball to the present day has managed to maintain its image as a male sport and bastion of masculinity. Even with the changes in the Little League rules, few girls have participated in Little League baseball. The organization, as well as many parents, have encouraged girls to participate in Little League softball, however. Softball is seen as an acceptable female version of baseball.

Even at the college level, women's softball is, and has been seen as, an acceptable substitute for women. It was only in the spring of 1989 that a woman played National Collegiate Athletic Association (NCAA) baseball. No semi-professional or professional women's baseball teams currently exist. But semi-professional or professional women's softball teams have existed in fair numbers since the 1920s. Women's baseball teams have basically been non-existent, even though women were playing baseball before they were playing softball. To a large extent women have been socially conditioned to see participation in baseball as a male endeavor and have accepted that condition. This book examines the history of women's participation in baseball and tries to account for how baseball has managed to remain a masculine domain, given its history of female participation.

1

An Unlikely Convergence: Victorian Ladies and the National Sport of Baseball

The second half of the 1800s set the stage for an unlikely convergence. A small group of Victorian ladies left their parlor couches, their smelling salts, and their feminine frailty behind to participate in the new national pastime of baseball, both as spectators and as players.

Their participation was in complete antithesis to the role of the ideal woman. Envisioned as the weaker sex, women were seen as biologically frail and in need of protection. Like porcelain dolls, they were to be treated with special care and were expected to be pure and chaste. Having children was the primary function of married women, and all their energy needed to be conserved for their reproductive role. The "true" woman was expected to devote her life totally to her husband and to motherhood. Her domain was the home. Strenuous activity of any kind was to be avoided. Sports and outdoor activities were male preserves. Women's roles were separate and distinct from men's. By the mid-nineteenth century the Victorian women, according to Gerber, "by avoiding exercise and cultivating a pale face and an incapacity to do work, . . . gave the appearance of gentility."[1]

With this accepted gender-role ideology and concept of gentility, it seems incongruous that women actually played baseball during the Victorian era. The image of the frail, Victorian lady stands in sharp contrast to the healthy, robust sportswoman. But in some respects the incongruities between the Victorian ideals of womanhood and the sports reality are a mirror image of the personage of Queen Victoria, for whom the era was named. For Queen Victoria was anything but the "true woman"—the woman of the Victorian ideal. "Queen Victoria was strong willed and directly involved in the affairs of a powerful state. Yet women of the era—credited to

Victorian mores—were expected to be passive, gentle, soft spoken, delicate, and unobtrusive."[2]

It was the Victorian era, 1876 to 1900, that provided unprecedented opportunities for American women. American society was undergoing rapid social and economic change as the result of industrialization, urbanization, massive immigration, and the depression of 1873. Additional factors that were especially conducive to allowing women's participation in sports were the women's suffrage movement, the establishment of women's colleges, the invention of the safety bicycle, technological changes that provided women with more leisure time, and changing medical attitudes about health and fashion.

As William O'Neill states, "For the country as a whole the 1890's were years of crisis and uncertainty. . . . For organized women, however, the nineties was a time of growth and accomplishment."[3]

Between 1880 and 1900 women entered the labor market in all areas. It was not just the poor immigrant woman who worked, but educated women as well. "In 1890, 36 per cent of all professional workers were women, and in 1950 they made up 40 per cent of the total. The degree of sexual segregation in 1960 was about the same as in 1900."[4]

On the other hand, a number of factors supported and reinforced the Victorian ideal that the woman's role was in the home. Writers of the time emphasized the importance of this role, medical theories stressed that women were of the weaker sex and that their existence revolved around their reproductive organs, and ladies' fashions restricted movement. The style of wearing corsets with whalebone stays laced as tightly as possible to achieve an hourglass figure with the ideal eighteen-inch waist realigned internal organs, constricted breathing, limited mobility, and led to fainting spells. Dresses with tight bodices and voluminous skirts reaching to the floor made any physical movement strenuous. This lack of mobility coupled with physical problems associated with organ and spinal realignment reinforced the myth that women were physically weak.

Medical opinion also supported and reinforced the image of women as weak and in need of special care. Doctors believed that if women overexerted themselves, all sorts of calamities could befall them, from nervous exhaustion to defective offspring. An interesting challenge to these views was the fact that immigrant women worked long hours and continued to be robust. This contradiction would eventually lead many doctors to revise their opinions and promote limited exercise as necessary for good health.

Some doctors in the latter half of the 1800s were beginning to realize that many of women's health problems were due not to a weak physique but to tight corsets and lack of exercise. They began to advocate moderate exercise for women. Physical educators such as Dioclesian Lewis were designing gymnastics programs for women and were at the forefront of encouraging women to participate in walking, skating, and other forms of exercise. The founders of the first women's colleges endorsed these ideas and required all students to exercise. This emphasis on exercise helped to pave the way for women to participate in sports. These changes were taking place just as baseball was entering its Golden Era in the 1880s.

By the late 1800s, to be American was to love baseball. Baseball had come to typify all that was good about America. Many believed that baseball taught children (especially those of immigrants) traditional American values; that community pride also came from belonging to local baseball clubs.[5] Baseball was the great assimilator of the masses.

Baseball had captured the spirit of the nation and was the national sport. In 1889 Mark Twain proclaimed, "Baseball is the very symbol, the outward and visible expression of the drive and push and struggle of the raging, tearing, booming nineteenth century."[6]

Baseball began as a gentile, social event played by private men's clubs. "Tea was served, the ladies were invited, gentlemanly conduct on the part of the contestants prevailed."[7] Proper sportsmanship was more important than winning, and the ladies were there to encourage and support their men.

During the Civil War, soldiers were introduced to the game, and it became popular with the masses. A Christmas Day game in 1862 drew a crowd of 40,000 soldiers.[8] The democratization and popularization of baseball changed the game and made it professional. Some clubs charged admission, and star players were recruited and paid. Baseball was becoming a business. By 1870 there were at least five salaried teams and in 1871, the National Association of Professional Base Ball Players became the first professional league.[9]

Professional baseball players in the 1880s were seen as ruffians who lacked the Victorian social graces. Begun as an upper-class men's club sport, baseball had spread to the masses and become rougher and less gentile.

Based on statistics published in a *New York Times* editorial on August 30, 1881, baseball had also become a dangerous sport. "It is estimated by an able statistician that the annual number of accidents caused by baseball in the last ten years has been 37,518, of which 3 percent have been fatal; 25,611 fingers and 11,016 legs were broken during the decade in question, while 1,900 eyes were permanently put out and 1,648 ribs were fractured."[10]

Professional baseball had its opponents. There were those who opposed playing games on the Sabbath, those who worried about the drinking behavior of the crowds, and those who were concerned about the gambling influences. It was because of these negative aspects that men invited women to come to the ball games. The men believed that the presence of ladies at sporting events would act as a purifying element. In the presence of a lady, men would have to act like gentlemen and refrain from uncouth language and rowdiness. The *Ball Players Chronicle* declared that the presence of ladies "purifies the moral atmosphere of a base ball gathering, repressing . . . all outbursts of intemperate language which the excitement of a contest so frequently induces."[11] Ladies' Days modeled after those of the Knickerbockers, an upper-class gentleman's club, became fashionable. The Knickerbockers in 1867 had designated the last Thursday of the month as Ladies' Day and encouraged their members to invite their wives, daughters, and girlfriends to come watch the ball games.[12]

Professional baseball clubs in the 1880s encouraged women fans, or "krankets," as they were called, to come out to the ball park. The baseball magnates thought that their presence not only would improve crowd behavior but would be a big boost for attendance. At that time only about 10 percent of spectators were women. Husbands were often reluctant to bring their families to games because of the rowdy behavior of fans. According to Benjamin Rader, "Until the twentieth century professional baseball was unable to rid itself completely of its association with the Victorian underworld of entertainment."[13] The Athletics and the Orioles in 1883 were the first professional teams to officially designate Thursday as Ladies' Days. Other teams immediately followed. Some set aside special ladies' sections where only ladies and their escorts were allowed. Smoking was usually prohibited.[14] In the 1880s Chris von der Ahe, the president of the St. Louis Browns, added another amenity: ladies' toilets.[15]

Women fans were catered to because they were seen as pretty ornaments, virtuous defenders of the moral order, and worshippers of the stronger sex. A letter to the editor of the *Baseball Magazine* exemplifies this view. "Why shouldn't women be let into the games free of charge? . . . A woman adds interest to everything. Wouldn't there be a big turn-out, though, if a lot of pretty girls sat in the grandstand and waved their handkerchiefs when a good play was pulled off? . . . Admission of women would tend to eliminate foul language, and make the game cleaner in every way."[16]

By 1909 the presence of women at games had become so popular that the National League decided to discontinue Ladies' Day. It assumed that the ladies would come regardless of Ladies' Day and free admission. But the financial benefits of Ladies' Days were such that they were restored in 1917.[17]

By the 1900s the popular press wrote about a number of women celebrities who were baseball fans. Lulu Glaser, the comic opera prima donna, was a Pittsburgh Pirate fan. She was quoted as saying, "Anyone with any real blood in his or her . . . veins cannot help being a fan. . . . Being a true American and being a fan are synonymous."[18] Her statement echoed the national belief that Americanism and baseball were one.

Although her enthusiasm for baseball was restricted to the accepted role of female fan, she did state that "I just love baseball. . . . If I were a man I would surely try to get out and make good with one of the big league teams."[19]

Mabel Hite, actress and wife of Giants player Mike Donlin, declared, "There is nothing I delight in more than sitting in the grandstand. . . . I'd rather be a baseball player than a worker in any other profession under the sun."[20]

Stella Hammerstein, the actress daughter of Oscar Hammerstein, was also an avid Giants fan. Supposedly, she was often late for theater performances because she was at a game.[21]

Trixie Cadiz of the Ziegfield Follies also declared herself a New York baseball fan. But she said that her first loyalty was to her hometown team, the Philadelphia Athletics.[22]

In 1909 the wife of Frank Chance, the manager of the Chicago Cubs, urged women to come out to the ball park for two reasons: one, to put a damper on the men's rowdiness; and two, to improve their health. She was quoted as saying, "If more women would forsake their bridge, whist and pink tea, sofa cushions and kimonos, and turn out to watch the cleanest sport in the world, there would be more . . . robustness among our sex." She believed that women who rooted for the home team would increase their lung power and have to see the doctor less often.[23]

But certainly men were not advocating that women be players. Being a fan was a passive activity that didn't threaten the sexual order. Albert G. Spalding stressed the sentiment of many men when he said women should be encouraged to participate in baseball as spectators but not as players. Golf, tennis, and even basketball were sports that women might be able to play, but baseball was just too strenuous for them. As spectators they could use " 'smiles of derision for the Umpire' who gave an unfavorable call, or resort to 'perfectly decorous demonstrations when it became necessary to rattle the opposing pitcher.' "[24] In this way, they could aid the men in the game.

At least Spalding gave credit to the female fans as being knowledgeable about the game. Many were more concerned about the love-crazed women fans in the early 1900s. Unfortunately, it was this type of female "groupie" that the public has often come to associate with baseball rather than the serious student of the game.

By the late 1800s baseball was the rage. Both men and women were avid fans. It was the major form of entertainment. Every town had at least one ball field and a home team. Males of all ages played the game. Everyone was consumed with the sport. It was only a matter of time before women would want to try their hand at playing the game. But first they had to be freed from the mystique of ill health and the belief that exercise was too taxing for their constitution.

In order for that to happen, the image of the "true woman" had to be transformed to that of the "new woman." This transformation occurred for several reasons. First, there was concern that many immigrant women who worked in the factories were actually physically stronger and healthier than many upper-middle-class and upper-class women. Second, there was a growing realization among doctors that exercise was healthy and that tightly laced corsets were detrimental to women's health. Third, women's colleges were founded with the philosophy that exercise was a necessary component for a healthy mind and body. Fourth, upper-class country clubs were established in which women could participate in tennis and other sports. But it was the establishment of the first women's colleges during the second half of the nineteenth century that was the major impetus for changing beliefs about the appropriate roles for women, changes in fashion, the importance of exercise for health, the acceptance of sports for women, and the opportunities for women to play baseball. Vassar College had baseball eights in 1866 and nines in 1876. Smith College had teams in 1879, and Mount Holyoke College in 1891.

Once college women began playing sports and baseball, upper-class women soon followed. Country clubs and private athletic clubs became places for wealthy women to play tennis, cricket, and golf and to go riding and yachting. Elizabeth Barney in 1894 in the *Fortnightly Review* declared that all over the country men and women were establishing country clubs and sporting clubs. In the East, ladies' athletic clubs had sprung up. Some, such as the Berkeley Ladies' Athletic Club of New York, were connected with the men's club, but others such as the Staten Island Ladies' Club were independent ladies' clubs.[25]

The safety bicycle was invented in 1894, and by the 1890s bicycling had become a popular activity for many women. "Bloomers," which Amelia Bloomer had unsuccessfully tried to introduce in the 1850s, now became fashionable for bicyclists.[26]

Professional opportunities for women to play golf and tennis soon became available. In 1885 the first national golf championship for women was held, and in 1887 the first tennis championship.[27]

Exercise and sports also became a middle- and working-class activity as these women began to emulate the upper classes. Professional walking, called pedestrianism, became a competitive sport in 1876. Competition often stretched over a six-day period, and large crowds came out to cheer the women on. Two women, Ada Anderson and Lulu Loomer, became famous for walking 3,000 quarter miles in 3,000 quarter hours. These events became more and more commercialized, with prize money being offered. Promoters changed the image of these events to freak shows when they had the women wear "strategically placed 'embarrassing bows.' " Public outcries ensued about the sensuous nature of attire, and rules on proper dress were enforced as a result. Promoters lost interest and the events disappeared in the 1890s.[28]

A few opportunistic promoters capitalized on the novel idea of women's baseball teams. The earliest of these were the Dolly Vardens of Philadelphia in 1867. These black women players wore red calico dresses as uniforms.[29] The name no doubt came from the fashion term *Dolly Varden*, which referred to a heavily made-up, corseted woman. The Dolly Varden image was based on a character of that name in a Charles Dickens novel, *Barnaby Rudge*, published in 1841. The Dolly in that novel was a plump, buxom working-class flirt whom men found irresistible.[30] Needless to say, the games the Dolly Vardens played were more theatrical events than sporting events. In general, the public disapproved of the women players.

Although commercialism of women's sports was seen as a problem, sports for women in general by the 1890s were becoming acceptable in colleges, public and private schools, private clubs, and community programs. As Betty Spears stated, "After centuries of constraints there appeared to be a frenzy of sport activities among women."[31] A new sporting woman was replacing the frail indoor type.

Changes were also occurring in depictions of women in popular magazines. Charles Dana Gibson's pen-and-ink drawings of Penelope appeared in *Life* magazine in the 1890s. The athletic looking Gibson girl replaced the heavier, corseted Victorian hourglass figure. She was tall, slender, beautifully proportioned, and simply groomed with a patrician air. During the day she wore a skirt and shirtwaist, during the evening an elegant evening dress with little jewelry. She played croquet and golf. She came to symbolize the new, more athletic American woman. This image of womanhood became the standard for advertisers as well. Women all over the country began to emulate her mannerisms and fashion.[32]

As unlikely as it seems today, some women at the end of the Victorian period were playing baseball. These early pioneers dared to challenge the Victorian image of femininity. They were instrumental in dispelling the myth perpetuated by the "cult of the true woman" that women were too frail to exercise. It was the exclusive Eastern women's colleges, populated with the daughters of the wealthiest families, that gave women their first opportunity to play.

NOTES

1. Ellen Gerber, "Part I: Chronicle of Participation," in *The American Woman in Sport*, ed. Ellen Gerber, Jan Felshin, Pearl Berlin and Waneen Wyrick (Reading, Mass.: Addison-Wesley, 1974), 11.

2. Joan Paul, "Conflicts between the Victorian Pedestal and the Tomboy" (Paper delivered at Southern District, American Alliance for Health, Physical Education, Recreation, and Dance, National Association for Girls' Women's Sports, Orlando, Fla. 21 Feb. 1981), 3.

3. William O'Neill, *Everyone Was Brave: A History of Feminism in America* (New York: Quadrangle/New York Times Book Co., 1971), 146–147.

4. Ibid., 148.

5. Steven Riess, *Touching Base: Professional Baseball and American Culture in the Progressive Era* (Westport, Conn.: Greenwood Press, 1980), 7.

6. Dale Somers, *The Rise of Sports in New Orleans: 1850–1900* (Baton Rouge: Louisiana State University Press, 1972), 115.

7. Tristram Coffin, *The Old Ball Game: Baseball in Folklore and Fiction* (New York: Seaview Books, 1981), 87.

8. Jack Selzer, *Baseball in the Nineteenth Century: An Overview* (Cooperstown, N.Y.: Society for American Baseball Research, 1986), 6.

9. Ibid., 7.

10. Irving Leitner, *Baseball: Diamond in the Rough* (New York: Criterion Books, 1972), 128.

11. Quoted in Harold Seymour, *Baseball: The Early Years* (New York: Oxford University Press, 1960), 328.

12. Ibid.

13. Benjamin Rader, *American Sports: From the Age of Folk Games to the Age of Spectators* (Englewood Cliffs, N.J.: Prentice-Hall, 1983), 122.

14. Seymour, 329.

15. David Voigt, *America through Baseball* (Chicago: Nelson-Hall, 1976), 20.

16. Letter from W.C.C., Minot, North Dakota, *Baseball Magazine*, Aug. 1908, 42.

17. Riess, 28.

18. Lulu Glaser, "The Lady Fan," *Baseball Magazine*, Sept. 1909, 22.

19. Ibid., 20.

20. Mabel Hite, "On Just Being a Fan," *Baseball Magazine*, Nov. 1908, 24.

21. E.W. Dunn, "Stella, the Stellar Star," *Baseball Magazine*, Sept. 1908, 58.

22. Orel Geyer, "A Fair Fan," *Baseball Magazine*, Nov. 1908, 24.

23. Ira Smith and H. Allen Smith, *Low and Inside* (Garden City, N.Y.: Doubleday and Co., 1949), 109–110.

24. Donald Mrozek, *Sport and the American Mentality, 1880–1910* (Knoxville: University of Tennessee Press, 1983), 144.

25. Elizabeth Barney, "American Sportswoman," *Fortnightly Review* 62 (Aug. 1894): 264.

26. Richard Swenson, "From Glide to Stride: Significant Events in a Century of American Women's Sport," in *Women's Athletics: Coping with Controversy*, ed. Barbara J. Hoepner (Oakland, Calif. DGWS Pub., 1974), 44–45.

27. Betty Spears, "Chapter 1 Prologue: The Myth," in *Women and Sport: From Myth to Reality*, ed. Carole Oglesby (Philadelphia: Lea and Febiger, 1978), 10.

28. Roberta Powell, "Women and Sport in Victorian America" (Ph.D. diss., University of Utah, 1981), 71–72.

29. Court Michelson, *Michelson's Book of World Baseball Records* (Chicago: Adams Press, 1985), 84.

30. Lois Banner, *American Beauty* (New York: Alfred A. Knopf, 1983), 119–120.

31. Spears, 10.

32. Evelyn Swenson, *Victorian Americana* (Matteson, Ill.: Great Lakes Living Press, 1976), 57.

2

Baseball at the Early Women's Colleges

The elite Eastern women's colleges sometimes referred to as the "Seven Sisters"—Smith, Wellesley, Mount Holyoke, Vassar, Radcliffe, Bryn Mawr, and Barnard—had a tremendous impact on societal perceptions of women's roles and sports. The "new woman," the educated, independent, athletic type who was a product of these schools, represented a radical departure from the "true woman," the weak, passive, frail, dependent woman of the Victorian ideal.

The early women's colleges were patterned after the men's. The founders, pioneers in their time, believed that women should receive an education equal to that of men, but in separate institutions so as to meet women's special needs and to preserve women's femininity. They also believed that in order to have a healthy mind, it was necessary to have a healthy body. Exercise in the form of calisthenics or physical education was required of all students. Very progressive for their time, these views had many opponents.

Some opponents believed that a college education would destroy women's femininity. Other authorities, basing their opinions on the prevailing knowledge about women's physiology, stated that trying to educate women like men was pure folly. Medical evidence showed that "45% of women suffered from menstrual cramps, and another 20% suffered from assorted ills. Thus for physiological reasons, 65% of the women would require the college program to be adjusted for them. Also it was reported that overstudy would give the girls brain fever. They would be weak and unable to have children."[1] The educated, athletic, robust, healthy, competitive woman of the liberal arts college was the antithesis of the Victorian ideal.

Parents who sent their daughters to these schools had to be progressive in their thinking and willing to put their trust in the educators. Their acceptance of the physical education philosophy meant that by the 1890s sports for women, and especially baseball, had become part of college life. But these sporting activities were viewed as social events rather than as strenuous competitive sports that men played.

Mount Holyoke College, the earliest of the women's colleges, began as a seminary in 1837 and became a four-year college in 1861. The other "Seven Sisters" developed shortly thereafter—Vassar in 1865, Smith and Wellesley in 1875, and Bryn Mawr in 1885. Radcliffe and Barnard both originated as parts of men's colleges. Radcliffe began as an annex to Harvard in 1878, in 1894 becoming a separate college. Barnard started as an annex to Columbia in 1889 and in 1900 became a separate institution.[2]

Although all the colleges were established to create educational opportunities for females that were equal to those for males, the motivations of the individuals who founded them were very different. For example, Mary Lyon, the mother of Mount Holyoke College, was a deeply religious woman who felt a need to develop a seminary that would educate women for God's calling. It was her religious calling, not a desire for modernizing women's roles, that led her to seek an endowment to establish Mount Holyoke Seminary (later, Mount Holyoke College).[3]

Having worked on her brother's farm, Mary Lyon believed in fresh air and exercise as necessary for health. Therefore she required all students to exercise by walking, doing calisthenics, and engaging in domestic work. In her *Book of Duties* she wrote, "The young ladies are required to walk one mile per day till the snow renders it desirable to specify time instead of distance, then three quarters of an hour."[4]

Matthew Vassar, a wealthy brewer who founded Vassar College in 1861, had a very different motive. Vassar had no heirs and wanted to leave his money to a worthy cause that would bear his name. Founding a women's college met this need. Vassar felt that Victorian women suffered from a lack of exercise. He spoke of the feminine image of the period as one in which "feminine beauty . . . too often blooms but palely for a languid or a suffering life, if not for an early tomb."[5] To protect women against failing health, he proposed that the college have a gymnasium with the latest apparatus so that the girls could develop healthy bodies.

The college program included light gymnastics patterned after those of Dr. Dio Lewis. Swimming, skating, gardening, and other feminine sports and games were to provide for good health as well as appeal to students.[6] The catalog stated that every student was required to wear a light and easy fitting dress for exercise, which was optional at other times. This suggested that this form of dress was appropriate for everyday wear.[7]

Henry Fowle Durant, founder of Wellesley College in 1875, was a crusader for women's rights. He stipulated that the faculty of the college as well as the president should be female.[8] He believed that college education was the means for women to become more equal to men. He also stressed the necessity of physical exercise so that women would be healthy and could develop to their fullest.

So it is clear that from the beginning, women at most of these schools were encouraged to complement their studies with exercise, especially with outdoor activities such as boating and ice skating. The physical and social aspects were encouraged, but not the competitive side, which was considered a male component. Many activities that might have been considered masculine, such as ice hockey and baseball, were accepted for health reasons and because it was believed that team sports developed character, camaraderie, and discipline.

Coincidentally, the founding of the first women's colleges occurred about the same time as the origin of professional baseball. From 1869 with the establishment of the first professional baseball team, to 1890 there was rapid growth in professional baseball, so that by 1890 there were seventeen white and two black professional leagues.[9]

By the 1880s baseball was in its Golden Era and was the national sport. The "baseball fever" that affected the nation also caught the fancy and imagination of college women. They too wanted to play the game. Their athletic role models were their brothers who were playing baseball at Yale, Williams, and Amherst. To these girls baseball was an exciting social and physical activity that got them out into the fresh air. It also offered a great deal more in terms of fun and competition than the physical exercise programs that were in vogue at the women's colleges they attended.

Although physical educators and college instructors were in general agreement that strenuous exercise was not appropriate for women, they allowed these girls to play baseball for two reasons: First, they were happy to see that the women wanted to exercise, since gymnastics classes were not always that well received; and second, they saw the activity as primarily a social one. Baseball started as informal games between dorms or houses on campus. Anyone who wanted to participate could.

In order to be allowed on women's campuses, even informal pick-up games had to be seen as feminine. The upper-class model of the private men's clubs and exclusive men's colleges was adopted, not the professional model.

A letter by Ruth Lusk, Class of 1900 at Smith College, explains the female version. She writes, "Someone remarked to President Seelye if he didn't think 'it was unladylike for us to be playing baseball just like men.' President Seelye asked the man if he had ever seen us play. The man said 'No.' Then President Seelye said, 'You wouldn't say they played like men.' "[10]

The uniforms of the girls left little doubt that this was a female version of the sport. The girls wore long dresses with high necks and long sleeves. Although the uniform was a definite hinderance to running or sliding into bases, it did offer some unique advantages for trapping or stopping the ball. One such strategy was to catch or stop low balls with one's skirt. (Incidentally, the "cap catch" was not outlawed in the men's game until 1873.) Although the uniforms were uniquely female, the rest of the equipment was standard. They used a regulation hardball, baseball gloves, and a face mask for the catcher.

On the whole the women's colleges with independent and largely separate identities such as Vassar, Smith, Mount Holyoke, and Wellesley were to provide greater opportunities for women to participate in baseball than schools such as Barnard and Radcliffe, which were annexes to men's colleges. This was primarily because the behavior of the girls was less likely to come under male or public scrutiny. With their separate campuses secluded from the view of outsiders, the colleges offered a unique environment for women to develop largely in a world of their own.

Vassar had the earliest baseball teams with baseball eights in 1866 and baseball nines in 1876. Smith had teams in 1879, four years after it opened; Mount Holyoke, in 1891; and Wellesley, in 1897. The other three were much later in fielding teams—Barnard, 1910; Radcliffe, 1915–1916; and Bryn Mawr by 1925.[11]

When baseball began at Vassar College, the teams were composed of eight rather than nine players. The June 1866 *Vassariana* lists the Laurel Base Club and the Abenakis Base Ball Club.[12] Early yearbooks and the student newspaper make no other reference to the baseball clubs until 1876, when the October 1876 *Vassar Miscellany* mentions that the baseball clubs have been consolidated and reorganized.[13]

A picture in the Vassar archives indicates that the first Vassar nine, the Resolutes, was formed in 1876. (See photo 3.) They wore caps and long-sleeved, full floor-length dresses with a band around their waists carrying the team name.

Sophia Foster Richardson, in recalling the so-called spontaneous introduction of baseball clubs in 1876 at Vassar, said that she believed that the catalyst for their formation was the Vassar female physician, Dr. Webster, who was "wise beyond her generation."[14]

She explained:

> The public, so far as it knew of our playing, was shocked, but in our retired grounds and protected observation . . . , we continued to play in spite of a censorious public. One day a student, while running between bases, fell, with an injured leg. We attended her to the infirmary, with the foreboding that this accident would end our play of baseball. Not so. Dr. Webster said that the public would doubtless condemn the game as too violent, but that if the student had hurt herself while dancing the public would not condemn dancing to extinction.[15]

During the spring of 1877, baseball matches were played every Saturday afternoon. Somewhat later, matches between faculty and students were played on Founder's Day.

Not a portrait

Not a portrait

E. Tyler shows us how easy it is to make a three-base hit.

P. King, reaching home-plate by a slide which no one else has ever been able to imitate.

1. Some fielding techniques, drawn by Gertrude May Cooper, Smith College Class of 1906. *Courtesy of Smith College Archives, Smith College.*

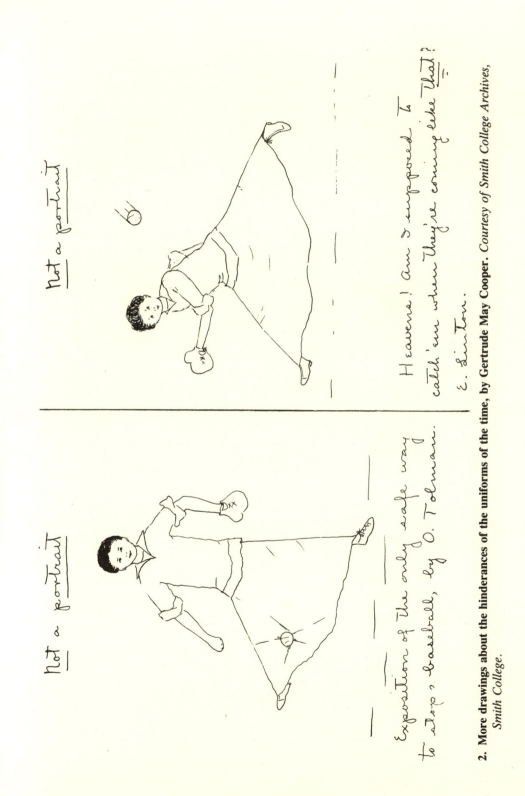

not a portrait

Exposition of the only safe way to stop a baseball, by O. Tolman.

not a portrait

Heavens! Am I supposed to catch 'em when they're coming like that?
E. Linton.

2. More drawings about the hinderances of the uniforms of the time, by Gertrude May Cooper. *Courtesy of Smith College Archives, Smith College.*

3. The Resolutes, Vassar College's first baseball "Nine," circa 1876. *Courtesy of Special Collections, Vassar College Libraries.*

The *Daily Eagle*, November 11, 1895, reported on the first women's field day in the country, which was held at Vassar. The event was closed to outsiders. The various classes competed against each other in track and field events. The contestants wore gym suits, while most of the spectators wore bicycle skirts.[16] One of the events was the baseball throw, for which records were kept over the years.

An article in the Vassar archives from the early 1900s titled "The Vassar Girl in Athletics" brags about the superior accomplishments of the girls.[17] And the *New York Herald*, Sunday, June 18, 1911, magazine section, had a feature article on Miss Dorothy Smith of New York, who broke two records on field day at Vassar and received her athletic letter. The headline read, "Vassar's Champion Athletic Girl." The reporter was especially impressed by her establishment of a new baseball throw record of 204 feet 5 inches.[18]

But the reporter was not as impressed by Vassar's baseball teams. He wrote, "Vassar, like several of the other girls colleges, has its own baseball teams. The girls belonging to the college nines play regularly and practice hard. Yet it must be admitted that few are good at the game."[19] Miss Smith explained to this reporter that the reason for their limited skills was that they lacked competition. Interscholastic sports were not allowed, and so the girls could play only among themselves.

Vassar was not unique in its refusal to allow intercollegiate sports. The other "Seven Sisters" had similar policies.[20] In general, sports activities were acceptable as long as they were not too strenuous or too competitive. The faculty and parents didn't take the girls' sports activities seriously. Baseball was seen as a relaxed, low-key activity that got the girls out in the fresh air.

In 1879 Smith College also had intramural baseball teams. Eventually, there were interclass matches, interhouse matches, and even an annual faculty-student game.

A letter from Minnie Stephens, Class of 1883, to her classmates indicates how important baseball was in establishing sports at Smith.

> Perhaps you have never really heard how Smith College happened to get the athletic field. . . . Way back in Seventy Nine, I was more or less active and full of fun. It seemed to me that we ought to have some lively games in the way of wholesome exercise, so I got a few friends together and we organized a base ball club. We had no place to play except on the lawn in front of the Hubbard House.[21]

A March 10, 1892, Boston *Herald* headline proclaims, "Smith Girls Play Ball." The freshmen beat the sophomores by a score of 29–9, but some interference led to some of the scoring against the sophomores. "In the first inning the sophs got in two runs, owing chiefly to the fact that the

centre field caught in her dress skirt." There were also a few mishaps to
dresses in the second inning, in which the game was delayed and some pins
were applied.[22]

There are other letters in the Smith archives written to parents or for
the school archives which describe playing inter-house baseball. Two are
especially informative. One is from Ruth Lusk, Class of 1900.

> The spring of 1898 and 1899—Dickinson House had a baseball team called
> White Squadron. Other houses had teams too, and we played inter-house
> games. The ball our team used for practice was a regular hard ball and had
> been used in an Amherst-Williams game where Amherst was the Victor—
> 4–0 I believe.[23]

The second is a letter of April 20, 1908, from Margaret Townsend, Class
of 1911, addressed to her parents urging them to send her a baseball glove.
"Please ask Morgan [older brother] if he has a baseball mitt he can send
me. We are practicing all the time now, and trying curves, and playing
with a real baseball."[24]

In November 1916 the three upper classes held a "Smith World Series."[25]
By 1930 Smith College was touted as having the best outdoor athletic
facilities, which included a baseball field.[26] In the 1930s there is also mention
of a custom of a "traditional" father-daughter baseball game during com-
mencement week under the auspices of the Athletic Association.[27]

Baseball became an organized sport rather than a club sport at Smith
in 1916, and it is listed as a major sport in the 1917 *Student Handbook*. It
is difficult to tell when baseball ceased to be played on the campus. The
1946–1947 *Student Handbook* lists softball rather than baseball. But equipment orders suggest that around 1940, softball equipment was being ordered. This would suggest that baseball was played for a considerable
period at Smith and yet no one in later years seemed to be aware of it.[28]

The *Mount Holyoke*, of June 1891 states that the first official baseball
club has been established.

> Our first base ball club, organized during the spring term, has flavored the
> average conversation with "strikes," "innings," "home runs," etc. The dia-
> mond is in the quadrangle, and with the slope above fitted out for spectators,
> the Greeks would have thought it an ideal theater. Already the members
> have gone through most of the experiences naturally connected with the
> game, though disabling the umpire is a pleasure in store for the future. The
> organization was completed so late that they will not play in the inter-col-
> legiate league this year, but doubtless next season, they will compete on
> equal terms with nine other colleges.[29]

In future years no record could be found of intercollegiate play or even
the existence of such a league. Again information is contradictory because

although this is the first official record of baseball at Mount Holyoke, pictures in the archives show women playing baseball in the mid–1880s.

Like Mount Holyoke, Wellesley College also formed a baseball club. It was established in 1897 as a social sport for "pleasure players."[30] It is interesting that the women at these colleges considered it very important to stress the sport as a social activity and to downplay the competitiveness. This probably enabled them to play the sport without the onus of being engaged in a male activity. It also encouraged women to come out for the sport regardless of their skill level.

Baseball continued as a club sport at Wellesley until 1911, when baseball became part of the physical education program. Instruction and physical education credit were given for baseball from 1911 to 1935.[31] After 1935, baseball was dropped.

Newspaper articles in a Boston paper state that the first baseball season at Wellesley was in 1914, but this is probably the first season that the program received publicity. One article is titled "Girl Players in Pitching Duel: Wellesley College Juniors Beat Seniors in Indoor Baseball Game." Miss Hoyt, the junior class pitcher, receives praise for her overall playing ability. "Miss Hoyt proved to be a star, for in addition to pitching what was—for girls—'airtight ball,' she knocked out a three-base hit and fielded her position like a major league veteran."[32]

The article goes on to mention that six of the girls received "W's," letters for their playing. This suggests that baseball was well received by the athletic department and the administration of the school.

The annual field day festivities also included a baseball game. A newspaper article announces the upcoming field day to be held November 2, 1914. The writer states, "Each afternoon on the college athletic field skirted prototypes of Tris Speaker, Ty Cobb and Joe Wood are striving to master the fine points of the game."[33]

Barnard and Radcliffe have a much later history of baseball. Baseball was officially added to Barnard's list of approved sports by the athletic department in 1910, when class teams were formed. Even though baseball was well established on the campuses of Vassar, Smith, Mount Holyoke, and Wellesley, the Barnard decision received caustic criticism from *The Reach Official American League Guide for 1911*, which stated in no uncertain terms, "We hold, and we know, that base ball is not a game for any woman, not even the most masculine of the sex."[34]

The Cincinnati *Enquirer*, March 23, 1910, provided a much more objective view: "The Barnard girls will play on a diamond of regulation size with bags, mitts, bats and other accouterments from a regulation sporting goods house. They will play genuine baseball with all its complications." There were some modifications; no stealing was allowed, and the ball was slightly heavier and had to be pitched underhand, which was common in men's baseball through the 1870s.[35]

Although the press made a big issue of Barnard women playing baseball, it was not an important issue on campus. No mention of baseball is included in the 1910 through 1912 course announcements for physical education. The only mention of baseball was in the *Barnard Bulletin* of Wednesday, April 5, 1911. The article states: "Baseball began with a rush last Monday. . . . The girls settled down to work immediately with a great deal of enthusiasm."[36] That Saturday a game was played between a freshman team and an upper-class team.

The following spring is the next time the *Bulletin* makes a reference to baseball. The Barnard women's team challenged Teacher's College to a game. But Barnard was unprepared for her opponent and lost 3–10 in the five-inning game. Although announced as part of the physical education program in 1910, baseball at Barnard remained very low key and never developed a large following. Apparently if a group of girls was enthusiastic about putting together a team, the administration approved. The physical education department did not make baseball a major sport.

Byrn Mawr in Pennsylvania is the only one of the "Seven Sisters" that didn't have established baseball teams in the late 1800s or early 1900s. Baseball was probably played in 1925. According to Caroline Rittenhouse, the college archivist, "In the short handwritten history of athletics at Bryn Mawr, baseball is mentioned only once as an alternative spring sport. Nothing other than that appears in the catalogs or yearbooks."[37] There is always the possibility that baseball was played informally.

Some early women's colleges that were not part of the Seven Sisters also had baseball teams. Wells College in Aurora, New York, had teams in the 1870s; Mills College in Oakland, California, had teams in 1872; Wheaton College in Norton, Massachusetts, had teams in 1900; Pembroke College, the women's college of Brown University in Providence, Rhode Island, had teams in 1905; Agnes Scott Institute in Decatur, Georgia, had teams in 1905, one year before the school became a degree-granting college; Skidmore College in Saratoga Springs, New York, had teams in 1916; Hollins College in Hollins College, Virginia, had teams in 1917; Goucher College in Baltimore, Maryland, had teams around 1920; Rockford College in Rockford, Illinois, had teams around 1923; and Randolph-Macon Women's College in Lynchburg, Virginia, had teams in the 1920s.[38]

Ironically, although baseball was thought of as a man's game, it was not an issue on most women's campuses because it was primarily student-organized and remained to a large extent outside the physical education program. Even when baseball was included within the physical education program, the emphasis was more on the social and health aspects of participation than on competition. Games were usually played between classes or between faculty and students for the sheer fun of the game rather than as hard-nosed competition. Any girl who wanted to participate could. In most instances games were a private, intramural affair played on the women's campus and the public was not invited.

It was basketball, rather than baseball, that became the catalyst for

eliminating women's competitive sports on campuses. Basketball, introduced in 1892 at Smith College, quickly became a popular and highly
competitive game played by women on campuses throughout the country.
Pressure from the students to make it an intercollegiate sport brought
opposition from the physical education teachers. Products of the Victorian
culture, the female teachers worried about women's sports becoming similar to men's sports. Lucille Eaton Hill, director of physical training at
Wellesley College, summarized their concerns when she stated: "Fiercely
competitive athletics have their dangers for men, but they develop manly
strength. For women the dangers are greater, and the qualities they tend
to develop are not womanly."[39]

In 1923 the Women's Division of the National Amateur Athletic Federation was formed. It drew up a platform of resolutions for governing
female athletics. Basically, it called for programs of physical education that
would stress universal participation rather than the participation of a select
few. It felt that women's sports were becoming too elitist and believed that
individual records and the winning of championships should be discouraged
and that the emphasis should be on physical fitness.

According to Dudley and Kellor, some of the reasons cited by physical
educators for making women's sports less competitive were these:

- Girls take things so seriously and the members of the defeated team cannot
  concentrate on studies for several days, especially where prizes are offered.

- Their behavior is generally demoralizing to the school; they try every means
  to meet in the library, halls and lavatory and talk games, of course.

- We have hundreds who would like to use the gymnasium but are unable
  to do so after school because the members of the team monopolize it.[40]

The platform the educators proposed was adopted at the Conference on
Athletics and Physical Recreation for Women and Girls, April 6–7, 1923.
Most women's sports organizations accepted the platform.[41] Its acceptance
basically meant the elimination of intercollegiate athletics for women and
of highly competitive sports. Play days in which girls could participate in
many events became the norm. As part of track and field events there was
often a baseball throw competition and interclass team competition. But
the emphasis was on universal participation rather than on elite athletes
who played on intercollegiate teams. The idea of making baseball an intercollegiate sport disappeared forever. A few women's colleges managed
to play a few games with other colleges, although the majority of their
games were informal ones played among girls on their own campuses.

Wheaton College and Pembroke College (the latter earlier known as
the Women's College of Brown University) both had an early tradition of
playing either high school or college teams in their area. And interestingly
enough, when other women's colleges succumbed to the 1923 physical

education decree that women should not play intercollegiate sports, these schools ignored it. The intercollegiate game that received the most publicity was the one between Pembroke and Wheaton played on May 11, 1928. The *Providence Journal* headline read, "Pembroke Pounders and Wallopers from Wheaton to Clash in Baseball." It was reported that the Pembroke team had been secretly practicing for three weeks for the big game. Their secret weapon was their pitcher, Ethel Martus, who "throws a ball with a powerful right hand, has a flock of snappy little curves, which her teammates believe will out the reputed heavy hitting Wheaton Wallopers."[42]

Newspapers from three states covered the game and it was reported that motion pictures were taken. At the end of seven innings Pembroke defeated Wheaton 21–8. The two teams cheered for each other and then went to Miller Hall for ice cream.[43]

The Women's College (Pembroke) was next scheduled to play Jackson College, and Miss Frances Dennett, director of physical education, announced that "the diamond game will be a permanent part of the Women's College athletic program."[44] But the Brown University archives contain no mention of intercollegiate games in later years.

According to Káren Lamoree, archivist of the Farnham Archives, the women's history archive at Brown University, baseball reached its greatest popularity in the 1920s and peaked in 1928.

The 1890s and early 1900s had been years of dramatic change that provided new opportunities for women. College education for women gained acceptance, the number of women who entered the professions increased dramatically, women entered sports and were active in baseball, and women fought for the right to vote. But in 1920 when the battle for suffrage was finally won, complacency set in.

Between 1890 and 1910, a Vassar professor recalled, women students "proudly . . . marched in militant processions and joyfully, . . . accepted arrest and imprisonment for the sake of 'Votes for Women,' free speech and to help a strike. By the 1920's, however, going to college had become an act of conformity rather than deviance, and the atmosphere of special purpose began to evaporate."[45]

The women's colleges dropped the sciences, and "marriage" became the number one goal. Women's opportunities again declined, and there was a return to the status quo. Women's intercollegiate sports were basically banned, with the emphasis now placed almost entirely on physical education and play days. And although some colleges continued to have interclass baseball games even into the 1930s, women's baseball had seen its day.

In the 1920s the sporting-girl role disappeared from college campuses, but it found new acceptance in the society at large. Companies, organizations, and local communities began to provide opportunities for women to participate in team sports. As competitive sports for women were dying on college campuses, highly competitive professional and amateur sports were becoming the norm in the society at large. In fact, the period from 1917 to 1936 has been referred to as the "First Female Athletic Era."[46] It is during this period that sports became commercialized and some athletes became exploited. In the process some women found opportunities to play semi-professional and professional baseball.

NOTES

1. Betty Spears, "The Emergence of Women in Sport," in *Women's Athletics: Coping with Controversy*, ed. Barbara J. Hoepner (Oakland, Calif.: DGWS Pub., 1974), 27.

2. Helen Horowitz, *Alma Mater: Design and Experience in the Women's Colleges from Their Nineteenth-Century Beginnings to the 1930s* (Boston: Beacon Press, 1984), 19.

3. Ibid.

4. Persis McCurdy, "The History of Physical Training at Mount Holyoke College," *American Physical Education* 14 (March 1909): 145.

5. Spears, 27.

6. Harriet Ballintine, *History of Physical Training at Vassar*. Paper in Vassar Archives.

7. Ibid.

8. Joanna Davenport, "The Eastern Legacy—The Early History of Physical Education for Women," in *Her Story in Sport: A Historical Anthology of Women in Sports*, ed. Reet Howell (West Point, N.Y.: Leisure Press, 1982), 360.

9. Ted Vincent, *Mudville's Revenge: The Rise and Fall of American Sport* (New York: Seaview Books, 1981), 157.

10. Ruth Lusk, Class of 1900, letter to Rachael M. Studley, Class of 1901, Smith College Archives.

11. *Vassariana*, Vol. 1, No. 1 (June 1866): 4; Sophia Foster Richardson, "Tendencies in Athletics for Women in College and Universities," Reprinted from Appleton's *Popular Science Monthly* (Feb. 1897): 1; Maida Goodwin, Smith College Archives Specialist, letter to author, 16 June 1988; *Mount Holyoke*, Vol. 1, No. 1 (June 1891): 9; Victoria Summers, "The Historical Development of the Undergraduate Program in Health and Physical Education at Wellesley College." A Special Project Submitted for Hygiene 323, Graduate Seminar in Hygiene and Physical Education, Wellesley College (June 1939) 75; *Barnard Bulletin* (April 5, 1911): 2; Jane Knowles, Radcliffe College Archivist, letter to author, 17 June 1988; Caroline Rittenhouse, Bryn Mawr College Archivist, letter to author, 14 July, 1988.

12. *Vassariana*, Vol. 1, No. 1 (June 1866): 4.

13. *Vassar Miscellany* (Oct. 1876).

14. S.F. Richardson, "Tendencies in Athletics for Women in College and Universities," *Popular Science* (Feb. 1897): 517.

15. Ibid., 518.

16. "First Woman's Field Day: Open Air Athletics at Vassar," *Daily Eagle*, 11 Nov. 1895.

17. "The Vassar Girl in Athletics," circa early 1900s, Vassar Archives.

18. "Vassar's Champion Athletic Girl," *New York Herald*, 18 June 1911, Sun. magazine sec.

19. Ibid.

20. Karen Kenney, "The Realm of Sports and the Athletic Woman: 1850–1900," in *Her Story in Sport: A Historical Anthology of Women in Sports*, ed. Reet Howell (West Point, N.Y.: Leisure Press, 1982), 111.

21. Minnie Stephens, Class of 1883, letter to her classmates, Smith College Archives.

22. "Smith Girls Play Ball," Boston *Herald*, 10 March 1892.

23. Ruth Lusk letter to Rachael M. Studley.

24. Margaret Townsend, Class of 1911, letter to her parents, 20 April 1908, Smith College Archives.

25. Mary Carson, "A History of Physical Education at Smith College" (M.A. thesis, Smith College, 1951), 55.

26. Emmett Rice, John Hutchinson, and Mable Lee, *A Brief History of Physical Education*, 5th ed. (New York: Ronald Press, 1969), 300.

27. Carson, 111.

28. Smith College *Student Handbook* for 1917 and 1946–1947; Maida Goodwin, Smith College Archives Specialist, letter to author.

29. *Mount Holyoke*, Vol. 1, No. 1 (June 1891).

30. Victoria Summers, "The Historical Development of the Undergraduate Program in Health and Physical Education at Wellesley College" (Thesis, Wellesley College, 1939), 88.

31. Ibid., 75.

32. "Girl Players in Pitching Duel: Wellesley College Juniors Beat Seniors in Indoor Baseball Game," Boston newspaper, 1914, Wellesley College Archives.

33. Article in Boston newspaper, 1914, Wellesley College Archives.

34. "Base Ball Not for Women," in *The Reach Official American League Guide for 1911*, ed. Francis Richter (Philadelphia: A.J. Reach Co., 1911), 169.

35. "Base Stealing: Will Not Be Allowed in Barnard College Girls' Games," Cincinnati *Enquirer*, 23 March 1910.

36. "Baseball," *Barnard Bulletin* (5 April 1911): 2.

37. Caroline Rittenhouse, Byrn Mawr College Archivist, letter to author.

38. Temple R. Hollcroft, "A Brief History of Wells College" (Written for the seventy-fifth anniversary of Wells College and read at the observance of this anniversary, 15 Oct. 1943), 7; "A Glance Backward," *The Chimes*, 1914–1915, unnumbered page; "A Baseball Game at Wheaton," *Rushlight*, Vol. 47, No. 11 (June 1902): 103; Editorials, *The Sepaid*, Pembroke Women's College magazine, Vol. 6, No. 1 (Dec. 1905): 36; Deborah Gaudier, Agnes Scott College Archivist, letter to author, 26 March 1992; Elizabeth Foye, Skidmore College Archivist, letter to author, 11 Aug. 1988; Anthony Thompson, Hollins College Archivist, letter to author, 21 July 1988; A.H. Knipp, *History of Goucher College* (Baltimore, 1938), 477; Joan B. Surrey, Rockford College Public Services Librarian, letter to author, 26 Oct. 1989; Harold Seymour, *Baseball: The People's Game* (New York: Oxford University Press, 1990), 516.

39. Ellen Gerber, "Part 1: Chronicle of Participation," in *The American Woman in Sport*, ed. Ellen Gerber, Jan Felshin, Pearl Berlin, and Waneen Wyriek (Reading, Mass.: Addison-Wesley, 1974), 69.

40. Gertrude Dudley and Francis Kellor, *Athletic Games in the Education of Women* (New York: Henry Holt & Co., 1909), 151.

41. Alice Sefton, *The Women's Division National Amateur Athletic Federation: Sixteen Years of Progress in Athletics for Girls and Women, 1923–1939* (Stanford, Calif.: Stanford University Press, 1941), 77–79.

42. "Pembroke Pounders and Wallopers from Wheaton to Clash in Baseball," *Providence Journal*, 11 May 1928.

43. "Women's College Defeats Wheaton, 21 to 8, in First Baseball Contest," *Providence Sunday Journal*, 13 May 1928.

44. "Pembroke Pounders."

45. William Chafe, *The American Woman: Her Changing Social Economic and Political Roles, 1920–1970* (New York: Oxford University Press, 1972), 92.

46. Mary Boutilier and Lucinda San Giovanni, *The Sporting Woman* (Champaign, N.Y.: Human Kinetics, 1983), 33.

3

Women's Own Semi-Professional and Professional Baseball Teams in the Late 1800s and Early 1900s

In the late 1800s women's sport participation became more acceptable for the masses because of upper-class women's involvement in sports both at the Eastern women's colleges and at country clubs. Students at Eastern women's colleges had proven the harbingers of doom and ill health wrong. Not only did they do academic work similar to that done by men at men's colleges but they also participated in regular physical exercise and played sports. Rather than becoming debilitated, they flourished on the mental and physical stimulation.

The society pages showed upper-class women yachting and playing croquet, tennis, and golf. There were pictures of men and women socializing together at their country clubs. The strict sex-role segregation that middle-class and working-class women experienced was absent. Middle-class and working-class women began to emulate the upper classes and to copy their leisure patterns. The severe social sanctions against women engaging in sports began to disappear, and young girls had new freedom to play in the open air. In 1894 Elizabeth Barney wrote, "The girl who went fishing, climbed trees, and jumped fences was no longer inevitably looked upon as a tomboy or regarded with severe disapproval."[1]

Acceptance was not universal, however, for there were still writers and others who believed that sports and college were not appropriate for ladies. Articles in ladies' magazines debated the pros and cons. In 1912 the *Ladies Home Journal* ran a four-part series on the effects of college on women. The author, Edith Rickert, surveyed hundreds of female college graduates

from the years 1849 to 1909 to determine what effect a college education
had on them. The first article examined the question "How did college
affect your health?" The responses of the alumnae were overwhelmingly
positive toward both a college education and college athletics or exercise.[2]

Testimonials were given as to the benefits of athletics to health. However,
the author of the article warned parents that college was not for every girl.
Parents should make sure that their daughter was mentally and physically
fit before sending her off to college. Even for fit girls there was the danger
of losing one's femininity. She especially warned parents about permitting
their daughters to participate in sports or track and field contests. "In the
keenness of competition. The girls not only vie with one another, but they
also have even the idea of coming as nearly as possible to the standards
set by men. It is one more futile effort to ignore differences of sex."[3]
Rickert preyed on the fear of many Victorian parents that exercise might
make their daughters less feminine and hurt their marriage prospects.

Fortunately, the women who attended and later graduated from these
colleges ignored her warnings. Many of them became teachers in public
and private schools and involved their students in physical exercise. For
example, 82.5 percent of graduates of Mount Holyoke from 1838 to 1850
taught school. Although most taught only until they married, which was
usually less than five years from the time they graduated, 26 percent taught
for ten years or more.[4] So the influence of the "Seven Sisters" physical
education philosophy was pervasive.

Athletics, and especially baseball, became part of many school and community programs. The popularity of baseball crossed sex, class, and color
lines. Socially prominent upper-class women formed private baseball clubs
and women from middle- and lower-class backgrounds played on their own
semi-professional and professional teams.

An article in the *Baseball Magazine* in 1908 gave the public a glimpse
of Philadelphian socialites playing baseball. The author of the article asked
the readers, "Perhaps you think that the game of baseball is a strictly
masculine thing. Or perhaps, your knowledge goes a bit further, and in-
cludes a collection of 'pie-faced' females, in spotted uniforms who travel
through the bush country as 'professional' ball-players."[5]

Then the writer disclosed the startling fact that Clement A. Griscom, a
shipping magnate, had a baseball diamond at his summer home, Dolobran,
so that the daughters of his friends could play baseball. His wife, according
to the author, "entertained royalty and royalty has entertained her, but
baseball has claimed her for its American own." She even organized baseball parties at her home, which have become quite the rage. Hundreds of
guests hustled "to their seats with all the eagerness of kids who have killed
off a grandmother to attend the game."[6] The ladies were enthusiastic
rooters at these events, yelling out baseball jargon to the dismay of some
of the more proper ladies and gentleman.

Baseball was seen as an acceptable pastime for the daughters of the upper class, even though professional baseball players were thought of as lower-class ruffians. This is because proper manners were stressed and tea was served at the games; these were social events. With pride and admiration, upper-class mothers and fathers watched their daughters play. As was true with the women's colleges, the girls played out of public view, and therefore without fear of public sanction.

Proper dress and decorum were very important components of these games. One baseball club in Pensacola, Florida, in 1867 had a rule that if a player got entangled in her hoop skirt and fell, she was immediately expelled from the club.[7]

Promoters as early as the 1860s realized the financial potential from the novelty of having ladies' teams play mens'. The first teams were organized purely as publicity stunts. The sensationalism of having pretty, feminine, young ladies of good reputation playing against powerful, muscular men was considered enough of an attraction to draw crowds regardless of the women's skills. Although the games were billed as sporting contests between the sexes, promoters recruited girls on the basis of attractiveness rather than skills. The emphasis was on entertainment. The motivation to make a profit by putting on a good show was not that different from the owners of men's barnstorming teams. Promoters of men's teams also promised to put on a good show and often the financial backing for men's road teams came from theater owners and managers. Some of the players in the off-season even worked as actors or circus performers. The line between sport and entertainment was blurred. The most widely circulated baseball journal, the *New York Clipper*, began as a sporting and theatrical review.[8]

The bottom line was that women's baseball teams were organized for financial reasons and not for the love of sport. The opportunity for women to play professional baseball was not the result of equality, but rather the result of a few opportunistic businessmen who saw a way to make a quick dollar.

A letter dated December 28, 1903, in the archives of the Baseball Hall of Fame at Cooperstown indicates the importance of financial considerations. Mr. Kunkel, the manager of a Texas Bloomer Girls' team, wrote to Mr. Herrman, a promoter, about arranging games for the team. He stated, "We ask you if you want to make some money, this is one of the best ways to make it, you get the games for us, we would like to play every day ball, you can make about three hundred dollars clear money yourself every [week] if you get the games and I know you can get the games."[9]

Mr. Kunkel described the team as being composed of seven girls and four boys, one of which had only one arm. Although he stressed the novelty of having girls and a one-armed player, he also carefully listed the teams they had defeated. He realized that novelty alone would not make the team successful.

Promoters and owners realized the importance of having feminine looking players. Publicity stressed that the players were proper young ladies
and the fact that their uniforms were dresses reinforced this image. Owners
knew the public would not come out to the ball park to see women who
were considered of ill repute or actresses. An 1883 *New York Times* article
carefully explained how the management had selected the players for the
two opposing women's teams, the Blondes and the Brunettes. The players
had been chosen from a pool of 900 applicants in which variety actresses
and ballet dancers had been "positively barred."[10] The managers' truth-
fulness about the recruitment process is somewhat questionable based on
an ad that ran in the *New York Clipper*, September 22, the day of the
game. The ad said, "Wanted two young ladies with experience, or those
who can play fife or drum preferred."[11]

Much later an advertisement probably for the Blondes and the Brunettes
appeared in the *Sporting and Club House Directory of 1889*. The ad read,
"Young Ladies Base Ball Club and Revival of the Ancient Grecian-Roman
Open-Air Pastimes for Women. Wanted at all times young and handsome
girls who can play ball. Liberal salary and all expenses paid to the right
people." Unfortunately, the directory also claimed among its list of clubs
the 900 most respectable brothels in Chicago.[12]

Although owners of women's baseball clubs stressed the respectability
of the clubs and the girls, the image of the female ball player was not
particularly savory. At best they were considered in the same category as
actresses. Promoters, however, were able to attract young women by promising good wages and travel. Parents and husbands of girls who were recruited often were not happy about it.

Harry H. Freedman, an 1880s promoter, was accused of recruiting
women for a profession considerably older than that of baseball—prosti-
tution. While Freedman's team of "buxom beauties" was playing in New
Orleans, the police received a number of complaints from parents accusing
Freedman of enticing their daughters to leave home to join his baseball
team. Freedman was eventually arrested on the charge of being a "dangerous and suspicious character."[13]

But it was not just parents who voiced concern about these traveling
teams. Ministers, righteous Victorian ladies, and others complained about
the sinful nature of these girls and the impropriety of their bloomer outfits.
In Freeport, Long Island, in 1905 when it was rumored that a traveling
Bloomer Girls' baseball team was coming to town, the women in the
community became incensed. Supposedly they threatened their husbands
with divorce if they dared attend the game. Needless to say, the game was
cancelled. The town elders congratulated the women for preserving the
moral good and attacking the wickedness of the big city.[14]

The earliest record of a women's professional ball team is 1867, when
a black women's team, the Dolly Vardens, was formed in Philadelphia.

Their uniforms were red calico dresses, and they played with a mush ball of yarn.[15] In 1883 there is another record of two black ladies' teams competing against each other.

The date of the earliest white ladies' baseball team is difficult to establish. The National Baseball Hall of Fame library has an illustration of a female baseball club at Peterboro, New York, playing a game on July 3, 1869, before a large crowd. The caption under the picture reads, "The Last Illustration of Women's Rights." The women are wearing bloomer-style uniforms with baseball caps. On their feet are fashionably high leather shoes laced above the ankle with a small heel and a pointed toe. It is assumed that this is an amateur game, but it could have been semi-professional.[16]

The first of the women's professional barnstorming teams to gain widespread publicity were the Blondes and the Brunettes in 1875. These were the brainstorm of Frank Myers, S.B. Brock, and Thomas Halligan. One team consisted of nine blondes and the other, nine brunettes. The teams were established for purely financial reasons. An article in the *New York Clipper*, September 18, 1875, stated, "[The owners] under the impression that there is money in it, propose to give exhibitions in the principal cities."[17]

The first game was played on September 11, 1875, in Springfield, Illinois, and was promoted as "the first game of baseball ever played in public for gate money between feminine ball-tossers." The girls were reported to be of "reputable character" and to have "shown some degree of aptitude in ball-playing." The game was adapted to the females. The distance between the bases was 50 feet instead of 90 feet, the bats were slightly smaller than those used by men, the ball was lighter, and the game consisted of six innings. The Blondes beat the Brunettes 42–33 in a high scoring game with much action and many errors. The teams were fairly evenly matched because in the next game in Decatur, Illinois, the Brunettes won 41–21. The newspaper reporter conceded that the troupe contained some pretty fair players but stated "the attraction is the novelty of seeing eighteen girls prettily attired in gymnastic dress" playing baseball.[18]

In 1879 a women's team with uniforms similar to those of the Blondes and Brunettes played at the New Orleans Fair Ground. One wonders if the promoters were Myers, Brock, and Halligan. The *New Orleans Picayune* reported that "their handling of the ball . . . is characteristic of the feminine sex—a side and hip throw."[19] They may not have played well, but they were paid well. Each girl received $10 for the game.[20]

The next wave of publicity, in 1883, was for two teams also called the Blondes and Brunettes. These teams, however, were based out of Philadelphia rather than Springfield. The publicity emphasized the theatrical and compared their games to classical Greek and Roman outdoor gymnastic exercises. Their costumes were Greek-like dresses. Exhibition games were played in Philadelphia and in New York. The game in Philadelphia was played on August 18 in Pastime Park before a crowd of 500. The *Philadelphia Inquirer* did not consider the game particularly newsworthy and devoted only six lines to it, listing the name of the teams, the crowd size, and the score.[21]

The *New York Times*, however, considered the game a major event and a long article appeared on August 19. Although the article described the game as "a ridiculous exhibition," it did help to bring out the curiosity seekers for the game scheduled in New York City on September 1. According to the sportswriter the girls' throwing skills were so unpredictable that even the players watching could not contain their laughter. The regulation diamond was too large for the girls. Most of the girls were unable to throw the ball the distance from the pitcher to second, let alone from first to third. If the ball was thrown directly to them, they managed to catch it; but if it came fast and hard, "their courage failed, and they got out of the way without delay." Although the girls' skills on the diamond were limited, the reporter admitted that they had had only ten days' practice and that their playing would look better on the half-sized diamond in New York.[22]

Needless to say, with all the publicity that the Philadelphia game received, the New York crowd was even larger than the Philadelphia one. Fifteen hundred people came out for the game at the Manhattan Athletic Club. The two teams played a five-inning game, with the Brunettes defeating the Blondes 54–22. The reporter for the *New York Times* was again extremely caustic. He called the game "a base-ball burlesque" and said that the crowd laughed themselves hungry and thirsty. As to the girls' playing, he said, "They played base-ball in a very sad and sorrowful sort of way, as if the vagaries of the ball had been too great for their struggling intellects. At the bat most of them preferred to strike at the ball after it passed them. Then it generally passed the catcher. . . . The girls displayed an alarming fondness for making home runs on three strikes." Their inept playing excited the audience. He continued, "It was original and excited rapturous applause. Often when the fielders could not stop the ball in any other way they sat down on it. This was at once effective and picturesque, and never missed gaining a great howl of applause." He was equally damning as to the male umpire's skills and actually complimented the girls on knowing the rules of the game.[23]

As well as crediting the women with knowing the rules, he somewhat reluctantly admitted that the two pitchers and the two catchers for the teams were skilled players. He said, "Four of the girls had become expert—for girls. These were Misses Evans, P. Darlington, Moore, and Williams comprising the batteries."[24]

The teams continued to play exhibitions in major cities throughout the United States well into December. In St. Louis and Pittsburgh in November, the teams played five men's teams from the Delaware and Allegheny Clubs instead of playing each other. In St. Louis the game score was so disastrously lopsided that when the girls played in Pittsburgh, the men had to play with a handicap. The men had to bat one-handed, could have only five men in the field, and had to make all stops, catches, and throws left-handed.[25]

News of the girls' woeful skills traveled as far away as England. An English reporter for the *Pall Mall Gazette* of London remarked with disdain that American ladies pay too much attention to attracting the male eye and not enough to being sporting women. He said, "In England such an accusation would be repelled with scorn; but in America they evidently make no secret of it."[26]

American women were unlike their British counterparts in clinging to the Victorian ideal of femininity. Sports historian John Betts has remarked that by the end of the 1800s, English girls enjoyed being referred to as "open-air types" while American women still clung to the Victorian ideal of "pallid cheeks, narrow waists, and frail wrists."[27]

Not all women players had the abysmal skills of the Blondes and Brunettes and a team called the "buxom beauties." Some women had skills comparable to men's. In Huntsboro, Alabama, a club called the Mrs. Jane Duffy Club beat a local men's club by a score of 20–11.[28] A Philadelphia girls' team on December 24, 1884, defeated a men's club, the Mutual Baseball Club of Jackson, Mississippi, by a score of 13–11.[29] In 1883 a twelve-year-old girl in Pottsville, Pennsylvania, was credited with being able to pitch as well as the average male amateur pitcher.[30]

The 1880s goes down in history as a period of bizarre baseball. The public craved baseball in any form, and promoters were quick to capitalize on the public's enthusiasm by staging all kinds of unusual baseball exhibitions. In New York City in 1884 a game was played on ice in Central Park.[31] In Baltimore on July 13, 1883, two games between Our Boys and the Newington Clubs were played in the water. The team at bat stood on shore and hit to the opposing team, which fielded in the water. "The first base and the right fielder stood knee deep in water, the batter and pitcher were up to their waists, while only the head and shoulders could be seen of the left fielder. The bases were life-preservers anchored in the water."[32]

By the 1890s the public had grown tired of novelty exhibitions. Having pretty female players was not enough to attract the crowds. The public wanted to see serious baseball games with close scores. In women's baseball the emphasis shifted from women's teams playing each other to women's teams playing against men's teams. The public now insisted on seeing a real battle between the sexes on the field. Although the women still played in feminine attire—skirts and bloomers—it was important that they were seen as skilled players.

Being able to play baseball with some degree of expertise was important and many promoters emphasized how their female players were equal to men. One Tennessee promoter became so carried away with the idea of equality that he claimed the girls on his Bloomer Girls' team "were equally talented at playing baseball and chewing tobacco."[33]

The 1890s heralded a new age in women's baseball, with teams springing up across the country. On September 20, 1890, *The National Police Gazette* announced that W.S. Franklin had organized a barnstorming team of "bright and buxom ladies." They wore striped dresses belted at the waist, polka dot scarves around their necks, dark stockings, and ankle-high laced leather shoes. On their heads were matching striped baseball caps. They were so skilled that they annihilated the men's teams everywhere they went on their cross-country tour. In fact, Franklin claimed that the team had proven so successful that he was trying to organize other young lady baseballists.[34]

Franklin's Young Ladies Baseball Club Number 1 played against a number of men's teams throughout 1890–1891. They even played an exhibition game against the New York Giants.[35] Franklin was a clever promoter who somehow managed to have a highly competitive team. This was the case even though his ads for female players stressed appearance rather than skills.

The fact that his team was so competitive against men's teams makes one wonder if he had a few male ringers on the team dressed as women. Debra Shattuck believes that he did. From the picture of the team (see photo 4), it is difficult to tell. Shattuck has pointed out, however, that some or all of these women could be men dressed in women's clothing. The players who are most suspect are those whose last names could also be a male's first name, such as Effie Earl, May Howard, and Nellie Grant.[36]

For all Franklin's claims of the team's popularity, the Young Ladies Baseball Club was not always well received. Ministers preached sermons against the impropriety of girls playing, and the press was often very critical.[37]

In 1891 an enterprising team from Chicago, the Chicago Ladies, barnstormed throughout Nova Scotia. The team was competitive enough to beat men's teams in Amherst, Annapolis, and Middletown,[38] but their playing drew mixed reactions. In Truro and New Glasgow, there was stiff resistance to their playing. The Truro *Daily News* reported that a group had tried to get the mayor to ban the team from playing in Truro. In New Glasgow, a minister at a local prayer meeting verbally attacked the team. Despite the controversy, the games were played. The local press also criticized the team, saying the games were shams because the women had no skills. After this rather unpleasant start, the team was greeted by a crowd of 3,000 in Halifax. In Moncton they were so well received that it was reported in the local paper that town officials were going to invite them back the next year.[39] Colin Howell, a Canadian sports historian, credits

4. **Young Ladies Baseball Club Number 1 of 1890–1891.** *Courtesy of National Baseball Library, Cooperstown, N.Y.*

the Chicago Ladies with generating so much interest in women's baseball that teams were organized in the Maritime provinces.

About this same time teams called Bloomer Girls began to appear throughout the United States. According to Furman Bisher, a sportswriter, they got their name from Adelaide Jenks Bloomer, a pioneer suffragette, and not from the baggie pants called bloomers.[40] The name Bloomer Girls was a generic one in that teams of this name were in Boston, Texas, Chicago, New York, and other cities. These teams barnstormed from town to town playing any men's amateur or semi-professional team that would book them. This was now serious baseball. Many a promoter used a little creative dishonesty to make sure their teams were competitive. They hired one or two male ringers whom they passed off as females. The men often played catcher, pitcher, or shortstop. In the trade they were known as toppers because they usually wore a curly wig. Young men barely of shaving age were the preferred recruits.

The manager of the New England Bloomer Girls was heard to brag that he had a player, Clarence Wortham, who made "as handsome a girl as any boy on the team." Since the team played many of its games at night under gaslights, it may have been fairly easy to keep the fact that there were men on the team a secret.[41] It is interesting that promoters apparently had little trouble finding males who were willing to play. This seems amazing, especially in the early years when the women's uniforms were dresses. With the rigid gender role segregation, one would think that there would have been a great deal of stigma attached to playing as a woman. Apparently financial incentives were enough to convince many young men not to worry about public scorn.

In later years, some of these toppers, or ringers, even used the Bloomer Girls' teams as stepping stones to the professionals. For example, "Smokey Joe" Wood and Rogers Hornsby were two very successful major leaguers who got their start playing women's baseball.[42]

Joe had only good things to say about the quality of the women's playing. He mentioned how impressed he was with the skills of some of the players. "There was one girl, Ruth Egan, who was real good. . . . She played first base with a catcher's mitt, but she could really catch the ball.[43]

Joe Wood went on to become a major league pitcher. In 1912 he became one of a few pitchers to win thirty games in a single season and to win three games in a World Series. If there had been a stigma attached to playing women's baseball, Joe Wood established that it was a legitimate role for men. In fact Rogers Hornsby, who later played for a Bloomer Girls' team, stated that he was merely following in Joe Woods's footsteps.[44]

Not everyone took this view. An article in the *Nashville Banner*, September 9, 1910, stated that Mr. Mingua was desperately trying to locate his son, Earl, fourteen, who was believed to be playing second base on a

Bloomer Girls' team in Kentucky. The headline read, "When Father Locates Earl the Bloomer Girls Will Need Another Player."[45]

Although there were opportunities for the men to jump from women's baseball to major league ball, it wasn't the case for the women. Even women who received excellent news coverage, such as Maud Nelson of Chicago Bloomer Girls fame, were never asked to major league tryouts. The idea of women being able to play major league ball was never taken seriously.

In 1892 and 1893 the Boston Bloomer Girls and the New York Champions played baseball around the country.[46] The Chicago Bloomer Girls played games throughout the Midwest starting in 1899. Sports articles on the Chicago Bloomers appeared fairly regularly from 1899 until 1911 in the Cincinnati *Enquirer*. Reader interest in women's baseball must have been sufficiently high to warrant the paper to follow the team.

Clippings from the period 1899 to 1900 in the Cincinnati *Enquirer* indicate that the Chicago Bloomer Girls' team played local men's teams throughout the Midwest. Based on newspaper accounts in the Cincinnati *Enquirer*, attendance ranged from 1,200 to 3,000 people.

Although the women lost most of their games, the scores were usually very respectable, and in most instances the reporter's dispatches from around the country commented on the excellent skills of the women. Toward the end of the summer of 1900 the pitching skills of Maud Nelson attracted attention, and some men found to their chagrin that they couldn't get a hit off her. The team began to get a few wins and the game scores became closer. Maud Nelson had a fairly long career. After playing for the Chicago Bloomers from 1899 to 1902, she became a pitching ace with the Star Bloomer Girls Base Ball Club of Indianapolis, Indiana. (See photo 5.)

The *Boston Herald* on August 23, 1903, carried the headline "Woman Plays Great Ball: Miss Neilson, Although Her Team Lost, Struck Out Seven Men in Five Innings and Hit Hard." "One thousand people attended the game in Lewiston, Maine in which Miss Neilson pitched for the Star Bloomers—a team composed of six women and three men—against the Athletics."

Although her name is misspelled, there is no doubt that Maud Nelson was the star of the game even though her team lost 9–8. She is the only player mentioned in the article by the reporter. "The feature of the game was the pitching, batting, and fielding of Miss Neilson. She made three base hits, and had four put outs and four assists and made no errors. In the five innings she pitched she struck out seven men."[47]

But not everyone was enthusiastic about men's teams playing women's. The University of Tennessee forbid its students from playing with the Chicago Bloomer Girls' team. When five students were reported to have

5. Star Bloomer Girls Base Ball Club. *Courtesy of National Baseball Library, Cooperstown, N.Y.*

participated in a game on June 13, 1900, they were immediately expelled. Two of the alleged players were seniors who were scheduled to graduate the following week.[48]

On October 7, 1905, the Chicago Bloomer Girls played the Cincinnati Stars and lost by a score of 5–18. The manager, Schmelz, was undaunted by the loss. He announced that this was the last game for two years for the Bloomers in the United States, as they were going on world tour. They were scheduled to play in Australia, Cuba, and perhaps even England. The press also failed to dwell on the loss, although it was noted that they lost because of weak batting. The press raved about their fielding. " "Manager Schmelz certainly has a jewel in Miss Day at first base. She is without doubt the greatest lady ball player in the business, and deserves all the nice things that have been said by the press throughout the country about her. Darling at short and McKenzie in the outfield could give some of the stars of the Central League cards and spades and beat them out. They also know how to hit the ball." Judging by the articles in the Cincinnati papers, the women were considered serious players and not just novelties.[49]

Articles in the Cincinnati *Enquirer* indicate that various Bloomer Girls teams were playing in Cincinnati in 1911. A July 29, 1911, article announced that the original Bloomer Girls, "the club that this year has been the talk of the Eastern part of the United States," was to play the Union Printers. A sellout crowd of 2,000 was expected. The press did not underestimate the skills of the girls.[50]

One season the Boston Bloomer Girls bragged that in twenty-eight consecutive road games against men's teams they had never been defeated.[51] This was quite a record and indicated that women's baseball teams had come a long way.

But not all women's baseball teams were professional; there were also amateur clubs. These clubs were formed by women just for the enjoyment of playing. Usually the women's families were very supportive. For example, the August 19, 1904, edition of the Cincinnati *Enquirer* reported that the married ladies of Flat Rock, Indiana, challenged the single ladies of Shelbyville to a game in 1904. Both teams were composed only of women. They were the wives and daughters of the local merchants. The ladies' names were listed with their husbands' occupations. For example, "The battery for the married women consisted of Mrs. Willetta Ensley, wife of William Ensley, merchant of Flat Rock, as pitcher and Mrs. Ella Nading, wife of Walter Nading, the banker, as catcher."[52] The reporter had nothing but praise for the women's skills as did the husbands, boyfriends, friends, and neighbors who made up the crowd.[53]

The Hickey and Clover clubs played against each other at Forest Hills in 1903. Each team was composed of five women and four men. Miss Rose Duffy, the manager of the Hickey Club, advertised that she would like to hear from other mixed teams of women and men to arrange games. The

Hickey Club, according to the *Boston Herald*, August 31, 1903, had two
excellent players. "Miss Conry has no equal as a pitcher among any of the
girl players around Boston, and there are few men who can twirl a faster
ball or furnish a better assortment of curves."[54]

In 1918 a New York Bloomer Girls team wore uniforms similar to men's.
By this time it was expected that some of the players on the team would
be men and no attempt was made to disguise them. (See photo 6.)

By the end of the 1920s most of the women's teams had disappeared
and the number of amateur and semi-professional men's teams had declined. The country had changed. Transportation had improved. There
were more forms of competing entertainment. Radio broadcasts of professional baseball games drew fans away from their local teams. Babe Ruth
became a national hero and replaced the hometown heroes of an earlier
period. At the turn of the century every small town had had at least one
baseball team and a city as small as 30,000 often had as many as six teams,
many of them sponsored by merchants and local clubs.[55] As opportunities
for young men to play ball declined, it was only natural that women's
barnstorming teams would prove less profitable. Ladies' ball clubs had
reached the peak of their popularity in the late 1880s and early 1900s.

A few highly competitive Bloomer Girls teams, however, managed to
survive and persisted into the 1920s and 1930s. The women on these teams
were highly skilled, and the press took their playing seriously. An article
in *Literary Digest*, July 28, 1923, proclaimed that the Kansas City Bloomer
Girls had defeated one of the best men's semi-pro teams in New Jersey.[56]
A New York Bloomer Girls team, managed by a woman, Margaret Nabel,
continued to play until 1935. The team of mostly females often had a few
key men in the positions of catcher, pitcher, and shortstop. In 1932 they
billed themselves as the undefeated female champs and claimed that in
more than twenty years they had never been beaten by another female
club. The women were recruited from the five boroughs. According to
Billie Taylor Rota, a star on the team, it was not difficult to recruit good
players because young girls like herself had grown up playing baseball.
According to her, girls back then did not play softball, they played baseball.
So there were many young women with excellent skills.[57]

The New York Bloomer Girls drew large crowds wherever they went.
They were considered serious contenders and good entertainment. Admission to the games was a quarter. To survive financially the women's as
well as the men's semi-professional teams had to have a certain spontaneity
and unpredictability. In a game with the men's Level Club in Plainfield,
New Jersey, on May 23, 1932, the coach of the men's team, John O'Keffe,
pulled a surprise maneuver. He put the team's midget mascot, Nittoli, in
the game as a pinch hitter. Nittoli managed to get a single, and when he
stole to second the crowd went wild. The men eventually won the game
11–9, but the highlight of the game had been Nittoli.[58]

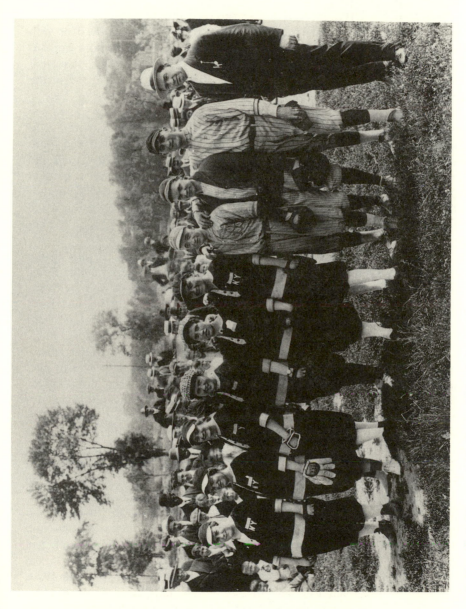

6. New York Bloomer Girls Team. Male pitcher on the team (tallest, in uniform) David Koske, the rest are unknown. *Courtesy of National Baseball Library, Cooperstown, N.Y.*

The team traveled to the games in their own cars, and the girls were usually paid about $5 a game. As Billie (Taylor) Rota said, it was the Depression and the money seemed pretty good because she made $20 a week at her desk job.[59]

The New York Bloomer Girls' twenty-year winning streak against other women's clubs fell August 22, 1932, when the girls lost to the Cos Cob Club girls' team 11–6 in Connecticut. The game was played before a crowd of 2,500. A news clipping states, "Miss Taylor playing first base, managed to bring in a home run which took some of the sting of defeat out of the game."[60]

The New York Bloomer Girls also played against black men's semi-pro teams. On September 16, 1932, they played the Jersey City Colored Athletics.[61] Apparently, playing against black teams was accepted and there were no protests. What is interesting about this is that Allington's All Americans, a barnstorming team that played in the 1950s, met vehement opposition to their playing a "colored" team in Texas in 1956. Several of the players on Allington's team stated that a riot almost broke out when they arrived to play the black team in Jasper. The game had to be cancelled.[62]

The New York Bloomer Girls ended their 1932 season by playing the Philadelphia Athletic Girls in what was billed as the Eastern Female Baseball Championship title. The Philadelphia team had recently won the Pennsylvania women's baseball title by defeating the Philadelphia Bobbies. Both teams played with an all-female lineup. The New York Bloomer Girls held onto the title with a decisive win, 14–5.[63]

The New York Bloomer Girls' last season was 1935. Edna Duncanson, a native of Gaspereau, Nova Scotia, was the only Canadian ever to play for the New York Bloomer Girls. In an interview she said, "My biggest thrill in life was being accepted on a team that went undefeated in twenty-five years of play." So the legend that the team had never lost a game to another women's team continued despite the Cos Cob defeat. The team that year traveled in two open touring cars and played local men's teams. Duncanson remembered playing the House of David. Everywhere the team went there were large crowds. She said: "Both men and women, young and old, turned out to watch the games. The bleachers were always full." Apparently even with the crowds it was no longer financially lucrative and at the end of the season a dynasty ended. Duncanson returned home and continued to be active in sports, participating in basketball, softball, and bowling.[64]

Another famous women's team still operating in the 1920s and 1930s was the Philadelphia Bobbies. In 1925 the team toured Japan playing exhibition games against men's B club teams from Japan University, Tedai Club Tokyo Dental University, Medical Toteshu Shiyochiku Kinema, and several other teams.[65]

There were thirteen girls on the team, ranging in age from thirteen to twenty-three. Most of the girls were from the Pennsylvania area, but one was from Virginia and another from Illinois. The team played the majority of their regular-season games against men's teams from Pennsylvania to Virginia. Rarely did they play other women's teams. On occasion they did play against the New York Bloomers. The girls on the team were Leona Kerns, Nellie Schenk, Florence Eakin Straub, Alma Nolan, Loretta Jester Lipski, Edith Houghton, Sarah Connely, Jenny Phillips, Fereba Garnett Pattison, Agnes Curran, Edith Ruth, and Nettie Gans Spangler. Two former major leaguers, Earl Hamilton, a Pirates pitcher, and Eddie Ainsmith, a Washington catcher, sometimes made up the battery.[66]

On September 23, 1925, they left Philadelphia for a barnstorming tour that would end in Seattle, where they would board the ship *President Jefferson* for Yokohama. Along the way the Bobbies played games in Fargo, North Dakota; White Fish, Montana; and Wenatchee, Everett, Tacoma, and Seattle, Washington. Each host town entertained the girls with sightseeing, dinners, and dances. The girls had a marvelous tour. The diary of Nettie Gans Spangler contains only one negative comment and that is about the men on the Seattle team. She wrote, "I was spiked, kicked in the mouth and [got] two bruised fingers." Obviously, chivalry was dead.

In Japan, the local newspaper was as curious about the American girls as Nettie and the others were about the Japanese. The headline in the Japanese paper read, "Women's Team Look like 12 Year Olds and One Member Is Six Feet Tall, but They Are Lovely and Cute." The reporter went on: the "group of young and vivacious sports women were all wearing sports shoes instead of high heels and all members look like real sports persons."

After being graciously entertained by the Japanese for a few days, they played their first games with Japan University. The Bobbies lost both games, the first 0–6, the second 1–2. The team posted its first win when they defeated a team of Japanese actors. In Osaka they were victorious over the Foreign Language team in a 6–3 game and against the Dental College team in a 1–0 game. They also played a third game in Osaka, but neither the name of the team nor the score was recorded in Nettie's diary. The tour then continued to Kyoto where the team played to a large crowd and two of the Bobbies suffered injuries. One girl broke a finger and the other sprained her ankle. Again no score is given. Next they played two games in Kobe, one with a Young Men's Christian Association (YMCA) team and the other with a Canadian Academy. Again Nettie fails to record the scores. She seems more interested in the dinners, sightseeing, and other happenings.

Upon the team's return home, Philadelphians welcomed them with much fanfare. Nettie wrote: "PHILADELPHIA AT LAST! There were crowds of people at the gate when we got off the train. Of course, photographers were there to take our pictures." For girls such as Nettie Gans Spangler and Edith Houghton, baseball offered tremendous opportunities to travel, to meet influential people, and to learn about the world. Edith Houghton, the Bobbies' shortstop, went on to become the first and only woman to scout for major league baseball. She was hired by the Philadelphia Phillies in 1946.[67]

Women on the numerous Bloomer Girls teams paved the way for a few talented women players to make the transition from women's ball to men's. And at the turn of the century several women actually became stars on men's teams.

NOTES

1. Qtd. in Karen Kenney, "The Realm of Sports and the Athletic Woman, 1850–1900," in *Her Story in Sport: A Historical Anthology of Women in Sports*, ed. Reet Howell (West Point, N.Y.: Leisure Press, 1982), 108.

2. Edith Rickert, "What Has the College Done for Girls?" *Ladies Home Journal*, Jan. 1912, 12.

3. Ibid.

4. Helen Horowitz, *Alma Mater: Design and Experience in the Women's Colleges from Their Nineteenth-Century Beginnings to the 1930s* (Boston: Beacon Press, 1984), 27.

5. Roy Somerville, "Feminine Baseball De Luxe," *Baseball Magazine*, May 1908, 18.

6. Ibid., 19.

7. Ted Vincent, *Mudville's Revenge: The Rise and Fall of American Sport* (New York: Seaview Books, 1981), 95.

8. Ibid., 100.

9. Christ Kunkel, letter to Mr. Herrman, 28 Dec. 1903, NBHFL.

10. "A Base-Ball Burlesque: Blondes and Brunettes Toying with the Bat," *New York Times*, 23 Sept. 1883.

11. Ad in the *New York Clipper*, 22 Sept. 1883.

12. Qtd. in Gerald Gems, "Early Women's Baseball: A Case in Subjugation and Transformation," *Base Woman*, Jan. 1989, 2.

13. Dale Somers, *The Rise of Sports in New Orleans, 1850–1900* (Baton Rouge: Louisiana State University Press, 1972), 119.

14. Robert A. Smith, *A Social History of the Bicycle* (New York: American Heritage Press, 1972), 105.

15. Court Michelson, *Michelson's Book of World Baseball Records* (Chicago: Adams Press, 1985), 84.

16. Illustration, "The Last Illustration of Women's Rights—A Female Base-Ball Club at Peterboro, NY," 3 July 1869, NBHFL.

17. "The Female Baseball Club," *New York Clipper*, 18 Sept. 1875.

18. "Blonde vs. Brunette," newspaper clipping, 1875, NBHFL.

19. Somers, 119.

20. Ibid.

21. *Philadelphia Inquirer*, 20 Aug. 1883.

22. "Girls at Baseball: A Ridiculous Exhibition at Philadelphia Park," *New York Times*, 19 Aug. 1883.

23. "A Base-Ball Burlesque."

24. Ibid.

25. "Noteworthy Contests of 1883: Novelties," *New York Clipper*, 29 Dec. 1883.

26. Ibid.

27. John Betts, *America's Sporting Heritage, 1850–1950* (Reading, MA: Addison-Wesley, 1974), 219.

28. "Novelties," *New York Clipper*, 29 Dec. 1883.

29. "Base Ball, The Female Nine at Jackson," *New Orleans Daily Picayune*, 24 Dec. 1884.

30. "Novelties."

31. David Voigt, *American Baseball: From the Commissioners to Continental Expansion* (University Park: Pennsylvania State University Press, 1983), xiii.

32. "Novelties."

33. Larry Keith, "Not Every Bloomer Held a Girl," *Sports Illustrated*, 4 Jan. 1971, E3.

34. Gene Smith and Jayne Smith, eds., *The National Police Gazette* (New York: Simon & Schuster, 1972), 119.

35. Bob McCoy, "Keeping Score," *Sporting News*, 5 July 1982.

36. Debra Shattuck, "Playing a Man's Game: Women and Baseball in the United States, 1866–1954" (M.A. thesis, Brown University, 1988), 42.

37. Source unknown, NBHFL.

38. Colin Howell, "Baseball, Class and Community in the Maritime Provinces, 1870–1910," *Histoire sociale–Social History* 22 (Nov. 1989): 278.

39. Ibid., 278–279.

40. Furman Bisher, "Girls of Summer: An All-Female Lineup for Sun Sox?" *Boston Sunday Herald Advertiser*, 6 July 1975.

41. Keith, E3.

42. Michael Gershman, "Smokey Joe's Shining Season," *Sports Heritage*, Sept./Oct. 1987, 47.

43. Ibid.

44. Ibid.

45. "When Father Locates Earl the Bloomer Girls Will Need Another Player," *Nashville Banner*, 9 Sept. 1910.

46. Diane Pavlovich, "Baseball Should Be Open to All People," *Collegiate Baseball*, 26 Feb. 1988, 4.

47. "Woman Plays Great Ball," *Boston Herald*, 23 Aug. 1903.

48. "Played Ball," Cincinnati *Enquirer*, 14 June 1900.

49. "To Tour the World," Cincinnati *Enquirer*, 7 Oct. 1905.

50. "Typos and Bloomer Girls," Cincinnati *Enquirer*, 29 July 1911.

51. Keith, E3.

52. "Bloomer Girls, Outdone by Ladies of Shelbyville, Ind.," Cincinnati *Enquirer*, 19 Aug. 1904.

53. Ibid.

54. "Teams Made up Mostly of Girls to Play Baseball at Forest Hills," *Boston Herald*, 31 Aug. 1903.

55. Robert Smith, *Baseball in America* (New York: Holt, Rinehart & Winston, 1961), 199.

56. Keith, E3.

57. Billie Taylor Rota, interview with author, 7 May 1990.

58. "Levels Defeat Bloomer Girls," Plainfield, N.J., *Courier-News*, 23 May 1932.

59. Rota interview.

60. "Bloomer Girls Lose While 2,500 Watch," Greenwich, Conn. *Daily News–Graphic*, 22 Aug. 1932.

61. "Michaels and Taylor Oppose Colored A's," *Hudson Dispatch*, 16 Sept. 1932.

62. Interview with various players, AAGBL reunion, 24 Oct. 1991.

63. "Bloomer Girls Retain Crown," *Bayonne Times*, 26 Sept. 1932.

64. "Folks," *Atlantic Insight*, May 1989, 38.

65. Information on Philadelphia Bobbies' 1925 Japanese tour from articles in Japanese newspaper *Asashi*, Oct. 1925, translations by Aida Diétz, Falls Church, Virginia, and from Nettie Gans's Japanese tour diary, NBHFL.

66. Harry Roberts, "Phillies to Get Woman's Angle in Hunt for Talent," newspaper article, Feb. 1947, NBHFL.

67. "Woman Scout," *Base Woman*, Oct. 1987, 4.

4

Turn-of-the-Century Women Pioneers in Men's Minor and Major League Baseball

By the 1900s the status of women ballplayers was changing. Now there were women who had grown up playing baseball and were knowledgeable about the game. Six women of this period managed to participate as full-fledged members in the world of male baseball. Four were players: Lizzie Arlington, Alta Weiss, Lizzie Murphy, and Josie Caruso; one was an umpire, Amanda Clement; and one was an owner, Helene Britton.

LIZZIE ARLINGTON, PITCHER, 1898

Elizabeth Stride or Stroud, whose professional name was Lizzie Arlington, was probably the first of the woman "phenoms." She had grown up in Mahanoy City, Pennsylvania, a coal mining area, and had learned to play ball from her father and brothers. When she was twenty-two, she was discovered by Captain William J. Conner, owner of the Philadelphia Reserves. It was the end of the 1898 season and he was looking for a crowd pleaser. Supposedly he paid her $100 a week to finish out the season.[1]

In her first game for the Philadelphia Reserves on July 2, 1898, she pitched four innings and played second base against the amateur Richmond Club. It was reported in the Philadelphia *Inquirer*, July 3, 1898, that "Captain Conner is very proud of his new star and sees millions in her, but he was sorely disappointed at the size of the crowd."[2] Fewer than 500 attended the game, and Conner quickly lost interest in his new star.

Ed Barrow, president of the Atlantic League, then hired her to pitch in minor league exhibition games as a ploy to increase attendance. She played her first and what was to be her only regulation minor league game on July 5, 1898, for Reading against Allentown. Billed as "the most famous lady pitcher in the world," she made her entrance on the field in a carriage drawn by two white horses. It was purely P.T. Barnum, and even Barrow admitted that he "used circus tricks now and then to coax in customers." Ironically, with all the fanfare she pitched only the last inning of the game. Again she failed to be a big attraction. Only about 1,000 spectators came to the game.[3]

The Reading *Eagle* described her playing as follows: "She went about it like a professional even down to expectorating on her hands and wiping her hands on her uniform." The newspaper was quick to remark that she might be good for a woman but couldn't make it among professional players, although it was conceded that she would be able to compete with amateurs.[4]

The Hartford *Courant* stated, "She plays ball just like a man and talks ball like a man and if it was not for bloomers she would be taken for a man on the diamond, having none of the peculiarities of women ball players."[5]

Unfortunately, her scheduled appearance with the Hartford Club was cancelled, and future Atlantic League games never occurred. Hired as a promotional gimmick, she was no longer needed when the crowds did not materialize.

An article in the Cincinnati *Enquirer,* June 12, 1903, documents that another woman also tried to play professional ball. Miss M. E. Phelan inquired about playing center field for the all-male Flora Baseball Club of Indiana. Having played for a number of women's teams, she believed she would be an asset for drawing crowds. She wrote, "A lady in your club would prove an attraction and would justify your team paying the salary I would ask—$60 per month and expenses."[6] It is not known if she was hired or if any other women attempted careers. Three women, however, had celebrated careers on men's teams. Alta Weiss played baseball for sixteen years from 1907 to 1922, Lizzie Murphy for eighteen years from 1918 to 1935, and Josie Caruso for three years from 1929 to 1931.

ALTA WEISS, PITCHER, 1907–1922

Alta Weiss, an outstanding player of the early 1900s, is another excellent example of the importance of male sponsorship. The middle child of three daughters, Alta was the apple of her father's eye. From early on her father encouraged her to play baseball and treated her like a son. He worked hard to develop her athletic ability.

Dr. Weiss played an instrumental role in planning Alta's education and athletic life. Even though Alta was a full-time student in the winter months and played baseball only in the summer, he made sure her pitching skills did not get rusty in the off-season. He had a gymnasium built onto his barn so that Alta could practice in the winter. John Berger, an employee of Dr. Weiss's who was a good baseball player, practiced with her all winter.[7] To develop her physique, he had the gymnasium equipped with body-building equipment, basically treating her as an athlete in training.[8]

Her father was a showman who worked hard to market his daughter's baseball image. He established a folklore around her extraordinary pitching ability. "He swore that when she was less than two years old, she hurled a corncob at the family cat with all the follow-through and wrist-snap of a big league pitcher."[9]

He was very successful in promoting her, and in 1907, at seventeen, she became the star pitcher for the Vermilion Independents, a men's semi-pro team in Ohio. "Special trains were run from Cleveland and surrounding towns to accommodate the more than 13,000 fans who attended Vermilion's final seven games of the 1907 season." She was hailed as the "girl wonder."[10]

Alta had a complete pitcher's repertoire—fast ball, curve, knuckler, and sinker. She is quoted as saying, "It's a little indelicate to say it, but I also learned to throw a spitball. . . . I chewed gum during a game to make sure I had an abundance of saliva. For a girl, I had a pretty good fast ball and I had control except with the knuckler and the spitter. I never knew how they would break."[11]

At the end of the season her father realized his daughter's economic potential and bought half interest in the team and changed the name to the Weiss All-Stars. With an eye for publicity, he changed the team uniforms to white for the men and black for Alta. Usually he had Alta pitch five innings and then play first base the other four.[12] (See photos 7–11.)

The press loved her and enjoyed making her a celebrity. Harry P. Edwards, the sporting editor of the *Cleveland Plain Dealer*, extolled her extraordinary ability. "Without a doubt she is a phenom for I saw her pitching against some of the best semi-professionals in Cleveland and she was very effective against them. She seemed to have everything that any amateur pitcher has and fields her position well in addition to having a good baseball 'noodle.' "[13] "On May 22, 1908, the Cleveland Press taunted its American League club with an eight-column banner line, 'If the Nap Pitchers Can't Win Regularly, Why Not Sign Alta Weiss to Help?' "[14]

Alta was a pioneer not only on the ball field but also in medicine. She was the only female in the Class of 1914 at the medical school at Columbus, Ohio. She maintained a medical practice while playing baseball until 1922. From 1925 to 1946 she practiced medicine in Norwalk, Ohio. Upon her father's death in 1946, she returned to Ragersville to take over her father's medical practice.[15]

Although Alta Weiss occupied what in her day were seen as masculine roles, there is no evidence that she considered herself a feminist. "The abundant source material on Weiss makes it clear that she was not using

7. **The Weiss All-Stars.** *Courtesy of Ray Hisrich.*

8. Alta Weiss. *Courtesy of Ray Hisrich.*

9. Alta Weiss in a studio shot. *Courtesy of Ray Hisrich.*

10. Alta Weiss, pitching, 1902. *Courtesy of Ray Hisrich.*

11. Alta Weiss, 1908. *Courtesy of Ray Hisrich.*

baseball to further the cause of women's rights. She simply loved the game and thrilled . . . to play it."[16]

She also did not see her career as opening the door for other women to play baseball. In fact, she held very traditional views about women's roles. She did not feel that women had the ability to play ball. Alta Weiss no doubt saw herself as an exception to the rule, but she was still a product of her cultural environment and accepted the paternalistic view that women were the weaker sex.

LIZZIE MURPHY, FIRST BASE, 1918–1935

Lizzie Murphy, billed as "the queen of baseball" and as "Spike Murphy, the best woman baseball player in the country," came from a very different social background than Alta Weiss. The daughter of a mill hand, Lizzie was working class. She was born and brought up in Warren, Rhode Island, and was one of seven children, five girls and two boys. Although her father did not envision a professional baseball career for her, he was supportive and proud of her athletic accomplishments. She was an all-around athlete and excelled as a skater, swimmer, and long-distance runner as well as a ball player.[17]

There was no corncob in her background, but she could throw a mean stone at an early age.[18] In recalling how she developed her throwing arm, Lizzie once stated: "When I was at an age when kids threw stones at cats and hens. . . . I guess I hit the mark as often as many of the boys."[19]

At eighteen she decided that she had to make a decision about baseball. She went to watch a game and apparently decided then and there that it was her destiny to play baseball. She first joined a Warren amateur baseball team and played at whatever position she was needed—usually shortstop, first, second, or third base. It was said that "in addition to being the star woman baseball player of Bristol county, she is as versatile a player as any big league utility man." But it was not only her versatility that was appreciated. She also had a powerful bat. Her batting average was higher than that of many of the men on the teams they played.[20] She played for three summers, and when her skills improved, she moved up to Eddie McGinley's Providence Independents. With them she barnstormed throughout New England.[21] After that she played throughout Canada and New England for Carr's All-Stars.[22]

Based on descriptions from clippings in her scrapbook, Lizzie was an exceptional player. "[She] fielded her position in perfect fashion, whose pegging to the bases was quick and accurate, a batter with a sure eye and plenty of muscle, and a base runner without peer, an excellent player."[23] In fact, in an interview in 1913 she claimed that she had never been struck out.[24] (See photo 12.)

The financial rewards of her playing days are difficult to judge because she refused to discuss her salary. It is assumed, however, that when she played with the Warren semi-pro team she made $55 per week and her salary increased substantially by the time she played for Carr's All-Stars. She also supplemented her salary by selling postcards of herself to fans who came to watch her play. She once stated that she made $22 selling cards to a crowd of less than 1,000 in Worcester and around $50 selling to a crowd of 6,500 in Dorchester, Massachusetts. Obviously, she was not afraid to promote herself.[25]

Coming from a poor background, Lizzie knew the value of a dollar and was not about to have any baseball manager take advantage of her financially. In her first semi-professional game, the gate was $85. It was standard procedure to split the proceeds among the players. To Lizzie's surprise the money was divided among the men and she received nothing. She took no action at the time and continued to go to practice as if nothing had happened. That Saturday when it came time to board the bus for the game, she refused. The manager pleaded with her to go because the public was expecting her. She explained that she was a professional and needed to be paid for playing. The manager was afraid that if his female phenomenon did not appear the fans might rebel. He was especially concerned because several hundred sailors were coming from Newport to see her play. So he agreed to pay her $5 a game plus a share of the gate.[26]

In later years when Lizzie had become well-known, she became selective as to which exhibition games she played. In order to get her to play, managers often had to give her a larger percentage of the gate, guarantee her a set amount from the sale of her postcards, or guarantee her a certain number of games at a set price. Baseball was a profession for Lizzie and her main source of income. But she was not mercenary and often played for charity events for nothing.[27]

As early as 1913, the 1913–1914 edition of the *Bristol, Warren and Barrington Rhode Island Directory* listed her occupation as "ball player."[28] So officially, by age twenty, she was a professional baseball player. At first people came to see her as a novelty. "But as she improved and became a star, the spectators came to see an expert ballplayer at work."[29] The fact that she was able to make her living as a professional ball player from 1918 to 1935 establishes that she was a skilled player.[30] When she played first base for Eddie Carr's All-Stars in the 1920s, she was advertised as the Queen of Baseball, the best woman baseball player in the country.[31] At first Eddie Carr got some backlash from the press for supposedly exploiting a young girl. Carr responded with "No ball is too hard for her to scoop out of the dirt, and when it comes to batting, she packs a mean wagon tongue."[32] Eddie Carr was understandably proud of his find. So much so that he had a picture of Lizzie on his letterhead. He was thrilled with both her drawing power and her playing. He once stated, "She was worth every cent I was paying her. . . . She swells the attendance, but most important, she produces the goods. . . . She's a real player and a good fellow."[33]

She was also very proud of the fact that Eddie Carr's All-Stars had some ex–major leaguers. She remembered playing with Mack Hollis, a former Rochester player; Artie Grace, who had played for the Boston Red Sox; and Phil Dolan. The team also played against the Cleveland Colored Giants, the Boston Braves of the National League, and other well-known teams.[34]

What Lizzie liked to boast about most was the fact she had played against the Boston Red Sox. On August 14, 1922, she played first base for the American League All Stars against the Red Sox in a benefit game at Fenway Park. Lizzie played two innings and her team won the game 3–2.[35] In recalling the game Lizzie remembered how unfriendly the American League All Star players were to her in the pre-game warmup. When she went into the game in the fourth inning, she knew there was a lot of resentment about her playing. Then her chance came to show everyone she really belonged in the game. McClellan, the third baseman, threw the ball to her at first. The throw was off-target, but Lizzie managed to get it for the out. She said that McClellan nodded his approval to the pitcher and after that everyone accepted her.[36]

Lizzie goes down in history as the first woman ever to have played against a major league team. In 1934 Babe Didrikson would add another first by actually playing for major league teams in major league exhibitions. Babe pitched a few innings for the Philadelphia Athletics against the Brooklyn Dodgers and for the St. Louis Cardinals against the Boston Braves.[37]

After all her years of playing baseball, retirement at age forty was a difficult disengagement for Lizzie. On several occasions in later years, she was asked to participate in various events that would commemorate her baseball career, but she refused. We will never know whether it was pride or bitterness or some other reason, but certainly in her later years she was disillusioned with the game she once loved.

Even though she had been a pioneer in her day, she never identified herself as a feminist. She did not realize her historical significance. In fact, she treated her playing career as an anomaly. When a sportswriter, Barney Madden, asked her in 1941 if she thought girls should play sports, she said, "Oh sure, if they don't overdo it. Softball is all right, baseball not so good. Too tough."[38]

But she never doubted her own ability to play nor seemed surprised that she was accepted. She attributed her success to her own confidence and hard work. "I never go into anything unless I feel sure I'm going to make good. Although those [baseball] days meant a lot of hard work, I feel that the sport, and the traveling from place to place were an education."[39]

Lizzie Murphy seems to have been a practical woman who played baseball because the opportunity presented itself and she loved the game.

12. Lizzie Murphy, first basewoman, 1918–1935. *Courtesy of National Baseball Library, Cooperstown, N.Y.*

Sexism or sexual harassment were not issues Lizzie Murphy thought about. When a reporter asked her in 1938 if she had any trouble with the men on the team, she replied no. Lizzie was not surprised that men swore or cursed nor did she feel threatened by it. She seems to have been totally unaware of larger women's issues and to have experienced little or no conflict between her baseball and feminine roles. A news article after she was married discussed how she loved being a wife and cooking for her husband. In the article pictures of her cooking are juxtaposed to pictures of her playing ball.[40]

Her obituary remembered her baseball days. When she died at age seventy on July 27, 1964, the *Providence Journal* described her baseball skills. "She fielded her position with professional ease and had a quick and accurate throwing arm. She was also an excellent batter with a sure eye."[41]

JOSIE CARUSO, 1929–1931

Dick Jess, a promoter, successfully launched the baseball career of Josie Caruso, whose given name was Josephine Parodi. In 1929 Dick Jess contacted a New York newspaper and stated that he was scouting Upper Manhattan and the Bronx for a good girl baseball player whom he could make into a diamond star. He was sure that there was a female Babe Ruth waiting to be discovered. That gal turned out to be eighteen-year-old Josephine Parodi. Jess quickly gave her the professional name of Josie Caruso, perhaps trying to draw on the fame of the very popular opera star of the time, Enrico Caruso. The team was billed as "Josie Caruso and Her Eight Men." Josie played first base. The team played other semi-professional and amateur teams throughout the East. One newspaper article stated that of the first nineteen games played that season, the team had won fourteen.[42]

A 1929 article in the New York *Mirror* reported that in her first season of play Josie signed a contract for $5,750 for a fifty-game schedule. According to her grandson, however, that was probably mostly media hype. He recalled that his grandmother, Josie Caruso, had told his mother, "I loved the game so much they knew I would play for nothing and that is basically what I received . . . very little . . . and we needed it with a large family and no father." Josie's father had died when she was twelve.[43]

Josie was well worth any money she was paid because she drew the crowds. An article declared, "Throughout the east, at all of the major semi-pro parks, Miss Caruso has shattered attendance records." A night game against the Pennsylvania Coal Miners B.B.C. on August 1, 1929, at the Polo Grounds, home of the New York Giants, drew a crowd of 3,500. The game set two historical records: It was the first game to be played

under lights at the Polo Grounds, and it was the first time a woman had
been in the lineup.[44]

A local sportswriter made the following comment about Josie's Polo
Grounds debut: "Josie Caruso, a buxom lass, played first base without an
error and drew a walk to score a run. She was the sensation of the tilt and
was cheered lustily by the Giants players who sat in civies back of the
dugout."[45]

At 5 foot 6 inches and 140 pounds, Josie Caruso was a well-built athlete.
Yet most articles discussed her femininity. One writer stated that she was
not like the usual run of professional girl players, who are tough looking.
"Josie is pretty and though she can't make the weight that [the] modern
girl is seeking still she is only 140 pounds. The girl is versatile. The same
strong hands that grip a bat so firmly are the nimble ones that manipulate
a milliner's needle so expertly. Dainty fingers that ripple over the keys of
a piano are the same ones that wrap around the leather and whizz the pill
on its way."[46]

There is no doubt that Josie Caruso was an exceptional ball player.
But because there were so few women who played professional ball, it
was easy to bill her as the best in the United States or the best in the
world, and many a sportswriter did just that. What is interesting is that
of all the numerous newspaper articles in her scrapbook not one compares
her skills to earlier players such as Arlington, Weiss, or Murphy. In fact,
not one mentions either her batting average or her fielding percentage.
Her skills are praised only in general terms. For example, one article
states: "Josie Caruso, a young girl, has made a baseball record that is
envied by some major-league players. Miss Josie is the outstanding girl
playing semi-pro ball today and besides is one of the highest salaried
players in semi-pro ranks. Miss Caruso plays first base as well as any
man in the game, . . . [and] proves a greater drawing card than a lot of
major leaguers."[47]

Josie became a national celebrity when she appeared in newsreels in
movie theaters across the country. But Josie soon put an end to her movie
career and refused to pose for any more cameras. She wanted her baseball
playing to speak for itself.

Josie's career lasted approximately three years, from 1929 to 1931, when
she married Joseph Menditto. Her career interests then shifted to raising
a family; she had two daughters and helped her husband run his printing
firm. To a large extent her baseball career faded into the background both
with the public and among her close friends. As her grandson said, "Grandmother never played up her career in baseball. . . . It was years before my
mother was aware of her mom's career. . . . Only upon the insistence of
my mom did she allow 'The Scrapbook' to be circulated to those chosen
few."[48]

AMANDA CLEMENT, UMPIRE, 1905–1911

While the presence of women players is amazing, perhaps more startling is the fact that a woman umpired at the turn of the century. Amanda Clement was the first official woman umpire in men's baseball. She umpired from about 1905 through 1911 for semi-pro teams in the Dakotas, Nebraska, Minnesota, and Iowa.

Umpiring in the late 1800s and early 1900s was a very dangerous profession. Fans, players, coaches, and journalists, all harassed the umpires and it was considered good fun. Venting your frustrations over the game on the umpire was even considered acceptable behavior. A.G. Spalding, the sporting goods entrepreneur and owner of the Chicago Cubs, stated publicly that fans who harassed umpires were merely expressing their democratic right to oppose tyrants.[49]

But the abuses were more than verbal. Expressions such as "kill the umpire," unfortunately, were not just idle threats. Several minor league umpires actually lost their lives and many minor and major leaguers were brutally assaulted by fans.[50] Soda, beer, and whiskey bottles often became lethal weapons when hurled by an angry fan. At Sportsman's Park in 1907 a bottle fractured the skull of umpire Billy Evans.[51]

James Johnstone, another umpire, wrote an article in *Baseball Magazine* in November 1908 describing how he too had been threatened on a number of occasions by unruly fans. What's interesting is that the behavior was so tolerated that even he claimed that he held no ill feelings. "Two or three rebellions against me are yet fresh in my mind and I think they always will be. But I carry no harsh feelings against the participants in these uprisings, for I know how the feeling runs in an audience on such occasions."[52]

Yet the incidences he spoke of were not minor. He recalled one instance when a player rushed from the bench and knocked him down so that he was severely hurt. A police wagon quickly whisked him off to jail, to protect him from the fans. But he still was not safe because an angry crowd swarmed about the jail. He said, "Word was passed around that they were going to lynch the umpire, but I felt no uneasiness."[53]

Three upstate New York newspapers all agreed that "1900 will go down in the baseball annals as the stormiest year in the history of the national game." The *Albany Journal* even went so far as to say it was sheer luck if any umpire escaped a slugging.[54]

But it was the journalists who really fanned the fires and made the life of an umpire miserable. Newspapers did not worry about libel suits or being objective. Yellow journalism sold papers, and umpire bashing was in. It was said that when fans in Albany threatened to throw one umpire in the Hudson River, the local reporter wrote that he needed a good dunking.[55] A *Clipper* reporter went so far as to write, "It is the proud privilege of every man seated . . . to hiss at and 'bullyrag' and abuse [the umpire] when he does not especially favor the local club."[56]

Club owners also encouraged fans to bait the umpires. They believed that the umpire's role as villain added to the gate receipts. In fact, many owners paid the fines of their players who were penalized for "kicking" (abusing) the umpire.[57]

It seems amazing that anyone would want to umpire during this time, but even more surprising that a woman would be recruited and hired. Yet in 1905 Amanda Clement not only became the first woman umpire but was accepted and held in high esteem by fans, players, and journalists. Several factors made this possible. The turn of the century witnessed a dramatic change in women's roles. The image of the "new woman" meant that women were engaging not only in athletics but also in many occupations outside the home. Women ball players, although a novelty, existed and helped to pave the way for the acceptance of an umpire. But more important, baseball was the national pastime. Competition from town to town and from club to club was fierce. Baseball was a serious business. Winning often became so important that paid "ringers" were recruited for the local "amateur" teams. Community pride often rested on having a winning team. Betting on local teams, semi-pro and professional, was rampant. Rumors often circulated that an umpire had been paid off by the home team. Therefore umpires, especially honest ones, were in great demand.

Baseball, however, was still a man's game. Playing baseball was a male rite of passage. Women were not accepted as baseball equals. Even exceptional players such as Arlington, Caruso, Murphy, and Weiss were seen as promotional gimmicks, as women "stars" in a man's game. This strict division of the sexes, however, operated in Amanda Clement's favor. It meant that a woman umpire could play a role that a man couldn't. Rowdy behavior, swearing, cursing in front of a woman, was seen as not only rude but unmanly. Consequently, a female umpire in many ways could receive more respect from players, managers, and fans than could a man. One headline of the time read, "She Can Umpire, There Are No Kicks, Because Players Are Gallant."[58] Another stated, "Her presence makes it certain the game will be clean of unseemly kicking and the use of questionable language on the part of players."[59]

A newspaper article in 1907 said that Miss Clement was so successful as an umpire that fans had never attacked her. "She has never been assaulted on the diamond, has never had any trouble with the crowd."[60] Amanda Clement confirmed the sportswriter's account. She said the worst thing a fan had ever done was to call her a "rube." But the fan's remark was ignored by the crowd, so it wasn't repeated.[61]

Amanda never received the sexual harassment that later women umpires such as Bernice Gera and Christine Wren in the 1970s and Pam Postema in the 1980s experienced. Bernice Gera met constant obstacles in trying to have an umpiring career. One school would not admit her because she was a woman, and then when she finally graduated from another school, no one would hire her. She finally got a job with the New York–Pennsylvania Class A League, but the president of the National Association refused to sign the contract. His refusal made the contract null and void. The reason given was that she was too short at 5 feet 2 inches. So she went to court. Mario Biaggi, her attorney, filed a complaint with the New York State Human Rights Commission. In November 1970 the commission ruled that the league discriminated against men and women of ethnic minorities of short stature. The ruling was appealed, and the State Court of Appeals upheld the original finding. On July 25, 1972, she officially signed with the New York–Pennsylvania League. She finally officiated at a minor league game in Geneva, New York, only to be harassed by the fans. It was all too much. At the end of the game, she burst into tears and declared that she resigned from baseball.[62]

Christine Wren in 1975 became the next woman to try her luck at minor league umpiring. She too experienced sexual harassment from the fans. Fans taunted her with "Go Home and Do the Laundry." Players asked, "Why . . . does a nice-looking broad like that want to be an umpire?"[63]

In 1988 Pam Postema, a successful minor league umpire, was passed over for the majors. Although many people felt that sex discrimination was at play here, the official baseball version was that she was not up to major league standards. Amanda Clement, amazingly enough, never had any of these problems. She was almost always treated with respect and considered a lady. She had strict standards for herself as well as for the players. Not only wouldn't she officiate if there was profanity, but she also would not work on Sundays.[64] Amanda was a pious Congregationalist. Always careful to maintain her ladylike image, when traveling alone for away games she usually stayed with local ministers.[65]

Players respected her, and most were courteous to her. In fact, Amanda often remarked how polite the players were. She said they said such things as "Beg your pardon, Miss Umpire, but wasn't that one a bit high?"[66] Apparently a woman umpire had a distinct advantage. Baseball ruffians who were accustomed to abusing the umpire melted into gentlemen.

Some sportswriters even suggested that there be more women umpires in order to keep the game civilized. Amanda Clement also believed that if there were more women umpires, the managers, players, and crowds would be less rowdy. She said, "If women were umpiring none of this [rowdyism] would happen. Do you suppose any ball player in the country would step up to a good-looking girl and say to her, 'You color-blind, pickle brained, cross-eyed idiot, if you don't stop throwing the soup into me I'll distribute your features all over your countenance!' Of course he wouldn't."[67]

Amanda thought umpiring was a good profession for a woman. She was quoted as saying, "There is no reason why a young woman cannot make a business of umpiring and be a perfect lady. I maintain that it is just as womanly as it is to play tennis. It certainly is healthful, and many a woman in poor physical condition would be benefited immensely if she could spend a summer out in the sun umpiring."[68]

But it was more than male chivalry that made Amanda a success. She also knew her stuff. She was an expert umpire who knew the rules and was impartial and fair. News article after news article reported on her extreme competence. "Miss Clement evidently knows her baseball book and knows it well."[69] "Miss Clement is absolutely fair."[70] "She thoroughly understands the fine points of the game, is the possessor of an 'eagle eye' and good judgment. . . . She is especially good on balls and strikes and on bases she has a habit of being right on the spot when the play is made. Altogether Miss Clement is declared to be the equal if not the superior of most of the league umpires."[71] "Her rulings command greater respect and give better satisfaction than those of the best male umpires."[72]

She was known for being so fair that at one tournament the crowds booed when the male umpire for the next day's game came on the field. They insisted on having Amanda. When the manager pleaded with them that the umpire came at great expense and had already been paid, the crowd took up a collection for the $15 fee. They then hired a car to pick up Miss Clement so she could umpire the game.[73]

The fans were not the only ones who loved Amanda; so did newspaper reporters. She was a newsman's delight. She made good copy, had a good sense of humor, was modest, and never let the publicity go to her head.

She was a heroine to most of the people of Hudson as well as throughout the Dakotas. The press was not only kind to her but also protected her. It was said that she often received more publicity for officiating than did many of the teams that played.[74] Of course, baseball promoters loved her drawing power and advertised her as the "Only Lady Umpire in the World" and the "World's Champion Umpire."[75]

The sportswriters got a kick out of the idea that this polite young lady could keep the peace among the uncouth and ruffian ballplayers. They wrote, "South Dakota has a woman umpire who is said to be about the best preserver of the peace in the whole northwest."[76] It is true that she was not intimidated by the players and knew how to exert her authority. Indeed, she once ejected six players from a game.[77] She was a woman of tremendous confidence and presence. One sportswriter was so impressed by how well she managed the game that he predicted that "her work seems to indicate that the woman umpire has come to stay."[78]

What is amazing about Amanda Clement's umpiring career is that she fell into it by chance. She claimed that her career began when she was asked partly as a joke to umpire a game between two lodges. She said, "I knew baseball however, and made good because I would not stand for their 'beefing' that day."[79]

The players and managers were impressed enough with her umpiring to invite her to umpire the next year. When a professional team came from Canton the following week, she umpired for them. She then went to Canton to ump the return game. After that she said, "I officiated in games between Hudson and Hawarden and Renville and Hawarden and after that—well my services seemed to be in demand."[80] Word quickly spread that she was a skilled umpire who was confident of her call and took "no beef" from the players. Her career was launched.

Since she was the first woman umpire, she had to set the fashion for woman umpires. In the early years she wore a long full skirt down to her ankles, a white shirt with black tie, and a baseball cap. She stored the extra balls in her blouse.[81] Later she wore the same style outfit without the tie and with UMPS emblazoned across her chest in large letters.[82] (See photo 13.)

As was fairly common during this period in baseball history, Amanda umpired from behind the pitcher's mound. In that way she could also watch the bases. In Amanda's era there still was only one umpire.[83] Umpiring from the mound was of course safer than standing behind the batter. She did not have to worry about getting hit by foul tips or players' spikes. But umpiring was still a strenuous activity. She was often out in the hot sun for nine innings or more and couldn't retreat to the dugout every other inning as the players did.

Her umpiring proved lucrative and paid for her college education. It was reputed that she made as much as $15 to $25 a game and that writers from the East urged her to go East and work for the major league teams there.[84] By the time her career ended, she was reputed to be one of the highest-paid umpires in the West.[85] It is estimated that she officiated at about fifty games a year.[86] Based on umpiring fifty games at an average of $20 a game, she grossed $1,000. We must consider this salary in comparison to 1910 incomes, when 96 percent of the working families earned less than $2,000 a year.[87] So this was not a bad income for a part-time job.

In 1905, when she started umpiring professionally, Amanda Clement was only seventeen years old. She was a student at Yankton Academy, where she was captain of the champion basketball team. She was also a champion tennis player.[88] In 1912, at age twenty-four, she set a world record for a woman throwing a baseball with a throw of 275 feet. While teaching physical education at Yankton College, she refereed basketball games and was probably the first to do so.

Her professional baseball umpiring career spans from 1905 to 1911 and was more or less a way to finance her college education rather than a full-time vocation. She did, however, continue to umpire special games until she was forty years old. After leaving the University of Nebraska in 1909

13. Amanda Clement, in her umpire's uniform. *Courtesy of South Dakota Amateur Baseball Hall of Fame, Inc.*

she pursued a career as a physical education teacher and taught and coached in South Dakota, North Dakota, and Wyoming.[89]

Amanda Clement in many ways epitomized the modern woman. She certainly felt no sex barrier. She was an all-around athlete and in many respects ahead of her time. She was the first woman baseball umpire and the first woman basketball referee.[90] It is said that during World War I she taught ballet to the football team at the University of Wyoming.[91] Ballet lessons for football players and power skating lessons for hockey players by female figure skaters are considered a recent innovation.

In 1929 she returned home to Hudson to care for her sick mother. For the five years she was in Hudson, she was active in all types of fields. She was a newspaper reporter, city assessor, justice of the peace, and she coached all types of children's teams. After that she went to Sioux Falls and practiced social work until 1966, when she retired. Amanda Clement led a very full and active life until she died in 1971 at eighty-three.[92]

In reminiscing about Amanda's life after her death her nephew remembered some of the times when she had played catch with him and his friends. He said that she threw the ball so hard that the boys "would often sneak indoors on the pretense of needing a drink of water. But instead . . . would pad their gloves with a sponge."[93] Apparently, she could easily have become another professional ball player rather than an umpire. At one time she had played first base on the Hudson, South Dakota semi-professional team with her brother, Hank.[94] She was a tall, well-built woman. At 5 feet 10 inches she made a good-sized ball player, since many players of that era were short.

Unfortunately, other young girls didn't follow in Amanda's footsteps. It was not until 1969 that another woman, Bernice Gera, attempted to become an umpire. Amanda Clement was never able to see her officiate. She died on July 20, 1971, at eighty-three, one year before Bernice Gera was finally permitted to officiate in a minor league game. By that time the days of Amanda Clement were forgotten. She had failed to pave the path for the acceptance of female umpires.

HELENE BRITTON, CARDINALS' OWNER, 1911–1917

Around the same time that Alta Weiss and Lizzie Murphy were playing semi-pro ball and Amanda Clement was umpiring, Mrs. Helene Britton became the first woman owner of a major league team, the St. Louis Cardinals. The other major league owners were not happy about having a woman in their midst. Although they came to respect her as a businesswoman, they never accepted her as a legitimate owner. To the bitter end the major league establishment maintained that ownership and management of a major league team was the proper domain of men only.

On September 25, 1908, Frank deHaas Robison, Helene Robison Britton's father, died and left the ownership of the Cardinals to his brother, M. Stanley Robison. When Stanley Robison died on March 24, 1911, Helene Britton, his niece, just thirty-two, inherited the team. She inherited 75 percent ownership with 25 percent ownership going to her mother.[95]

Although she was knowledgeable about the game, Helene Britton was still deemed unacceptable by the other owners because she was a woman (they did admit that she understood baseball, however). One magazine

14. Helene Britton, St. Louis Cardinals' owner, 1911–1917.
Courtesy of the Sporting News.

article even stated that she was a product of baseball. "[Of] her earliest years her recollections were all of base hits and outfield flies."[96]

Her family had originally owned another National League team, the Cleveland Spiders. In 1898 her father and his brother purchased the St. Louis Cardinals.[97] She had grown up around baseball and felt quite knowledgeable about the business. But Mrs. Britton was aware that a woman owner would be looked on askance, and so in her interviews she was careful to acknowledge that baseball was a man's game, but because of her background she was a capable exception to the rules.

> I can honestly say that I have always loved baseball. My father and uncles talked baseball ever since I can remember. My father insisted that I keep score. . . . I grew up . . . in an atmosphere of baseball. I even played it when a girl and I am glad to know that the game is played in a somewhat modified form in hundreds of girl camps and elsewhere by young ladies all over the United States. Played in that way, I believe it as a healthful and interesting diversion though I realize that any thing which resembles a professional type is distinctly a man's game. . . .
>
> I realize that my position as the only woman owner in the major leagues is a peculiar one. And I don't pretend to know the game as intimately from a playing stand-point as a man might do in my place. I appreciate the fact that baseball is a man's game, but I also appreciate the fact that women are taking an increasing interest in the sport.[98]

The first two years she owned the team, first Edward A. Steininger and then her attorney, James C. Jones, served as presidents. But she remained the real power behind the title.[99] Although she delegated authority and had men in the top positions, Mrs. Britton never failed to take an active part in the decision making. She had a great deal of self-confidence and believed not only in herself but also in women's right to vote and make decisions. She was an active suffragette.

In 1914 she appointed her husband as president and had Miller Huggins as manager, but she did not leave the affairs of the team to them. She retained her power of ownership.[100] She "ran the club for eight years, hiring and firing managers, making deals, and attending all league meetings."[101]

From 1911 to 1916 she participated in all the league's annual meetings which were held at the Waldorf-Astoria Hotel. She made it a point to sit in the first row and to appear in the annual picture. Her presence irritated such magnates as Charlie Ebbets of the Dodgers, Harry Hempstead of the Giants, and William Baker of the Phillies, but there was not much they could do about it.[102]

During the first year of her ownership the Cardinals not only rose to fifth place but also made a handy profit of $165,000. She was so delighted with her manager, Roger "Duke" Bresnahan, that she gave him a five-year contract. But their relationship quickly soured. He resented her interference, and she resented his lack of respect. In 1912 the rift became so great that she fired him. Through an out-of-court settlement he obtained $20,000 for breach of contract.[103]

It was at this point that she made her husband president. On the surface this arrangement seemed to work out well. A man she could trust implicitly was in the main position of authority and yet she could be the decision maker. In 1914 her husband offered the team a 20 percent bonus if they could finish the season in third place or higher. They went on to finish in third place. Everyone seemed to be happy and profiting. The Cardinals were now the highest paid players in the league.[104]

At one point, on the advice of her attorneys, she decided to sell the team. Delighted, the other owners tried to force her to sell on their terms. Much to the other owners' surprise she recalled her selling options and retained ownership of the Cardinals. A newspaper article declared, "Baseball may not be a game for a magnatess . . . but in the meeting room of the Waldorf-Astoria Hotel in New York, Mrs. Britton, calm but determined, stood her ground . . . [and] when the other owners attempted a force play she called in her selling options and returned home still in possession of the Cardinals.[105] The magnates were forced to buy the St. Louis Browns instead.

Helene Britton was not to be intimidated by the other league owners and sold her franchise when she wished and under her own terms. In February 1917 she sold the franchise to a group from St. Louis for $375,000.[106] The sale was probably precipitated by her marital problems. In 1916 she divorced her husband and assumed the presidency of the Cardinals, a position no other woman has ever held.[107] A year later she sold the team.

Although most of the evidence seems to suggest that the early women who participated in baseball had either direct male sponsorship or, as in the case of Helene Britton, inherited the position, none of these women was merely a puppet. They were all competent, determined, and enthusiastic participants and represented all socio-economic backgrounds. They were pioneers in their time and had the courage and determination to overcome the stigma against women in athletics. Except for Mrs. Britton, the women did not appear to be feminists or suffragettes. Their individual motivations were very different, but for most baseball simply represented a career choice.

NOTES

1. "Woman Players in Organized Baseball," *SABR Baseball Research Journal*, 1983, 159.

2. Ibid., 160.
3. Ibid.
4. Ibid.
5. Ibid., 161.
6. Debra Shattuck, "Playing a Man's Game: Women and Baseball in the United States, 1866–1954" (M.A. thesis, Brown University, 1988), 61–62.
7. Sesquicentennial Historical Committee, *Ragersville, Auburn Township, Ohio, 1830–1980: The Sesquicentennial Story of a Community* (Berlin, Ohio: Berlin Printing, 1980), 195–196.
8. Ibid., 190.
9. Ibid., 193.
10. Debra Shattuck, "80 Years Ago in Vermilion: A 'Skirt' on the Mound Stuns Baseball Fans," *Vermilion Photojournal*, 31 Aug. 1987, Sec. C.
11. Dover–New Philadelphia, Ohio, *Times Reporter* 30 July 1980, Sec. D.
12. Sesquicentennial Historical Committee, 196.
13. Harry P. Edwards, title unknown, *Cleveland Plain Dealer*, 22 March 1908, NBHFL.
14. Sesquicentennial Historical Committee, 197.
15. Ibid., 191.
16. Shattuck, "Playing a Man's Game," 66.
17. Elizabeth Williams, "Warren Woman Recalls Life as Baseball Star," Providence *Evening Bulletin*, 2 Feb. 1938.
18. Ibid.
19. John Hanlon, "Yesterday: Queen Lizzie Plays First Base," *Sports Illustrated*, circa 1969, E3, NBHFL.
20. "Warren Girl an Expert Baseball Player," *Providence Sunday Journal*, 27 July 1913.
21. Williams.
22. John Hanlon, "The Queen of Baseball," *Yankee Magazine* 49 (July 1985): 15.
23. Williams.
24. "Warren Girl an Expert Baseball Player."
25. Hanlon, "Yesterday," E3.
26. Dick Reynolds, untitled paper on Lizzie Murphy, 4–5, NBHFL.
27. Ibid., 6.
28. Shattuck, "Playing a Man's Game," 68.
29. " 'Lizzie' Murphy Larivee, 70, One-time Ballplayer, Dies," *Providence Journal*, 29 July 1964.
30. Ibid.
31. Hanlon, "Yesterday," E3.
32. Ibid.
33. Williams.
34. Ibid.
35. Reynolds, 1.
36. Ibid., 2.
37. Ibid.
38. Ibid.
39. Williams.

40. Ibid.

41. " 'Lizzie.' "

42. Douglas Noble, M.D., Paramus, N.J., letter to author, 27 June 1992; "Josie Caruso's Ball Team to Meet Inwood Firemen," newspaper article, Josie Caruso scrapbook.

43. "The Wonder Girl," New York *Mirror*, circa 1929, Josie Caruso scrapbook; Noble.

44. "Girl Baseball Star Refuses to Perform for Movie Cameras" and "Polo Grounds Draws 3,500 to Night Game," newspaper articles, Josie Caruso scrapbook.

45. "Polo Grounds."

46. Jacques, "Sport Uptown," newspaper article, Josie Caruso scrapbook.

47. "Josie Caruso to Lead Them against Inwood Tomorrow," newspaper article, Josie Caruso scrapbook.

48. Noble.

49. David Voigt, "America's Manufactured Villain—The Baseball Umpire," *Journal of Popular Culture* 4 (Summer 1970): 7.

50. John Thorn, *A Century of Baseball Lore* (New York: Hart Pub. Co., 1974), 18.

51. David Voigt, *American Baseball: From the Commissioners to Continental Expansion*, vol. 2 (University Park: Pennsylvania State University Press, 1983), 101.

52. Qtd. in James Johnstone, "Mobbing the Umpire," *Baseball Magazine* 1 (Nov. 1908): 35.

53. Ibid., 36.

54. Ed Brooks, "The Role of the Umpire in 1900," *Baseball Research Journal* 9 (1980): 76.

55. Ibid., 79.

56. Voigt, "America's Manufactured Villain," 8.

57. Ibid., 1–6.

58. "She Can Umpire: There Are No Kicks, Because Players Are Gallant," special dispatch to *Enquirer*, circa 8 Sept. 1907, newspaper clipping, NBHFL.

59. "Amanda Clement, the College Girl Who Has Umpired Many Games of Ball," newspaper clipping, Amanda Clement scrapbook.

60. "She Can Umpire."

61. Ibid.

62. Irving Leitner, *Baseball Diamond in the Rough* (New York: Criterion Books, 1972), 215.

63. David Voigt, "Sex in Baseball: Reflections of Changing Taboos," *Journal of Popular Culture* 12 (Winter 1928): 396.

64. Shari Roan, "The 'Lady in Blue': A Long Forgotten First," Fort Lauderdale *Sun Sentinel*, 8 July 1981.

65. Sharon Roan, "Yesterday: No One Yelled 'Kill the Ump' When Amanda Clement Was a Man in Blue," *Sports Illustrated*, 5 April 1982, M3.

66. Ibid.

67. "She Can Umpire."

68. Ibid.

69. Minneapolis newspaper, circa 1906 or 1907, Amanda Clement scrapbook.

70. "Gayville Ball Team Coming Back," newspaper clipping, Amanda Clement scrapbook.

71. "Amanda Clement, the College Girl."

72. "A Baseball Game between Hudson and Canton," Canton, S.D., 9 Sept. 1907, newspaper clipping, Amanda Clement scrapbook.

73. "Champion Lady Umpire of the World," newspaper clipping, Amanda Clement scrapbook.

74. Sam Cohen, *Connecticut Herald*, 9 July 1972, NBHFL.

75. Roan, "Yesterday," M3; Colin Kapitan, " 'Girl Umpire of Dakota' Etched Deep in Diamond Lore: Was YC Student," Yankton, S.D., *Press and Dakota*, circa 1964, Yankton College Archives.

76. "The Woman Umpire," newspaper clipping, Amanda Clement scrapbook.

77. Roan, "The 'Lady in Blue.' "

78. Minneapolis newspaper clipping, Amanda Clement scrapbook.

79. "Pioneer Female Umpire, Miss Clement Hopes to Secure a Minor League Appointment," 21 Oct. 1905, newspaper clipping, NBHFL.

80. "Girl Professional Baseball Umpire," Hudson, S.D., *Hudsonite*, newspaper clipping, Amanda Clement scrapbook.

81. Sam Cohen, " 'Retired' Lady Ump Wasn't First of Sex," *Connecticut Herald*, 9 July 1972, newspaper clipping, Amanda Clement scrapbook.

82. John Egan, "Hudson's Clement Distinguished as the Original Female Umpire," Sioux Falls, S.D., *Argus Leader*, March 1982, NBHFL.

83. Roan, "Yesterday," M3.

84. Roan, "The 'Lady in Blue' "

85. Roan, "Yesterday," M3.

86. Cohen.

87. Donald Mrozek, *Sport and the American Mentality, 1880–1910* (Knoxville: University of Tennessee Press, 1983), 51.

88. "Tennis Season Will Close Soon," newspaper article, Amanda Clement scrapbook; "Pioneer Female Umpire," 21 Oct. 1905.

89. Egan.

90. Kapitan.

91. Roan, "Yesterday," M3.

92. Egan.

93. Roan, "The 'Lady in Blue,' " Sec. C.

94. Ibid.

95. "Never Tell Her She Must," 6 Jan. 1916, newspaper clipping in Helene Britton file, NBHFL; Bill Borst, "The Matron Magnate," *SABR Baseball Research Journal*, 1977, 26.

96. Helene Britton interview, "My Experience as a League Owner," *Baseball Magazine* 18 (Feb. 1917):13.

97. Borst, 25.

98. Britton interview, 13.

99. Borst, 26.

100. Britton interview, 13.

101. Lee Allen, *The Hot Stove League* (New York: A.S. Barnes & Co., 1955), 191.

102. Borst, 26.

103. Ibid., 27.
104. Ibid., 28–29.
105. "Never Tell Her She Must."
106. Ibid.
107. Borst, 29.

5

Women Stars in Exhibition Baseball Games in the 1930s and 1940s

The Great Depression of the 1930s left thousands of people without jobs, and the prospects for economic recovery were gloomy. Although baseball attendance suffered, the major leagues were relatively unaffected. Minor league teams, especially in small cities, were not so lucky, and many struggled to remain financially solvent. Both major and minor league owners eagerly searched for ways to increase attendance.

Innovation became a key word. Major league baseball in 1933 instituted the first All Star game between the top players in both leagues. Larry MacPhail, general manager of the Cincinnati Reds, tried all kinds of promotional gimmicks from cigarette girls in satin pants, to female ushers, to red uniforms for the players. He introduced night games in 1935.[1]

But one of the greatest baseball innovators of all time was Joe Engel—owner, promoter, and president of the Chattanooga Lookouts, a class double A minor league team. He had been involved with vaudeville in the 1920s. A born showman, he was nicknamed "Barnum Joe" and was known for such antics as conducting elephant hunting safaris in his ball park[2] and for trading his shortstop, Johnny Jones, to the Charlotte Hornets for a 25-pound turkey. He then served the turkey to the Southern Baseball Writer's Association.[3] His greatest publicity stunt, however, came when he hit on the idea of having a woman, Jackie Mitchell, pitch an exhibition game against the New York Yankees.

JACKIE MITCHELL

Even though 1931 was a time of crazy fads, flag pole sitters, and dance marathons, Engel grabbed front-page news in almost every paper in the country when he signed seventeen-year-old Jackie Mitchell to the Look-outs. She was the first woman to ever sign a professional baseball contract. The rumor was that he needed to boost attendance and Jackie needed a new car. So a deal was struck.[4]

But it was not that simple. Two other people also played prominent roles. Jackie's father, who had developed his daughter's talent, was no doubt instrumental in getting Engel to use Jackie. Some believe that he approached Engel, rather than the other way around. Kid Elberfeld, head of the baseball school she had attended, also had an interest in her signing.

The announcement by Engel that a seventeen-year-old girl was going to pitch against Babe Ruth and Lou Gehrig of the Yankees grabbed national headlines. There was much hype around the event. It was reported that Engel had taken out a $10,000 life and pitching arm insurance policy on Jackie.[5]

Sportswriters loved the idea of a young girl pitching to the mighty Babe. Stereotypic versions of the frail young maiden going against the man of steel appeared in most newspapers. Citing that even the best of the male pitchers had a tough time against the Babe, they questioned how a seventeen-year-old girl who weighed only 130 pounds would fare.[6]

Two days after the game was announced, it was reported that the Memphis Chicks had tried to buy Jackie's contract for two players and cash. Engel reported that he turned down the offer because Jackie was just too good.[7]

The day before the big event reporters interviewed both Jackie and Babe Ruth. When asked if she thought she could strike out Ruth, Jackie replied with confidence, "Yes, I think I can strike him out."[8] Babe Ruth was not quite as ecstatic as Jackie about the game. He was quoted as saying that he didn't know what would happen if they let women in baseball. "Of course, they will never make good. Why? Because they are too delicate. It would kill them to play ball every day."[9] Ruth went on to say that he hoped it would be the last time he was ever called upon to bat against a female.

It was estimated that a crowd of 3,500 to 4,000 came out to see the game on April 2, 1931.[10] Clyde Barfoot was the starting pitcher for Chattanooga. He had previously played for both the Cardinals and the Tigers. After the first two Yankee batters got hits off him, Bert Niehof, the manager of the Lookouts, brought Jackie in as his replacement.

As she went out to the mound, Jackie remembered her father's words to her: "Go out there and pitch just like you pitch to anybody else." She still was very nervous, and it wasn't until she had the second strike on Babe that she really settled down. Years later she admitted that her youth and inexperience were also a blessing. "Honestly, I was just too young to know what was going on. Of course, it was exciting for me. But I just went in there and pitched like I had always been pitching."[11]

Apparently, Babe tipped his hat to her and reminded her that there was a batter on first before going into his famous batter's stance. She wound up according to one writer as if she were turning a coffee grinder.[12] The pitch flew over the plate, Babe swung and missed for a strike. Babe had a perplexed look on his face. The next two pitches were wide. Babe called for a new ball. Babe then swung and missed. On the next pitch, it was all over. Umpire Brick Owens called strike three and the mighty Babe was out. There was a roar from the crowd, and Babe gave an angry look to the umpire before walking to the dugout.

There is no doubt that Babe struck out that day. But some people believe that Babe cooperated good-naturedly.[13] The debate still continues to this day. According to other accounts he wasn't so good-natured. "Babe disliked the idea of being called out, and in seeming disgust kicked the dirt, called the umpire a few dirty names, gave his hat a wild heave and stomped off to the Yanks dugout."[14] A wire service report stated, "Ruth threw his bat against the dugout in disgust over being called out on strikes."[15]

Lou Gehrig then came up to the plate and met the same fate. One reporter said, "Lou Gehrig stepped up to the plate. His knees were shaking and he cut at three fast ones . . . and also sat down."[16] Tony Lazzeri, the third batter, got a base on balls and Jackie was retired. The Yankees went on to win the game 14–4.

Jackie expressed disappointment at having been pulled and said, "I still believe I might have won the game." She went on to say, "I think they [Ruth and Gehrig] are both fine men and great ball players. I see nothing strange about my striking them out, at least stranger things have happened. Not even the best batters can hit them all." She expressed tremendous optimism after the game and said that she expected to pitch for years to come and hoped one day to play in a World Series.[17]

Pictures of Jackie Mitchell with Babe Ruth and Lou Gehrig appeared in newspapers and magazines. (See photo 15.) Movie houses around the country showed the Universal Newsreel of Jackie striking out Ruth and Gehrig and walking Lazzeri. Jackie's moment of glory, however, was short-lived. Her plans to join the Lookouts on the road and to pitch in every city that had a league team came to an abrupt end. Baseball Commissioner Kenesaw Mountain Landis announced that women were banned from competing in baseball and that her contract was null and void.[18] Jackie's career as a player with the Lookouts ended.

On April 23 Engel officially announced that he had put her on the reserve list. Although she had not appeared in any regular games, she had been on the roster. He said that she would continue to have a role in the club doing promotional work.[19] But Jackie meanwhile returned to the Englettes, an all-girls baseball team that had been established the previous season with Engel as sponsor and her father as manager. No doubt the team was established to showcase Jackie, who had quickly become a pitching and

15. Jackie Mitchell with Joe Engel, Babe Ruth, and Lou Gehrig. *Courtesy of Chattanooga Regional History Museum.*

hitting star. She had had a seasonal batting average of .400 and was reported to have an uncanny knack at guessing a batter's weakness and placing the ball there.[20] Since the team played against men's semi-professional teams, Jackie's credentials had been established before she signed with the Lookouts.

In 1931 she also signed a contract to play with the Lookout Mountaineers, a professional men's basketball team.[21] In 1932 she returned to professional baseball when she joined the Greensboro, North Carolina, team of the Piedmont League for their road trips, but not their home games. From

1933 to 1937 she toured with the House of David, a men's barnstorming team known for its showmanship.

Unlike umpires Pam Postema and Bernice Gera, and NCAA college player Julie Croteau, Jackie said that she didn't experience any sexual harassment. Although it was true that the Greensboro manager had told the players not to cuss around her, there seemed to be no resentment to her playing. She was never heckled by other players or fans. In fact, fans greeted her enthusiastically and players treated her as family. Many players who lived in North Carolina invited her and her parents to come to dinner at their homes.[22]

Of course, a good question is, how could she play minor league ball if Landis had ruled her ineligible? There are several clues as to why this was possible. First, since the Piedmont League guides did not list her as a regular team member, she probably played off the books. Second, the Piedmont League was so low on the minor league circuit that no one paid much attention to it and it probably did not come to Landis's attention.[23]

In 1933 she signed to play baseball with the House of David, a team started by the religious cult of the same name. Except for Jackie, the players were all men, most with beards and long hair as in biblical times. With them, Jackie barnstormed across the country pitching an inning or so in both day and night games. They played mostly against men's minor league and semi-pro teams, but they did play one game against the Cardinals in St. Louis. Leo Durocher was their rookie shortstop at the time, and Jackie added him to her list of strikeout victims.[24]

She continued her baseball barnstorming for nearly five years, playing against such greats as Pepper Martin, Dizzy Dean, and Honus Wagner.[25] In the off-season she played professional basketball with an all-men's basketball team or toured on a team with Babe Didrikson. In 1937 at age twenty-three she retired from baseball and went home to Chattanooga to work for her father, who was an optometrist. She still continued to practice with some of the local men's teams, but her baseball days were over.[26]

Jackie maintained to her dying day that she thought she had legitimately struck out both Babe Ruth and Lou Gehrig and that Babe's anger at being struck out was genuine.[27] She recalled how after the second strike she had figured that Ruth would look for another one close and high. So she tricked him by throwing the next one straight down the middle with all the speed she could muster. Babe let the pitch go and the umpire cried strike three, and that's when Babe got mad.[28] According to her the only thing that the batters had been asked to do was to try not to hit the ball directly back to her on the mound, so she wouldn't get hurt.[29] She bragged, "I had a drop pitch. When I was throwing it right, you couldn't touch it."[30] "Better hitters than them [Ruth and Gehrig] couldn't hit me."[31]

Of course, there are those who claim that the strikeouts were merely a publicity stunt engineered by Joe Engel, who was known for his gimmicks. Since there was no objective reporting of the event, the controversy over whether Ruth and Gehrig were legitimately struck out or whether it was a publicity stunt still rages today.

There is no doubt that Jackie's playing hit a raw nerve among many male sportswriters and struck fear in the hearts of a few chauvinistic male fans. The *Sporting News* decried the "bawdy publicity" and said that the national game should be "treated with respect."

Absent from the news are any outcries from women about Jackie not being allowed to play. Women's consciousness had not yet been raised. In an interview in 1975 Jackie admitted that back then no one had heard of women's liberation. Although in retrospect, she said, "I guess you could say I was a pioneer in it."[32] In an interview with David Jenkins of the *Chattanooga News–Free Press* in 1982, she confided that when her baseball-playing career ended, she would have liked to have been an umpire. Even in 1982 she seemed resigned to her fate, "but back then they wouldn't let a woman do that either."[33] The idea that she should have or could have challenged the baseball establishment on this issue never entered her mind.

Jackie Mitchell certainly had legitimate baseball credentials. Prior to signing with the Lookouts she had completed Kid Elberfeld's Baseball School. Among the attendees were former Altanta player, Luke Appling, who was there doing a little pre-season training before reporting to the Chicago White Sox, and Jonah White of the Texas League. The players there claimed that she was "one of the most puzzling south paws they had ever faced." It was said that if she made it to the majors that she saw "no reason why she shouldn't command as great a salary as Babe Ruth now draws."[34]

One famous woman athlete at the time took Jackie Mitchell's pitching skills seriously. After the Lookout-Yankee exhibition game Babe Didrikson Zaharias refused to answer the challenge to appear in a pitching match against Jackie Mitchell.[35]

In 1952 Eleanor Engle, no relation to Joe, became the second woman to sign an organized baseball contract. Her signing with the Harrisburg, Pennsylvania Senators, a Class B minor league team, struck fear in the hearts of the men who controlled baseball. Their response was vitriolic. The Senators' manager, Buck Etchison, declared, "I won't have a girl playing for me. This is a no-woman's land and believe me, I mean it. She'll play when hell freezes over."[36] George Trautman, minor league president, declared her contract null and void and called the signing a travesty. He warned that severe penalties would be levied against any club that signed or attempted to sign a woman. Baseball commissioner Ford Frick agreed with him. An official ruling on June 21, 1952, banned women from playing either major or minor league baseball.

Jackie's baseball days were largely forgotten until 1975, when a writer rediscovered her and wrote of her 1931 feats. Several other writers wrote newspaper articles about her in the early 1980s.[37] This sparked the two highlights of her later years. In 1982, at age sixty-eight, she was asked to throw out the first ball on opening day at Engel Stadium for the game between the Lookouts and the Birmingham Barons. In 1984 she was guest of honor for the Atlanta Braves on Ladies' Day.[38]

She died January 7, 1987, at age seventy-three. Her obituary listed her full name as Virnie Beatrice "Jackie" Mitchell Gilbert. Her baseball days were remembered, especially the fact that she had struck out Babe Ruth, Lou Gehrig, and Leo Durocher.

In 1931 another aspiring woman player, Vada Corbus, attempted to play baseball only to find her hopes dashed.

VADA CORBUS

On April 10, 1931, the Missouri *Globe* announced that nineteen-year-old Vada Corbus, a catcher, and her brother Luke, an outfielder, were trying out for the Joplin Miners. A second news release on April 12 said that she would be playing in the opening game at Children's Field on April 30. On April 21 her picture appeared in the *New York Times*, and this sounded the death knell for her career. Apparently the advance publicity alerted baseball officials to Joplin's plans and her career ended before it started.[39]

Several other women, such as Babe Didrikson Zaharias, Frances Dunlop, and Betty Evans, had better luck.

BABE DIDRIKSON ZAHARIAS

Mildred Ella Didrikson, better known as "Babe" Didrikson, was the female athletic sensation of the 1930s and will probably go down in history as the greatest female athlete of all time. The boys in her neighborhood first recognized her amazing athletic ability, and because she hit so many home runs in their sandlot games, they nicknamed her "Babe" after Babe Ruth. Raymond Alford, a schoolmate and sports hero at Beaumont High School, recalled growing up with Babe. "I got acquainted with Babe first on the sandlots on Saturday. You know how kids get together. All the boys in the neighborhood'd come and Babe was *always* there. Let me tell you, she was the only girl, but she was also among the first to be chosen . . . . Ordinarily we didn't have anything to do with girls then. Babe was different. Once you saw her play, you didn't mind having her around."[40] Babe was a tomboy who played baseball, football, and basketball with her parents' encouragement.

Babe was born June 26, 1911, in Port Arthur, Texas. She was the sixth

of seven children of Norwegian immigrant parents. Growing up on Dou-
cette Avenue in the South End of Beaumont, Texas, in a poor, seedy
neighborhood, she learned to be tough and driven. But adversity made
her strong and single-minded in her pursuit of athletic greatness. Her life
mirrors the heroes of Horatio Alger's novels. Here was someone who went
from poverty and obscurity to become a world-class athlete and international celebrity because of hard work and perseverance.

In 1930 she dropped out of high school to become a stenographer for
Employer Causality Company of Dallas and to play basketball for the
Golden Cyclones, the company team. The company sponsored her for the
Amateur Athletic Union (A. A. U.) track and field championships in 1932.
In one afternoon she made women's sports history by breaking four world
records and winning six gold medals. One of those records was in the
baseball throw.[41]

In the 1932 Olympics in Los Angeles she gained international fame when
she won two gold medals. Besides excelling in basketball and track and
field, she was also a star in billiards, boxing, and tennis. But probably her
best sport was golf, where she won every major amateur title.[42] Among
her golf titles were the U.S. Amateur in 1946, the British Amateur in 1947,
the Ladies Professional Golf Association (LPGA) U.S. Women's Open
Championships in 1948, 1949, and 1950. In 1951 she was elected to the
Professional Golfers' Association (PGA) Hall of Fame.[43]

After the Olympics in 1932 Babe did various promotionals, and in 1933
she barnstormed across the country with Babe Didrikson's All American
basketball team. For this she was paid $1,000 a month—quite a salary
contrast to women working in the garment shops of New York, who averaged as little as $2.39 a week.[44]

In 1934 as a promotional gimmick Babe was hired by some major league
baseball teams to pitch in some of their spring training games in Florida.
Babe did not delude herself. She knew they wanted her for her name and
not her skills. In recalling a game she pitched for the Cardinals against the
Athletics, she laughingly admitted that her pitching was not up to major
league standards. "I always had pretty good control. . . . But I couldn't
seem to throw the ball past these major-leaguers."[45] And when Jimmie
Foxx came up to bat she remembered, "I . . . gave him one high, hard
one. . . . Foxx knocked it into the next county."[46] Paul Dean was way out
in the outfield trying to back her up and had to go clear out into the orange
grove to recover the ball.[47]

She had more luck when Connie Mack hired her to pitch for the Philadelphia Athletics against the Brooklyn Dodgers. She managed to strike
out the first two batters. But the sportswriter for the *New York Times* was
unimpressed. He labeled the feat "a bit of chivalry: both swung lustily at
a pair of strikes each, missing the ball by wide margins."[48]

Babe was a showwoman and loved playing to the crowd, but she hated not to have her skills taken seriously. Even when she played just for the fun of it, she played competitively and set high standards for herself. It was extremely important for her self-image to have people marvel at her athletic ability and to see her as a winner. Her ego demanded that she excel. Once during an exhibition at Yankee Stadium she missed a ground ball to the infield. This infuriated her. She ripped her skirt up the side to give herself more mobility, dug her feet in by the base, and had grounder after grounder hit to her to prove that she was a skilled infielder.[49] So although Babe knew that she was hired merely as a publicity gimmick to draw baseball fans, she still was out there to prove to everyone that she could play baseball.

She pitched in a number of other games, but the game she enjoyed the most was the one in Yankee Stadium where she pitched to Joe DiMaggio and batted against Spec Shea. Before the game she hit some golf shots and then took some infield practice. In the game when DiMaggio came up to bat she said, "All I was afraid of was that I might hit him with a pitch or that he might hit me with a batted ball."[50]

Later that spring Ray Doan, the same promoter who had previously signed her to play basketball, arranged to have her play baseball as a pitcher with the House of David touring team. They played against teams all over the country and always drew a big crowd. One of their most popular opponents was the Monarchs of the Negro League. Pepper Bassett remembered that Babe threw overhand as hard as a man.[51]

If her pitching was mediocre, her hitting was not. Emory Olive, a House of David teammate, remembered one of her hits. "Once at Logan Field in Chicago, we were playing in front of eight, nine thousand people and Babe she hit a line drive and scored, sliding into home in a cloud of dust. She won the game. The score was one to nothing."[52]

Other baseball credits of Didrikson included the fact that she could throw the ball farther than some major league outfielders (296 feet) and that in one game she hit three home runs and threw the ball 313 feet from center field to homeplate.[53]

Traveling with a men's team was always a problem for a woman. Babe solved this by traveling in her own car. She said, "I had the schedule, and I'd get to whatever ballpark they were playing at in time for the game. I'd pitch the first inning, and then I'd take off and not see them again until the next time."[54]

Her playing was purely a promotional gimmick to draw the crowds; she never really got to know the players or to feel a part of the team. From late spring to early fall the team played approximately 200 games. It was a lucrative arrangement in that she made about a $1,000 a month or more, but it was also a grueling existence, as Ruth Scurlock, an old friend from Beaumont, recalled. "This freakish circus travel she went through after the Olympics was terribly hard on her, physically and emotionally, but spiritually too. She was really drained. Her father and mother were ill a lot of the time. She must have felt such enormous pressure, and yet she had to go through with those demeaning travels and those ridiculous games."[55] Babe once lamented that she wasn't always sure "if the people were laughing with us or at me."[56]

Babe Didrikson was an individualist, a non-conformist when it came to traditional female roles, and a sportswoman, but she was not a feminist. She did not crusade for women's causes and had no interest in women's issues. A product of a lower-class background, her manner was rough. In order to succeed she had to believe in herself, and believe in herself she did. Rather than being embarrassed by her rough Texas upbringing, Babe revelled in it. She enjoyed shocking people and being seen as somewhat unconventional. On the golf circuit, she enjoyed making earthy remarks that often shocked the country club crowd but endeared her to the press and the public. Babe loved the limelight and loved the adoration of the fans. But as Betty Hicks, a professional golfer in the 1950s, was to lament by gaining publicity in this way Babe "helped to perpetuate a cruel myth about women athletes—the myth that we weren't quite women. This myth flourished in the '30s and '40s and was to become an enormous burden to those of us who were Babe's contemporaries in golf in the '50s."[57]

Babe, however, did not totally reject all of society's feminine conventions. She hated the fact that the press had referred to her as a "muscle moll." She wanted to be seen as a woman and not as a physical freak. Tremendously ambitious, Babe had tunnel vision concerning her goal of being a female athlete. She did what she thought she had to do to become a world-class athlete at a time when it was almost impossible to be considered feminine and a serious athlete at the same time. She realized that the world of competitive athletes was a rough business. Babe Didrikson died in Augusta, Florida, on September 27, 1956 from cancer. She was only forty-two.[58]

KITTY BURKE

The next woman to burst on the scene in baseball was twenty-five-year-old Kitty Burke, a nightclub blues singer. And burst on the field she did on July 31, 1935, at Crosley Field in Cincinnati. It was a night game between the Cincinnati Reds and the World Champion Cardinals. Over 30,000 fans attended the game, and it was estimated that 8,000 of them could not find seats and stood behind homeplate and along the base lines. Kitty Burke was standing approximately ten feet behind homeplate watching the game when she became incensed that Joe "Ducky" Medwick, the Cardinals left fielder, had scored to give the Cardinals a two-run lead over the Reds. When he came to bat in the eighth inning, Kitty began to heckle him by yelling, "You couldn't hit Freitas [the pitcher] with an ironing board." He screamed back, "You couldn't hit if you were swinging an elephant." Kitty waited until the Reds got up to bat. Then she ran up to Babe Herman, grabbed his bat, and went to the plate. The umpire yelled, "Play ball," and Paul "Daffy" Dean, the Cardinals pitcher, lobbed the ball to her. She hit it and raced off to first, where she was declared out. The whole thing was like something out of a cartoon. The Cardinals' manager then protested that the out should count and that it was the third out. He was overruled and Babe Herman came to bat. Herman hit a double and the Reds won 4–3.[59]

Kitty later said that when she went to the plate, she was determined to "sock one if I had to stay there all night."[60] So she goes down in the history books as the only woman to bat in a National League regular-season game even if was unofficial.

FRANCES DUNLOP

Frances "Sonny" Dunlop played for the Fayetteville Bears against the Cassville Blues in a class D minor league game in the Arkansas-Missouri League on September 7, 1936. Since there was no advance publicity, baseball officials failed to stop her play. She went hitless in three times at bat and met no action in right field. The *Fayetteville Daily Democrat*, September 8, 1936, wrote, "As far as it is known here, Miss Dunlop probably is the first girl in history to play an entire game of organized baseball."[61] Apparently that was her first and only game in organized baseball.

BETTY EVANS

Betty Evans was nicknamed "Bullet Evans" for her pitching skills as a softball pitcher. In 1948 she pitched an exhibition session in Portland Park, Oregon, for the Class AAA Pacific Coast Baseball League. She struck out six of nine players. Morris Bealle wrote, "Her feat of striking out six of nine near major leaguers still causes red faces in the American League when certain players think of it."[62]

CONCLUSION

With the exception of "Bullet Evans," all of the women in this chapter participated in baseball in the 1930s. It seems hard to believe that a period marked by economic uncertainty and social upheaval would offer women a unique opportunity to be a part of baseball. Certainly some would say that these women were exploited by men for purely economic reasons; that the novelty of women ball players was used by management to get publicity and to increase gate receipts. And there is no doubt that this was one important motive. But if it had not been for the 1920s, the Golden Age of Sports, women would not even have been considered for this role. The 1920s brought athletes national celebrity status. Sportswriters created a public interest in sports of all types and produced male and female sports heroes. In baseball Babe Ruth became a cultural hero. He symbolized the American ideal of success. Here was a poor, talented youth who made it to the top—a rags-to-riches story. Other male sports stars of the time were Knute Rockne in football, Bill Tilden in tennis, and Joe Lewis, Jack Dempsey, and Gene Tunney in boxing.

Women also proved that they could accomplish fantastic athletic feats. Gertrude Ederle, a New Yorker, not only became the first woman to swim the English Channel but also took two hours off the existing record beating all male records. Her record stood until 1964.[63] A Norwegian, Sonja Henie, set a record by winning gold medals in figure skating in the 1928, 1932, and 1936 Olympics. After her Olympic career ended, she starred in her own ice capades, the Hollywood Ice Review, and became a 20th Century Fox movie star. She made ten movies with co-stars such as Tyrone Power and Don Ameche.[64] It is estimated that she earned over $40 million.[65] And of course, Babe Didrikson, the Texan, who won two gold medals in the 1932 Olympics in Los Angeles was the perfect American heroine. The poor immigrant girl from the backwoods of Texas who made good. This was the stuff of which American dreams were made.

Cashing in on her popularity, major league promoters offered Didrikson $500 a night to do exhibition baseball games.[66] It was a good way to receive newspaper coverage and to get the fans to come out to the ball park. With few other opportunities available to her after the Olympics, Babe was willing to cash in on her fame. So it was of mutual benefit economically. Even though she was not trained in baseball and did not aspire to a baseball career, no one questioned her athletic ability. It was great sport to see her hit a few golf balls to the outfield, take third base practice, and pitch a few balls in the regular game.

Jackie Mitchell, Vada Corbus, and Frances Dunlop were entirely different than Babe Didrikson in that they were serious ball players who would have liked to have had professional careers. Although some minor league owners would have liked to have had a few women players as added attractions, the powerful men of baseball would not allow it. So the careers of Vada Corbus and Frances Dunlop ended abruptly. Jackie Mitchell fared slightly better, but her only day in the sun was April 2, when she went down in history as the pitcher who struck out Babe Ruth and Lou Gehrig. Kitty Burke was basically a baseball fan and an entertainer.

Baseball has since become more professional and less small-town. America has become more sophisticated. There will be no future Jackie Mitchells or Babe Didriksons to pitch against the majors. The crazy stunts of the 1920s and 1930s are now history. No women softball stars or ex–Little Leaguers will be offered the opportunity to pitch against batters of such fame as George Brett or Bobby Bonilla.

NOTES

1. Benjamin Rader, *American Sports: From the Age of Folk Games to the Age of Televised Sports*, 2nd ed. (Englewood Cliffs, N.J.: Prentice-Hall, 1990), 169.

2. "What Next: A Lady Ball Player," *Times Union*, 3 May 1970, Sec. C.

3. Lee Allen, *The Hot Stove League* (New York: A.S. Barnes & Co., 1955), 188.

4. Ibid., 189.

5. "Girl, 17, to Pitch against Babe Ruth for Chattanooga," 28 March 1931, newspaper clipping, NBHFL.

6. "Makes Debut Today against Babe Ruth, Jackie Mitchell," *Chattanooga News*, 2 April 1931.

7. Jack Orr, "The Girl Who Struck out Babe Ruth," June 1954, newspaper clipping, NBHFL.

8. William Jeanes, "High Jinks or High Skill? Jackie Mitchell Fanned Ruth and Gehrig in Her Pro Debut," *Sports Illustrated*, 4 April 1988, 131.

9. Qtd. in Cy Yoakam, "She Struck out Babe Ruth," *Sports Heritage*, March/April 1987, 25.

10. Allen, 189; David Jenkins, "Jackie Will Always Be 17," *Chattanooga News–Free Press*, 8 Jan. 1987, Sec. D.

11. Yoakam, 24–25.

12. Rud Rennie, "Jackie Mitchell Lasted for 3 Batters as Sluggers Turned Gag into Farce," *New York Herald Tribune*, 23 June 1952.

13. Morris Bealle, *The Softball Story* (Washington, D.C.: Columbia Pub. Co., 1957), 165.

14. "When Baseball's First Feminine Pitcher Struck out 'Mighty' Babe," *Chattanooga News*, 3 April 1931.

15. William Mann, "The Girl Who Struck out Babe Ruth," *National Enquirer*, 6 March 1982.

16. "When Baseball's First Feminine Pitcher Struck out 'Mighty' Babe."

17. Jackie Mitchell for United News, "Jackie Sure Mr. Ruth Was Mad at Umpire, Not Her: Girl Hurler Sees Nothing Strange about Striking out Bambino, Gehrig," 3 April 1931, NBHFL.

18. Bob McCoy, "Keeping Score: A Crafty Southpaw," 5 July 1982, newspaper clipping, NBHFL.

19. "Woman Players in Organized Baseball," *SABR Baseball Research Journal*, 1983, 159.

20. "Pro Baseball's First Girl Hurler Graduate of Elberfeld's School," *Chattanooga News*, 31 March 1931.

21. Betty Thomas, "The Day a Babe Struck out Ruth," *Chattanooga Life and Leisure*, July 1985, 24.

22. Yoakam, 90.

23. Ibid.

24. David Jenkins, "Jackie to 'Pitch' at Engel Stadium," *Chattanooga News–Free Press*, 11 April 1982, Sec. E.

25. Charles Moritz, *Current Biography* (New York: H.W. Wilson Co., 1947), 702.

26. Yoakam, 23; Jenkins, "Jackie to 'Pitch' at Engel Stadium."

27. "Girl Who Struck out Babe Dies in Fort Oglethorpe," *Chattanooga Times*, 8 Jan. 1987, Sec. D.

28. Mann.

29. Thomas.

30. McCoy.

31. Jeanes, 131.

32. Allan Morris, "Jackie Mitchell, Now Retired, Recall . . . She Fanned the Babe, Gehrig," *Chattanooga News–Free Press*, 9 July 1975, Sec. A.

33. Jenkins, "Jackie to 'Pitch' at Engel Stadium."

34. "Pro Baseball's First Girl Hurler Graduate of Elberfeld's School."

35. Ibid.

36. "Baseball Rules out Chattanooga Girl," 23 June 1952, newspaper clipping, NBHFL.

37. Yoakam, 90.

38. David Jenkins, "Jackie Mitchell a Winner in First Visit to Atlanta Stadium," *Chattanooga News–Free Press* 14 July 1985, Sec. E.

39. "Woman Players in Organized Baseball."

40. William Johnson and Nancy Williamson, *"Whatta-Gal": The Babe Didrikson Story* (Boston: Little, Brown, 1977), 35, 53–54.

41. Rader, 208.

42. "Babe Zaharias Dies at 42, Once Pitched for Cardinals," newspaper obituary, NBHFL.

43. Robert Markel, Nancy Brooks, and Susan Markel, *For the Record: Women in Sports* (New York: World Almanac Pub., 1985), 49.

44. Johnson and Williamson, 126.

45. Babe Didrikson Zaharias as told to Harry Paxton, *This Life I've Led* (New York: A.S. Barnes & Co., 1955), 183.

46. "Babe Zaharias Dies at 42."

47. Zaharias, 183.

48. Qtd. in Johnson and Williamson, 128.

49. Betty Hicks, "Babe Didrikson Zaharias, 'Stand Back! This Ain't No Kid Hitting,' " *WomenSports* (November 1975) 183–184.

50. Zaharias, 181.

51. Donn Rogosin, *Invisible Men: Life in Baseball's Negro Leagues* (New York: Atheneum, 1983), 137.

52. Johnson and Williamson, 129.

53. Moritz, 701.

54. Zaharias, 82.

55. Qtd. in Johnson and Williamson, 128–129.

56. Zaharias, 35.

57. Hicks, 28.

58. Betty Spears, "The Emergence of Women in Sport," in *Women's Athletics: Coping with Controversy*, ed. Barbara Hoepner (Oakland, Calif: DGWS Pub., 1974), 219.

59. Information compiled from newspaper articles: "Another Red Innovation," 8 Aug. 1935, NBHFL; "This Woman Did Bat in the Majors," *Albany Times Union*, 31 July 1985; "The Only Girl to Bat in the Major League," *National Enquirer*, 18 April 1986.

60. "This Woman Did Bat in the Majors."

61. Qtd. in "Woman Players in Organized Baseball," 161.

62. Bealle, 168.

63. Markel, 130.

64. Ibid., 74.

65. Wilbert Leonard, II, *A Sociological Perspective of Sport*, 3rd ed. (New York: MacMillan, 1988), 38.

66. Johnson and Williamson, 183.

6

Little League: Yes, Virginia, Little Girls Were Allowed to Play Baseball before 1974

It took a Supreme Court decision and an act of Congress to permit girls to play Little League baseball in 1974. Allowing little girls to play baseball with boys was heralded as a modern phenomenon. Many people gave credit to the women's liberation movement of the 1960s. Yet girls were playing baseball at Miss Porter's School, an exclusive girls preparatory school, as early as 1867, and Margaret Gisolo played American Legion junior baseball in 1928. But when the media discussed the issue of whether or not girls should be allowed to participate in Little League, no mention was made of these earlier players. How were girls barred from playing Little League, American Legion, and other forms of organized baseball?

In the late 1800s and early 1900s, girls at some of the most exclusive Eastern boarding schools such as Miss Porter's and Miss Hall's were playing baseball. Physical exercise such as walking and calisthenics had always been considered an important part of the curriculum, but these activities were not very popular among the girls. When some students suggested playing baseball, some headmistresses permitted it. In 1867 Miss Porter allowed the girls to form the Tunix Baseball Club with the stipulation that the games could not be seen from the road.[1] Although she worried about public reaction to their playing, neither Miss Porter nor her charges felt that by playing they were asserting women's rights. In fact, Miss Porter was a traditionalist. She believed that men's schools such as Yale taught men business and political skills and finishing schools such as her own taught girls to be useful wives.[2]

Although Miss Porter considered baseball just another form of physical activity for the girls, some parents did not. When some of the parents heard that Trinity College, a men's college in nearby Hartford, had challenged the girls to a game, they immediately wrote letters of protest.[3] The team was disbanded. But the spirit of baseball did not die. According to Isobell V. Hill's scrapbook, the team was active again the next season. It is not known if the club continued after 1868, although tintypes of an 1890 team and the 1902–1903 New Girl Old Girl game are in the library archives and there is also reference to an 1898 and a 1909 team. This suggests that baseball may have been played in intervening years as well.[4]

In 1905 two baseball teams were formed at Miss Hall's girls' school in Pittsfield, Massachusetts. The girls played in long pleated skirts with blouses with high collars. No doubt the outfits restricted movement and were hot on warm spring days.[5]

It is difficult to determine if baseball was played at other early girls' schools because no official records were kept. Letters, diaries, and alumnae reminiscences would be the only reference. Letters of inquiry to Rosemary Hall in Wallingford, Connecticut, Westover School in Middlebury, Connecticut, and the Emma Willard School (earlier the Troy Female Seminary) in Troy, New York, came back negative. A letter from Mrs. Hare, assistant librarian at the Masters School in Dobbs Ferry, New York, resulted in a more hedged response. Although she had found nothing to suggest baseball was played there, she was not sure that a more thorough search of memorabilia might not turn up something. It is likely that girls at other private schools also played the game.

Some form of baseball was played in many of the public schools in the early 1900s. For example in 1919 baseball was a girls' organized activity in New York's Public School Athletic League. A 1920 survey of Cleveland schools indicated that 91 percent of the high school girls played baseball.[6]

Baseball skills were part of a 1922 Playground Association Athletic Badge. Girls were awarded the badge on the basis of tests for balancing, running for speed, throwing a baseball for accuracy, throwing a baseball for distance, and demonstrating expertise in one of three games—baseball, basketball, or volleyball.[7]

In rural areas in the United States some girls grew up playing ball with their brothers and no one thought much about it. The role model for the athletic girl, or tomboy, was well established by the late 1800s with the character of Jo in Louisa May Alcott's *Little Women*. Although tomboys were exceptions, it was considered a stage that a few little girls went through and nothing to be concerned with. Margaret Gisolo was one such girl in Indiana.

MARGARET GISOLO: FIRST GIRL TO PLAY AMERICAN LEGION JUNIOR BASEBALL

What makes Margaret Gisolo's history unique is that she played American Legion baseball in 1928. One year later the rules were changed to exclude girls. From its beginning in 1939 Little League specified that the program was for boys only. It was not until 1974 that a court order opened Little League participation to girls. That decision coupled with Title IX paved the way for girls to play American Legion ball as well.

The American Legion junior baseball program was begun in 1925 with the specific intent of "extending athletic competition to more boys in America" and to "forward physical development, teach good sportsmanship, and make boys better American citizens."[8] In 1926, the first year of competition, fifteen states had established leagues; three years later all departments of the American Legion had teams.[9] The program was enthusiastically supported both by the American Legion posts and major league baseball. Beginning in 1928, under the leadership of Kenesaw Mountain Landis, the commissioner of baseball, $20,000 to $50,000 a year was contributed to the program. Part of this money was to be used for regional and national championships. The investment was a good one because by 1946 the American Legion program had produced more than 161 professional ball players.[10]

There is no doubt that American Legion junior baseball was conceived of as a boys' program and no thought was given to girls playing. The issue of girls playing became an explosive one in 1928 when the Blanford, Indiana, team defeated the Clinton, Indiana, team in the first game of the county championship. In the twelfth inning of a tied game Margaret Gisolo batted in the winning run to have Blanford win by a score of 8–7. Clinton immediately filed a protest stating that Blanford should have to forfeit the game because the team was ineligible because girls were not allowed to play.[11] They stated that the rule book said, "Any boy is eligible to play." A. V. Stringfellow, the person in charge of the local tournament, suspended Margaret for six days pending the outcome of the decision.[12] In the meantime the tournament officials passed the complaint on to the Indiana State baseball chairman, who in turn forwarded the complaint to the national office in Indianapolis.

By this time Margaret Gisolo was big news. Right after the game the headline in the *Hoosier Legionnaire* read, "Blanford Juniors Claim Girl 'Babe Ruth.' "[13] The local paper, the *Daily Clintonian*, said, "Girl Player Wins Game in 12th with Single."[14] The headline in the *Daily Clintonian* on June 20, 1928, read, "Will Blanford Have First Girl in a World Series?" It was a feature article on Margaret. Probably to the embarrassment of the Clinton Baptist junior team, the article went on to say that Clinton could "lay claim to the unique distinction of being the first ball club to ever be beaten by a safe hit off a girl's bat in a championship affair."[15]

The newspapers were well aware that the novelty of a girl playing would sell papers. Officials of the American Legion were also aware that the media could have a field day over the issue. Perhaps they worried about adverse publicity if they ruled her ineligible, or perhaps they thought that

16. Margaret Gisolo. *Courtesy of Margaret Gisolo.*

the publicity surrounding Margaret would be good for the program. No one really knows. But the American Legion went to great lengths to make sure the final decision was well thought out. Dan Sowers, the Americanism Commission director, decided the appropriate person to make the decision was Kenesaw Mountain Landis, the commissioner of major league baseball.[16]

Sowers met with Landis June 30, 1928. After that meeting he released this press statement:

> While the National Junior Baseball Program of the American Legion did not contemplate the participation of girls, . . . In view of the services of our women in the World War and The American Legion and the American Legion Auxiliary, it is held that Margaret Gisolo should not be barred on account of her sex.[17]

A Detroit newspaper headline read, "Good Decision." A media blitz had been set in motion. Newspapers across the country followed the progress of Margaret's Blanford team.

The Blanford team won the second game of the series 13–6 against Clinton to win the Vermilion County championship and to advance to the district playoffs in Terre Haute. Again Margaret was credited with outstanding play. "Covering the keystone sack adeptly, the Gisolo girl stabbed one out of the air to start a double play that retired the Baptist nine in the fifth frame, the only inning in which the Clinton nine was threatened.[18]

Still the decision was not final. A third game had to be played when officials discovered that one of Blanford's players was several weeks over the seventeen-years-of-age age limit.[19] The series then went to a third game, which Blanford won by a score of 5–2.[20]

Margaret by now was definitely the girl everyone wanted to see play. Terre Haute fans were so delighted at the chance to see Margaret Gisolo play that they set up a five-inning exhibition game with the Terre Haute Red Rovers.[21] Margaret pitched so that the Vigo champs would not gain an advantage by seeing Blanford's star pitcher.[22] Blanford won the exhibition game 7–5, and the "Terre Haute fans praised the girl's playing and credited the Blanford team with being a strong aggregation."[23] Blanford went on to win the district title against the Terre Haute Blue Devils 6–5 to advance to the sectional tournament. Margaret's fielding again was cited. "Margaret, holding down second base, handled six changes without a bobble to share fielding honors with Nelson."[24]

A Terre Haute, Indiana, July 9 newspaper headline read, "Boys Bank on Girl Slugger in Legion's Sandlot Tourney." The article went on to say, "Margaret Gisolo . . . prima donna of the diamond, will be the main attraction in the district finals of the American Legion's state junior baseball contest here."[25] Another news article read, "The little Italian maid is the cause of considerable disruption in the ranks of the tourney just because she can hit, field and run better than most boys her age."[26]

In a practice exhibition game with the Universal, Indiana, team, the Blanford Cubs decisively beat the Universal Juniors 12–2.[27] Blanford's winning streak was unbroken. The headline in the local paper read, "Margaret Has Perfect Day."[28] There was great speculation as to whether the Blanford team could continue its winning streak and win the sectional title. The Blanford players went on to beat Jasonville 7–3 and then Evansville 26–7 for the sectional championship. In the Evansville game Margaret won the sportsmanship award for her sectional tournament play. They now advanced to the state tournament having won the county, district, and sectional championships.

In the first round of the state tournament they beat St. Phillips, 17–3.[29] They then went on to win the state title against the Gary Yankees.

> Displaying a fighting spirit and comeback power that could not be denied, the Blanford Cubs defeated the Gary Yankees 14–12. . . . It was a powerful hitting attack unleashed by Sungali, Taparo, and Margaret Gisolo that carried the Cubs to their margin of victory. . . . Margaret Gisolo shined with unusual brilliance around the keystone sack, making two sensational catches of line drives, and featuring in one double play. The girl star has not made an error in seven games of tourney play.[30]

Margaret's Blanford team then played two exhibitions games against the Terre Haute All-Stars before going on to the regionals in Chicago. They won both games.[31] It seemed that the team was unbeatable.

Blanford town officials were so delighted with the team that they held a banquet for them at the Clinton Hotel before they left for Chicago. Local merchants collected $20 toward the purchase of new baseball shoes. The team left in a special Pullman car and three Pullmans were chartered by Blanford, Clinton, and St. Bernice fans for the trip to Chicago.[32] This was probably the biggest thing that had ever happened to Blanford, a coal-mining town of less than 1,000. The nine players, their coach, and their manager were local celebrities.

But they were not to be national champions. In the first game of the American Legion interstate regional baseball tournament in Comiskey Park, the Blanford Cubs lost 5–12 to Marine Post 273 of Chicago. The winning streak was over, and they were eliminated from the tournament. If they had won, they would have played the winner of the Ohio-Michigan game for the national championship. In four times at bat Margaret singled, walked, and sacrificed. She scored one run and batted in another. Her fielding was flawless. She made three fielding catches without an error.[33] The *Daily Clintonian* commented, "Margaret Gisolo, scintillating girl second baseman on a championship team in a boys' tourney, electrified the Chicago fans with her sensational playing around the keystone bag."[34] As the *New York Times* stated, "Margaret starred in defeat."[35] Her batting average for the seven-tournament games was .429. She fielded ten put outs and twenty-eight assists without an error.[36]

Margaret had become a national celebrity. Newspapers across the country ran articles on the team and featured her. Movietone News did a short sketch about her that appeared in all the theaters.

One sportswriter was so excited about Margaret that he suggested, "Perhaps it won't be long before some young lady will break into the lineup of a professional baseball team." His news release made it seem that women were a real threat. The headline read, "Girls Usurping National Sport: Suffrage Now Extends from Ballot Box to Baseball Diamonds." The headline was based on the fact that the season of 1928 saw three firsts for girls: Margaret Gisolo played in the American Legion junior baseball championships; Alice Buckman made the Griswold, Indiana, boys' high school team and became a star; and Carmela Yull, a fifteen-year-old New York girl, made the West Side Rangers team.[37] But the women's victories were to be short-lived.

Margaret Gisolo's fame, unfortunately, wasn't destined to pave the way for other little girls to play baseball. Although Margaret was only fourteen and the American Legion junior baseball program was designed for players through age sixteen, Margaret's career came to an abrupt end. In 1929 the American Legion barred girls from playing. Robert Bushee, department athletic officer of the legion and state tournament director, gave the reason for the rule change as purely financial. The American Legion could not afford the added expense of having female chaperones, especially since many girls would want to play, having heard about Margaret.[38]

Margaret and her parents accepted the decision, as did the public. There were no femininist groups to take up her cause. Although Margaret and her parents accepted the fact that American Legion baseball was for boys only, baseball continued to be an avenue of opportunity for Margaret. A few months after the American Legion decision she received a letter from the Pulaski Baseball Club Booking Agency asking her to play for a team made up of college girls and two or three men. In case her parents worried about her care, they were told, "We have a strong female with the Club as Chaperone of the Girls who will care for them as their own."[39] The team, the American Athletic Girls Base Ball Club, was based in Chicago and managed by Rose Figg. Margaret spent the 1929 season on the road with the team. She was just fourteen and had finished her sophomore year in high school.

The seasons of 1930, 1932, 1933, and 1934 she played for another Chicago barnstorming team, the All Star Ranger Girls Baseball Club, owned by Maud Nelson Olson, former Bloomer Girl star. They played local men's teams. In 1931 she played the first half of the season for the All Star Rangers and the second half for the Hollywood Movie Stars baseball team.

Margaret's playing never interfered with her schooling. She graduated in 1931 from Clinton High School and enrolled in Indiana State Teacher's College (ISTC) in Terre Haute. Unfortunately, ISTC did not have intercollegiate sports competition for women, so her sporting talents were confined to intramural play. During the summers, however, she was employed as a baseball player and earned money for college. In 1935 she received her B.S. degree in physical education and in 1942 received an M.A. in physical education with an emphasis on administration. In 1954 she joined the faculty of physical education at Arizona State University and developed the dance major for the school. In 1979 she received the distinguished teacher award from the Arizona State University Alumni Association.[40] In 1980 she retired as a full professor.

After her retirement she began playing tennis. The 1990 United States Tennis Association (USTA) *Tennis Yearbook* ranked her number two nationally in singles and doubles in the seventy-five-year-old age group. At seventy-six she still remains an outstanding athlete.

THE ADVENT OF SOFTBALL

Although Margaret Gisolo goes down in history as the first girl to play organized junior baseball, it was not unusual for girls in the 1920s to play sandlot baseball with their brothers. Softball, although invented in 1897, really didn't become popular until the 1930s. Softball as a sport for girls was just becoming established when Margaret played baseball. Softball got its foothold in 1926 when Gladys Palmer published a modified set of rules for girls' baseball. Although Palmer agreed that baseball as played by men was unsuitable for girls, she believed that a modified version had educational merit for girls.[41]

In April 1927 the Sub-Committee on Baseball of the National Committee on Women's Athletics of the American Physical Education Association met for the first time. At this meeting the 1926 rules were again slightly modified. This version of baseball with smaller base paths helped pave the way for softball to be accepted as an alternative form of baseball for women. Physical educators were adamant that women's sports should be less strenuous than men's and that women should not compete in interscholastic sports.[42] In trying to make sure that girls' games remained low key and that all girls could participate, they substituted play days for interscholastic competition. Along the way, softball became substituted for baseball in the school and community recreational programs.

It was during the 1920s that the transition from baseball to softball for girls became complete. In 1933 the Amateur Softball Association made the term *softball* official, and this name was substituted for the modified baseball games that girls had been playing.[43] Softball was now a sport distinct from baseball and came to be accepted as an appropriate female sport. Baseball was seen as a purely male sport.

As Darlene Mehrer lamented in 1987 on the one-hundredth anniversary of softball, "How, in one short century, has this ersatz sport [softball] so strangled the consciousness of the country in the grip of its flabby tentacles that the mention of women's *baseball* gets no reaction other than blank amazement?"[44]

The establishment of softball virtually ended girls' chances to participate in baseball. Because of this Mehrer said, "Happy Birthday, Softball, Wish You'd Never Been Born."[45] She equated the origin of softball in Chicago with other great Chicago tragedies. "Lots of things started in Chicago—the Chicago Fire, the St. Valentine's Day Massacre, the Black Sox Scandal. Softball fits right in."[46]

1939 LITTLE LEAGUE ESTABLISHED FOR BOYS ONLY

Certainly when Carl Stotz founded Little League baseball in Williamsport, Pennsylvania, in 1939, the idea of little girls playing baseball never entered his mind. The program was designed for boys ages eight to twelve for the purpose of "developing qualities of citizenship, sportsmanship, and manhood."[47] Manhood and baseball had become almost synonymous.

Because of World War II, Little League baseball really did not get started until the late 1940s. By the 1950s Little League had become an American institution. The 1950s also brought a resurgence of the Victorian image of femininity. The division between the sexes that had become blurred during the war was now distinct again. Women were envisioned as the frailer sex whose roles in life were as mothers and wives. Cheerleading was in, while active participation in sports for girls was out. Consequently, Little League baseball as a male prerogative was not to be challenged.

Donna Terry did manage to slip through Little League's masculine cracks in 1958, however. The team she joined played a game against the Little League All Stars. She was the only girl on a team composed of sons of U.S. Navy personnel stationed in Puerto Rico. Pitching in the first inning of the game, she struck out three players. In the second, she walked the first batter, struck out the second. Then the tell-tale sign of her femininity, her pony-tail, fell down her back. She was declared ineligible, and Little League barred her from playing baseball with boys in Puerto Rico. There was no protest, and she moved on to softball.[48]

On July 16, 1964, President Lyndon B. Johnson signed Public Law 88–378, which gave Little League a federal charter of incorporation and tax-exempt status. As a boys' organization Little League now had government recognition. By law Little League was to " 'promote Americanism' in thirty countries besides the United States and to file an annual report of its financial status and future goals with the Judiciary Committee of the House of Representatives."[49]

Little League was accepted as a boys' organization. In 1966, however, one spunky little girl, Charlene Rowe, in Charlotte, North Carolina, decided that if Little League would not let her play, she would form her own team. Her team took on all challengers. The following year she decided they needed a sponsor. So she called Phil Howser, president and general manager of Charlotte's Southern League Club. Mr. Howser said that he would sponsor the team if they would call themselves the Junior Hornets. Her mother claims her daughter did all this on her own. "Unknown to us, she called Mr. Howser and told him they needed a sponsor."[50]

Charlene apparently came by her talents naturally. Her father, Ralph Rowe, was a twenty-six-year veteran of baseball and coached Orlando Florida State.[51] Charlene had excellent skills. As her coach, Jack Williams, said, "She's as good as any of the boys. None of the boys we play against would dare kid her. They know they can't beat her."[52]

But it took until 1973 for parents of girls who wanted to play Little League to take up the gauntlet for equal rights. This is forty-five years after Margaret Gisolo played American Legion junior baseball and a decade after the women's liberation movement began in the 1960s.

It was the enactment of Title IX of the Education Amendments of 1972 amending the Civil Rights Act of 1964 that cleared the legal way for equality of opportunity in sports for women. Title IX states:

> No person in the United States shall on the basis of sex be excluded from participation in, be denied the benefits of, or be subjected to discrimination under any educational program or activity receiving Federal financial assistance.[53]

Psychologically, the Bobby Riggs and Billie Jean King tennis match of 1973 heightened public awareness of the issue of women in sports. Billed as the battle of the sexes, Bobby Riggs played on the promotional aspect that no woman could ever beat a man. The event received national press coverage and was televised across the nation. Male and female pride rested on the outcome. When Billie Jean King beat an aging Bobby Riggs handily, it was seen as a victory for women of all ages. It became a catalyst for piquing little girls' interest in sports and making their participation with boys seem possible.

It is estimated that between 1973 and 1974 fifty-seven lawsuits were filed against Little League, Inc., on behalf of girls.[54] Several of these were dismissed by state federal courts on the grounds that they lacked jurisdiction. Probably one of the most publicized cases was that of Carolyn King of Ypsilanti, Michigan. In 1973 Carolyn King, age twelve, tried out for Little League in Ypsilanti and was assigned to the Orioles. Her coach, Wayne Warren, made the statement, "This little girl had enough intestinal fortitude to come down to our tryout with all those boys, and I feel she deserves a chance." William Anhut, the president of the local chapter, upheld her right to play in defiance of national Little Leagues rules.[55]

Even before Carolyn had a chance to play, the national office of Little League revoked Ypsilanti's charter and said that it was sending officials from the national office to set up a new franchise with new personnel. Robert Stirrat, an official of the national Little League organization, argued that Little League was not discriminating against girls. Rather, Little League was acting in the girls' best interests by protecting them from harm. "We're not discriminating, . . . we just believe, from all available medical evidence, it's hazardous for boys and girls to play together in a contact sport like baseball."[56]

Taylor, the vice president of the local chapter, said that he couldn't understand how the organization could revoke the charter since she hadn't even played. The Ypsilanti local officials had voted 8–2 to allow Carolyn to play but had postponed her play until May 15 in order to gain support for her cause.[57]

The Ypsilanti chapter then sought a court injunction to stop action by the national organization. Little League, Inc., argued successfully that the Michigan courts had no jurisdiction over the case.[58] The town of Ypsilanti then started its own unaffiliated Little League program for boys and girls.[59] Similar cases were unsuccessful in Fairfax County, Virginia, and Portland, Oregon. The majority of cities dropped their protests.[60]

A ten-year-old California girl, Jenny Fuller, wrote a letter to President Nixon to complain that she hadn't been allowed to try out for Little League for two years. Her protest fell on deaf ears.[61] The issue, however, came before the Mills Valley City Council, which voted to deny Little League the use of town fields. Interestingly enough, the only vote against the resolution came from the female mayor, Jean Bernard. She commented, "There is very little difference between the sexes except in muscle power. Vive le difference!"[62]

In Ossining, New York, nine-year-old Elizabeth Cosin was told she couldn't try out for a team but that she could be its mascot.[63] Other girls challenged Little League's male exclusiveness, but it was the Maria Pepe case in New Jersey that finally brought about the rule change. In 1971 eleven-year-old Maria Pepe signed up to play Little League baseball in Hoboken, New Jersey. The national Little League headquarters contacted the Hoboken chapter and said that she was ineligible to play. If Hoboken permitted her to play, it would lose its Little League charter. Reluctantly, the local chapter told her she could not play.[64]

But, the issue didn't end here. The Essex chapter of the National Organization for Women (NOW) brought a class action suit in New Jersey state's Division of Civil Rights on behalf of Maria and any other girls who might want to play Little League baseball. NOW argued that Little League was guilty of sexual discrimination and that the organization was under the legal jurisdiction of Title IX because Little League used public recreational facilities (town fields) and in some instances town funds.[65]

The executive vice president of national Little League, Dr. Creighton Hale, argued that girls shouldn't be allowed to play for their own safety. He stated that girls have more fragile bones, slower reaction times by .002 of a second, and were physically weaker than boys.[66] Hale cited numerous medical studies to back up his claims.[67]

Dr. Sydney Cohlan, professor of pediatrics at New York Medical Center, countered this argument with the statement that "an active, competitive girl between 9 and 12 who wants to make the team is probably as strong and able as the average boy of that age. From 9 to 12 girls are as physically fit to play baseball as the boys."[68] As to differences in reaction time, Dr. Arthur Hohmuth, child psychologist, said that girls actually had a faster reaction time than boys from the ages of eight to twelve.[69]

Dr. Thomas Johnson, child psychologist from San Diego, testified that little girls and little boys should not be forced to play together because it would be bad for their mental health. He argued that nine- to twelve-year-old boys and girls preferred to be with their own sex.[70] This argument was struck down by Dr. Antonia Giancotti, a Hackensack, New Jersey psychiatrist, who claimed that mixed participation actually contributed to mental health.[71]

Miss Wenning of NOW pointed out that separation of the sexes was ridiculous. "We expect adult men and women to be able to work and function together on a cooperative basis. Yet all their growing up years they are separated and the differences between them are pointed out. They haven't been given the chance to cooperate as children, so how can they be expected to cooperate as adults?"[72]

Little League then switched the argument from one of the girl's safety to the fact that Little League was not a public accommodation and, therefore, not subject to Title IX. The court ruled against the league with one dissenting opinion. The majority opinion was that "Little League is a public accommodation because the invitation to play is open to children in the community at large with no restriction (other than sex) whatever. It is public in the added sense that characteristically local governmental bodies made the playing areas available to the local leagues."[73]

Although safety, medical concerns, and need of privacy were all cited as reasons that girls should not be allowed to play, the underlying reason was that men didn't want little girls to play. Yogi Berra probably summed up the emotional sentiment of many men when he said, "Why don't the girls play softball and shut up?"[74]

Fortunately, legal minds prevailed. Sylvia Pressler, the hearing officer, ruled November 7, 1973, in favor of girls being allowed to play Little League baseball. She said, "The institution of Little League is as American as the hot dog and apple pie. . . . There's no reason why that part of Americana should be withheld from girls."[75]

The case was then appealed to the Appellate Division, which on January 30, 1974, upheld the Division on Civil Rights order that Little League admit girls. But the decision didn't sit well with Little League supporters. Nearly all of the New Jersey Little League teams continued to refuse to permit girls to sign up and suspended operations.[76] A petition with 50,000 signatures protesting the decision was sent to the state legislature. Assemblyman Christopher Jackman introduced a bill to permit Little League to operate one year without girls regardless of the court ruling. The bill was barely beaten by a 39–38 vote.[77]

National Little League headquarters, bowing to legal pressure, finally backed down and said that it would "defer to the changing social climate" and let girls play. Peter J. McGovern, board chairman and chief executive officer of Little League, Inc., said a petition had been sent to the Judiciary Committee of the House of Representatives asking the committee to revise Little League's charter.[78] Congress changed the wording of the charter so that the word *boy* was replaced by *young people*. The purpose of the league was changed to read "to instill citizenship and sportsmanship" and the word *manhood* was struck.[79] It was a hard-fought battle, but girls had finally won the right to join Little Leagues across the country. Most Little Leagues in New Jersey and across the country complied with the ruling, but often reluctantly. Vincent Geloso of the Union, New Jersey, Little League said to the press, "Most of us didn't want the girls playing, but we figured, rather than penalize 500 boys by not having any baseball at all, we would let the girls play."[80]

Unfortunately, the decision came too late for Maria Pepe. She was then thirteen and too old to play.[81] However, her case paved the way for other little girls to play Little League and other forms of organized ball. But the numbers of girls who played were not as high as might have been expected because Little League quickly established a softball league, which siphoned off most of the girls.

Since 1974 there have been many firsts in Little League baseball. In 1974 Bunny Taylor, eleven, became the first girl to pitch a no-hitter in a Little League game.[82] In July 1979 Crystal Fields became the first girl to win the Pitch-Hit-Run Championship for nine- to twelve-year-olds. She won local, district, and divisional championships to get to the All-Star Game finals. There she compiled the winning score of 409 points for three categories of competition (hitting for distance, running a base path for speed, and pitching at a target).[83] In 1987 American Legion baseball got its first female coach. Nancy Dockter coached the McClusky, North Dakota, team.[84] In 1989 there were two firsts at the Little League World Series in Williamsport, Pennsylvania. Betty Speziale became the first woman umpire. She said, "This is the ultimate goal for umpires who've worked in the Little League. I set a goal to umpire in the Little League World Series, and I'm getting a chance to do that,"[85] Victoria Brucker, age twelve, became the first American girl to play in the Little League World Series. A European, Victoria Roche, was a substitute on the Brussels Championship team in 1984.[86]

Victoria's team from San Pedro, California, won the western regional championship to qualify as one of eight teams to play in the World Series. Victoria played first base and was the leading home run hitter in the tournament games with nine. Anthony Pesusich, a teammate, said, "They think, she's a girl, so they just pitch fastballs . . . and she just hits them out."[87]

A versatile player, in one regional game Victoria pitched four and one-third innings of no-hit baseball.[88] In another game her stepfather said that the opposing players laughed at her until she hit a home run, and then the pitcher intentionally walked her the next time she was up at bat.[89]

Although girls had won the right to play Little League baseball in 1974 and organizations such as American Legion junior baseball also changed their bylaws to admit girls, there were still some independent league hold-outs. And the battle was not over.

In 1983 eleven-year-old Jessica Meisner was declared ineligible to play for the Cranbury Athletic Association in Norwalk, Connecticut. The board voted that to let her play would violate the bylaws. The Cranbury Association, with approximately 400 boys, is one of two leagues in Norwalk not associated with the national Little League.[90]

When asked by a reporter if the bylaws could be changed, Vincent DePanfilis, president of the league, said that a change in the bylaws was a long procedure. It would have to be passed by both the rules committee and the executive board and could take up to two months. He continued, "My big concern is the potential negligence. What happens if she gets injured? How could we defend ourselves in court for allowing her to play?"[91]

It was *déjà vu*—a new twist on the 1973 Little League refrain of the importance of girls' safety. Only now the insurance company was laid to blame. But Jessica and her parents and her coach didn't give up. She took the field the next game, and after the first pitch the umpire stopped the game. She was declared ineligible and her team told it had forfeited the game. Her parents said that they would protest the ruling with the state Commission on Human Rights and Opportunities.[92]

John McMahon, the league commissioner who accepted her application, resigned. Mr. DePanfilis, the league president, reiterated the bylaws: "Page 10 is very specific. It says that players must be boys. It's in the bylaws." He then threatened to disband the whole organization. "We could abolish the corporation. I personally feel: forget it. If they want to make a big deal about it, let the city provide the baseball program for the kids."[93] It is difficult to believe that in 1983 some men would still see a little girl as a threat to masculinity and baseball.

Several days later the executive board met and by a narrow margin of 6–5 voted to revise the bylaws and to permit her to play. The reason given to the press for the change of heart was that the insurance company had said that it would cover her.[94]

The blatant discrimination against girls in baseball has now virtually disappeared for legal reasons, but more subtle forms still exist. Girls are strongly encouraged to play softball rather than baseball. If they do play baseball, they are often played less. Little girls are often put in the outfield "to protect them," so that they won't get hit by a ball. But as every Little Leaguer knows, left field is a lonely place. Unfortunately, less playing time often results in a self-fulfilling prophecy. The expectations for girls' performance are low, and because they don't get much playing time, their skills don't develop. As bench warmers they lose interest in the game and quit. This helps to perpetuate the myth that girls aren't really interested in the game.

The percentage of females in Little League was highest right after the 1974 decision. In 1977, it was estimated that nationally 1 percent of the players were girls. By 1980 the estimate was less than 1.0 percent (0.7 percent).[95] In 1987 the national estimate was about 7,000 girls, or about 1 per league. The estimate for Babe Ruth baseball was less than 1,000 out of 433,000 players on 23,000 teams. This amounts to 0.002 percent.[96] Certainly based on these statistics Little League, Inc., has never had to worry about an influx of girls. Little League baseball is still predominantly male, and the attitudes still reflect a male dominance. With the small percentage of girls who play Little League baseball, it is rare when a girl tries out for the high school team.

HIGH SCHOOL PLAYERS

In 1935, a fifteen-year-old sophomore, Nellie Twardzik, gained national publicity when she tried out for and made the Webster, Massachusetts, Bartlett High School boys baseball team. She beat out twenty-five boys to make the team. Newspapers referred to her as the "Babe Ruth" or "Babe Didrikson" of Webster. Bill King, an associated press sportswriter wrote, "Babe Ruth may be the greatest drawing card in the major leagues but,

17. The story of Nellie Twardzik, as told in the *Boston Post* on April 3, 1936.

as far as comparisons go, he is just another ball player when one considers the crowd appeal of 15-year-old Nellie Twardzik." It was estimated that there were as many as 1,500 spectators for games that used to bring less than 300.[97]

Nellie was already a seasoned first-basewoman before she joined the high school team. During the summer she played for the "Nellie's All Stars," her own all male team, coached by her brother, and the Dudley A. C. team.[98] She had also played for the Bates Shoe Company factory team in an exhibition game against the All Star Rangers, a midwestern girls barnstorming team, managed by Maud Olson (Maud Nelson of Bloomer Girls fame). Margaret Gisolo of American Legion Junior baseball fame and Rose Gacioch who would later play for the All American Girls Professional Baseball League, were members of the Rangers.[99]

During the summer of 1935, Nellie was recruited to play for the Watertown All Stars, a semi-pro team. Nellie, however, refused to accept any money for playing so as not to lose her high school amateur status. That fall, she was astonished to find out that the Bartlett High School coach George Finnigan barred her from playing. The reason he gave was that a boys' team was no place for a girl. He admitted that she was the best female player he had ever seen and was qualified to play.[100] A headline in the Newark *Evening Times*, March 17, 1936, read, "Complications, High School Team's Best First Baseman Is a Girl, and the Big Question Is What To Do About It."

But Nellie was luckier than Margaret Gisolo; her fellow high school students petitioned the school principal to let her play. The decision was repealed and she continued to play her junior and senior years.[101]

Because of the publicity generated by her playing, a number of other girls in Massachusetts tried out for their high school teams. None had the skills of Nellie and they soon vanished from the scene.[102]

After graduation, Nellie continued to play baseball for a number of men's semi-pro teams. In 1942, she married Navy Lieutenant James Thompson and retired from baseball to become a full-time housewife and mother.[103]

In 1973 Mori Irving, a seventeen-year-old catcher, wanted to try out for the Piscataway High School team. She was told that the New Jersey Interscholastic Athletic Association rules barred women from competing with men in contact sports. The American Civil Liberties Union filed a class action suit on her behalf asking the courts to declare the ruling unconstitutional.[104]

Mori Irving won her case, but it came too late. Although the courts ruled that she had a right to try out for the team, she declined the school's offer to join the team. As she said, "They have already had the try-outs, the cuts have been made and the team picked. . . . I want equal opportunity. . . . I don't want favoritism and I don't want to be discriminated against."[105] As a senior, she knew there was no next year.

In 1976 a high school senior girl sued the Tennessee Secondary School Athletic Association and won the right for girls to play.[106] No doubt there were other cases of girls who tried to play. In 1978 Robin Petrini pitched two innings for her high school varsity team in California. Local coaches said it was the first time a female pitcher had been used in an interschool game. According to the *New York Times*, there were no objections.[107]

She may have been the first pitcher, but she wasn't the first varsity player. In 1946 Jane Ashworth earned a varsity letter in baseball. She played second base for Westerly High School against Lockwood High in Warwick, Rhode Island.

Given the court cases of the 1970s, it is amazing that it took until October 11, 1984, for the Connecticut Interscholastic Athletic Association to agree to permit girls to play baseball. Prior to 1984, girls were allowed only to play softball. A revised ruling paved the way for girls to play hardball. It stated, "Baseball would ... be open to girls this spring because softball would no longer be considered comparable to baseball."[108] Yet there are still no high school girls' teams in Connecticut, and I know of no girls playing on boys teams. Softball remains the socially acceptable sport for girls, and it will probably stay that way.

In 1987 it was estimated that only 372 girls played Little League ball. Little League has carefully discouraged girls from playing hardball through its girls' softball league, which has grown to 270,000 members.[109] This has kept girls separate and different from boys. Little League has done all it can to make sure that it will be not be the feeder for channeling girls into high school baseball programs.

With so few girls in junior and senior high school baseball programs, the issue of a girl playing college ball seemed unlikely. But one girl, Julie Croteau, kept her love of baseball alive. She refused to be shunted into softball. Driven to succeed she worked hard to develop her baseball skills. Although it was a long, hard-fought battle, she eventually played high school varsity baseball and in 1989 became the first woman to play baseball for the NCAA.

JULIE CROTEAU: FIRST FEMALE TO PLAY NCAA BASEBALL

Unfortunately, even with court rulings allowing girls to play high school ball, the prejudice against women playing in high school didn't end. Julie Croteau, a seventeen-year-old first baseman from Virginia, couldn't make her Osbourne Park High School varsity team in 1987. Her family filed a sexual discrimination suit, which asked for $100,000 in damages and an injunction to let her play.[110]

The coach claimed that it wasn't a case of discrimination. Lots of boys who tried out didn't make it either. She just wasn't good enough. She came in second to last in the time trials.[111] As a sophomore she had made the junior varsity team but got very little playing time. Junior year she was cut. She claimed that she was told that the coach wanted her but the varsity coach, Ralph Ensley, ordered her and two other juniors cut.[112]

Julie recalled, "I wasn't one of the best players, but I was far from the worst. I believe that there were at least six people on the team, conservatively, that I was as good or better than. I should have been on the varsity."[113] Julie was not the only one to rate her ball-playing skills highly. Her Little League coach said, "As a first baseman, from a defensive point of view, she was one of the best."[114] Her Big League coach described her "as a young lady with a lot of heart and fortitude and the skills to go along with it. I think she's just as capable of playing first base as many of the boys."[115] A sixteen-year-old pitcher, Matt Cornwell, who played Little League with her, rated her playing an 8 on a scale of 10. He said, "I don't think I ever struck her out.[116]

In Little League she had a batting average of .300 and in Big League a fielding average of .975. Ross Natoli, a baseball coach at Catholic University, who had Julie in clinics, said: "She has average high school ability for boys. She's a line drive hitter, and she makes good contact. I'm seeing 70 to 80 high school games a year, and she has enough ability to make most high school teams."[117]

During the court hearing twelve boys from the team, unbeknownst to their coach, appeared and released a statement to the press saying that they didn't think she was qualified.[118] The court ruled that her case was not one of sexual discrimination. But was it?

As Tony Kornheiser, a sportswriter, said: "Only a fool would claim there isn't a general prejudice against women in serious team sports like baseball, basketball and football. Team sports are an avenue of the culture where men tend to see women in subservient, support roles—as cheerleaders, for example. They endorse women's rights to play and enjoy sports, but they want to keep those sports separate."[119]

Julie is no doubt a victim of that mentality. She worked hard to become a proficient baseball player. Julie began playing baseball at age six when her mother signed her and her male cousin up for Little League T ball. It was 1975, one year after the Little League decision. She went on to play Little League and Big League baseball. She also attended baseball clinics and camps. It was when she was in junior and senior high school that she really concentrated on perfecting her skills. During that time, she remembers, "I went to two baseball camps in Maryland and one in Virginia." It was at this point that she says she really began to start dealing with the fact she was a woman in a male sport and that there was a lot of resentment to her playing. She said, "I realize when I look back that there were a lot of girls when I started playing T ball. Almost half were girls and they disappeared as we got older and by the time we were twelve, they were pretty much gone."[120]

Her high school team, which she couldn't make, had a 4–13–1 record. So how outstanding a team could it have been? But Julie didn't let her disappointment at not being able to play varsity ball affect her desire to play. She continued to play Big League ball and that summer played for the Fredricksburg Giants, a semi-pro team in Virginia. The Giants play other Virginia semi-pro teams. The caliber of play is high because some of the players are on their way up to the minors or majors and others have recently been released.[121] Luckily for Julie her perseverence paid off and she got another chance. In 1989 she became the first woman to play baseball for the NCAA. As a freshman she played first base for St. Mary's College in Maryland, a Division III school.[122] She beat out fifteen males for a position on the team. She started in two-thirds of the games and had a .250 batting average.[123] It appeared that at long last Julie had finally succeeded.

Things went pretty well in her freshman year, but even at the beginning not all the media reports were positive. Mariah Nelson says that "when Julie was honored as Sportsperson of the Week on the *Today* show, anchor Bryant Gumbel said of her entry into college baseball, 'Is nothing sacred?' "[124]

But, alas, Julie's story doesn't have a happy ending. After the media attention subsided things changed. Some coaches began to make derogatory remarks and she began to get harassing phone calls. As a player Julie met all kinds of sexual harassment, from accusations' of being oversexed to accusations of lesbianism.

She resigned her junior year because of sexual harassment. Apparently, there had been a number of offensive sexist incidents, one of which was the reading aloud of pornographic magazine articles on the team bus. She said, "This sort of thing isn't just happening at St. Mary's; it's happening everywhere."[125]

Julie says when she spoke to the media about the incident and her resignation from the team, she wanted her experience to be a positive thing. She hoped that by talking about her experience things might change for other young girls who wanted to play. Instead, the media blew the bus incident out of proportion and made St. Mary's look bad.

Julie left St. Mary's College in the spring of her junior year. Her experience has left her disillusioned. Her world of baseball has been shattered and has left its scars. In a personal conversation she revealed that she didn't hear about the All American Girls' Professional Baseball League until her freshman year in college. She said, "I was so upset when I found out about this league. . . . I felt like I had been cheated. . . . If I had known about these women, . . . it would have been support, even if I had never met them."[126]

18. **Julie Croteau with her St. Mary's teammates.** *Courtesy of Julie Croteau.*

Sexual harassment shouldn't be an issue. Equality in the "male" sport of baseball, however, is a long way off. Unfortunately, the issue of sexual harassment in Julie's case will be brushed under the rug. Critics of women in baseball will cite Julie's poor third-season batting average as the reason for her quitting.

Although national news releases played up the fact that Julie was the first girl to play college ball on a men's team, there was at least one female before her. An April 14, 1951, article in the South Bend *Tribune* showed a picture of Margaret Dobson, nineteen, with her varsity baseball team-mates at Vanport College, Portland, Oregon. The caption read, "Oregon Coed Invades a Man's Domain." The article was titled "Margaret Plans to Ask Boys What They Do About Curves." In a game against Clark Junior College, Margaret played second base and apparently did a pretty good job. She "fielded two grass cotters faultlessly and handled three put-outs with dispatch. Sad to say, the official scorer was ungentlemanly enough to record one error against her." Her team won the game 10–7. She honed her skills by playing women's amateur softball for five years.· This was all prior to Title IX, and apparently she played without much fanfare. Her playing days have long ago been forgotten and have left no imprint on college ball. One has to wonder if there were others.

Will Julie's accomplishments also be forgotten? Does the fact of women playing baseball create such cognitive dissonance that the memory slips away? Certainly one would like to believe that there will be more Julies in the future and that their stories will be more positive. But the prognosis is poor.

Although Title IX makes it illegal to discriminate against girls and women in baseball, three factors will continue to prevent them from playing. First, junior baseball leagues such as Little League shunt girls off into softball. Second, most parents of girls still see softball as the acceptable female alternative to baseball. And third, since there are no girls' baseball leagues, girls must compete with boys and suffer both blatant and subtle forms of prejudice and discrimination. The exceptional few that dare to play Little League usually end their careers by age twelve. Without girls' feeder leagues, it is unlikely that many will play high school or college baseball. The girl who somehow manages to overcome the odds and try out will continue to be seen as an exception. The prognosis for women playing baseball in the minors or major leagues is dismal. Yet women played semi-professional baseball in the 1800s and even had their own major league, the All American Girls' Professional Baseball League in the 1940s.

NOTES

1. Grace Aspinwall Bowen Hardy, letter to the Alumnae Association, *Alumnae Bulletin of Miss Porter's School*, Spring 1939, 8.

2. Louise L. Stevenson, "Sarah Porter Educates Useful Ladies, 1847–1900," *Winterthur Portfolio* 18 (Spring 1983): 46.

3. "Kate Stevens Class of 1867," *When I Was at Farmington*, Chicago Chapter of Alumnae Association, 1931, 119.

4. Gloria Gavert, Archivist, Miss Porter's School, letters to author, 35 Oct. 1989 and 17 April 1991.

5. Madge Buerger, Executive Secretary Alumnae Association, Miss Hall's School, letter to author, 14 Nov. 1989.

6. Merrie Fidler, "The Establishment of Softball as a Sport for American Women, 1900–1940," in *Her Story in Sport: A Historical Anthology of Women in Sports,* ed. Reet Howell (West Point, N.Y.: Leisure Press, 1982), 530.

7. Emmett Rice, John Hutchinson, and Mabel Lee, *A Brief History of Physical Education*, 5th ed. (New York: Ronald Press, 1969), 303.

8. Tony Ladd, "Sexual Discrimination in Youth Sport: The Case of Margaret Gisolo," in *Her Story in Sport: A Historical Anthology of Women in Sport,* ed. Reet Howell (West Point, N.Y.: Leisure Press, 1982), 581.

9. Richard Loosbrock, *The History of the Kansas Department of the American Legion* (Topeka: Kansas Dept. of the American Legion, 1968), 82.

10. Richard Seelye Jones, *A History of the American Legion* (Indianapolis: Bobbs-Merrill Co., 1946), 266.

11. Ralph Burris, "The Story of Gisolo, Unique Legion Star," circa 19 July 1975, NBHFL.

12. Ladd, 583.

13. "Blanford Juniors Claim Girl 'Babe Ruth,' " *Hoosier Legionnaire,* 10 July 1928.

14. "Girl Player Wins Game in 12th with Single," *Daily Clintonian*, 20 June 1928.

15. "Will Blanford Have First Girl in a World Series?" *Daily Clintonian*, 20 June 1928.

16. Burris.

17. Qtd. in Ladd, 583–584.

18. "Blanford Wins County Series," *Daily Clintonian*, 22 June 1928.

19. "Girl Shortstop to Be Seen in Action at Sportland Park," *Daily Clintonian*, 22 June 1928.

20. "Foltz Pitches Blanford Cubs to 5–2 Victory," *Daily Clintonian*, 2 July 1928.

21. "Juniors Battle to Gain County Tourney Title," *Daily Clintonian*, 29 June 1928.

22. "Margaret Gisolo to Play before Terre Haute Fans," *Daily Clintonian*, 3 July 1928.

23. "Margaret Gisolo Shines in Game at Terre Haute," *Daily Clintonian*, 5 July 1928.

24. "Blanford Beats Blue Devils for District Honors," *Daily Clintonian*, 7 July 1928.

25. "Boys Bank on Girl Slugger in Legion's Sandlot Tourney," newspaper article, 9 July 1928, Margaret Gisolo scrapbook.

26. Larry Denning, "Blanford Girl Is Added Feature," newspaper article, 1928, Margaret Gisolo scrapbook.

27. "Blanford Cubs May Play Ball Opener Sunday," *Daily Clintonian*, 10 July 1928.

28. "Margaret Has Perfect Day," newspaper article, 15 July 1928, Margaret Gisolo scrapbook.

29. "Blanford Cubs Rap St. Phillips," *Daily Clintonian*, 26 July 1928.

30. "Blanford Cubs Win State Title," *Daily Clintonian*, 27 July 1928.

31. "Blanford Plays Hut All-Stars," *Daily Clintonian*, 3 Aug. 1928.

32. "Blanford Cubs Chicago Bound," *Daily Clintonian*, 7 Aug. 1928.

33. Extract from updated news release prepared by the American Legion, Dept. of Indiana, 1928.

34. "Blanford Falls before Illinois Junior Champs," *Daily Clintonian*, 10 Aug. 1928.

35. "Cleveland Legion Wins Final, 11–0," *New York Times*, 10 Aug. 1928.

36. Burris.

37. "Girls Usurping National Sport: Suffrage Now Extends from Ballot Box to Baseball Diamonds," newspaper article, NEA Service, New York, 11 Aug. 1928, Margaret Gisolo scrapbook.

38. "Legion Tributes Margaret Gisolo," newspaper article, 1929, Margaret Gisolo scrapbook.

39. L.L. Lucias, Business Manager, Pulaski Baseball Club, letter to Margaret Gisolo, 4 Jan. 1928.

40. Roberta Bender, "Goodbye Miss Gisolo (We Love You!)," *Arizona Arts and Lifestyle*, Summer 1980, 53.

41. Qtd. in Morris Bealle, *The Softball Story* (Washington, D.C.: Columbia Pub. Co., 1957), 165.

42. Ibid.

43. Ibid., 29.

44. Darlene Mehrer, "Happy Birthday Softball, Wish You'd Never Been Born," *Base Woman*, July 1987, 3.

45. Ibid.

46. Ibid.

47. Qtd. in Susan Jennings, " 'As American as Hot Dogs, Apple Pie and Chevrolet,' The Desegregation of Little League Baseball," *Journal of American Culture* 4 (1981): 82.

48. Jerry Izenberg, "The Girl Pitcher Who Took Puerto Rico by Storm," *New York Post*, 27 May 1983.

49. Lewis Yablonsky and Jonathan Brower, *The Little League Game* (New York: Times Books, 1979), 4.

50. Emil Parker, "Her Dad's in Game, Why Not Charlene?" newspaper article, Charlotte, N.C., 17 June 1976, NBHFL.

51. Qtd. in ibid.

52. Ibid.

53. Stephen Figler and Gail Whitaker, *Sport and Play in American Life*, 2nd ed. (Dubuque, Iowa: Wm. C. Brown, 1991), 311.

54. "Today Little League, Tomorrow Cooperstown-Feminist," Harrisburg, Pa., *The Patriot*, 14 June 1974, 44.

55. "Gal, 12, a Designated Little Leaguer," Ypsilanti, Mich., newspaper article, 3 May 1973, NBHFL.

56. Qtd. in Ricki Fullman, "Little League Balks as Girls Make Their Pitch," *Daily News*, 4 June 1973.

57. "Little League Bars Girl: Town to Fight," *New York Times*, 8 May 1973.

58. "Court Decision Is Awaited in Little League Test Case," *New York Times*, 30 June 1973.

59. Jennings, 83.

60. Ibid.

61. Ibid.

62. "Girl Ball Player Gets to First Base," *New York Times*, 20 June 1973.

63. Fullman.

64. Jennings, 81.

65. "Say It Ain't So, Flo," *Newsweek*, 24 June 1974, 75.

66. Robert Peterson. " 'You Really Hit That One, Man!' Said the Little League Boy to the Little League Girl," *New York Times*, 19 May 1974, Sec. 6.

67. "Discrimination Laid to Little League," *New York Times*, 10 Aug. 1973, N.J. pages.

68. "Not Out of Their League, Doc," *Sunday News*, 17 March 1974, Sec. C.

69. "Little League in Jersey Ordered to Allow Girls to Play on Teams," *New York Times*, 8 Nov. 1973, N.J. pages.

70. Ibid.

71. Ibid.

72. Joseph Treaster, "Girls a Hit in Debut on Diamond," *New York Times*, 25 March 1974, N.J. pages.

73. "Little League HQ Prodded on Girls," *New York Times*, 12 April 1974, N.J. pages.

74. "Insiders Say," New York *Daily News*, 25 May 1974.

75. Qtd. in "Little League in Jersey Ordered to Allow Girls to Play on Teams."

76. Walter Waggoner, "Byrne Declares 'Qualified' Girls Should Play Little League Ball," *New York Times*, 28 March 1974, N.J. pages.

77. Frank Deford, "Now Georgy-Porgy Runs Away," *Sports Illustrated*, 22 April 1974, 26.

78. C.C. Johnson, editorial, "We Believe . . . Little League Surrenders," *Sporting News*, 29 June 1974.

79. " 'Play Ball,' Senate Tells Girls: Little League Open to Them," Washington, D.C., News Bureau, 17 Dec. 1974, NBHFL.

80. Joseph Treaster, "Town's Little League Reluctantly Signs 3 Girls," *New York Times*, 27 April 1974.

81. "Little League in Jersey Ordered to Allow Girls to Play on Teams."

82. Lois O'Neill, ed., *The Women's Book of World Records and Achievements* (Garden City, N.Y.: Anchor/Doubleday Books, 1979), 567.

83. Lynn Ames, "Girls Playing Heads-Up Ball," Westchester Weekly, *New York Times*, 17 July 1977, Sec. 22.

84. Carolyn White, "Barriers Break Slowly in American Legion Baseball," *USA Today*, 3 Sept. 1987.

85. Jack Carey, "At Long Last a Woman Will Call the Shots," *USA Today*, 22 Aug. 1989, Sec. C.

86. "12-Year-Old Girl Breaks New Ground," *USA Today*, 22 Aug. 1989, Sec. C.

87. Ibid.

88. "Girl Makes a Hit, History in LL Series," *New York Post*, 24 Aug. 1989.

89. "Brucker Goes 1-for–2 in Debut," *Gannett* Westchester Newspapers, 24 Aug. 1989, Sec. B.

90. James Macenka, "Girl LL, To Play in League?" Norwalk, Conn., *The Hour*, 2 May 1983.

91. Ibid.

92. Ibid.

93. Ibid.

94. Ibid.

95. Jennings, 88–89.

96. Carolyn White, "Barriers Break Slowly in American Legion Baseball," *USA Today*, 3 Sept. 1987.

97. Bill King, "Nellie Is Babe Ruth of Webster," *Worcester Post*, 30 April 1935.

98. Bob Ahern, "Girl Athlete Will Play on Schoolboy Nine Wednesday," *Boston American*, 20 April 1935.

99. "Ranger Girls Defeated, But Show Real Class as Baseball Team," July 1934, newspaper clipping, Nellie Twardzik scrapbook.

100. "Girl Baseball Star Stirs School Wrangle by Her Presence on Bay State Boys' Team," *New York Times*, 17 March 1936.

101. "Pupils Petition For Girl Player," *Worcester Gazette*, 28 March 1936.

102. John F. Moulihan, "Girl Wants Position on School Nine," Worcester *Sunday Telegram*, no date; "Wants To Play on Boys Team," newspaper clipping, Nellie Twardzik scrapbook.

103. K. Baumeister, "Female 'Babe Ruth' Content with Home, Children Now," Worcester *Telegram*, no date, Nellie Twardzik scrapbook.

104. "Girl Goes To Bat against Ban in Sports," *New York Times*, 11 April 1973, N.J. pages.

105. Richard Phalon, "Girl Wins but Rejects the Right to Try out for Baseball Team," *New York Times*, 14 April 1973, N.J. pages.

106. Jackie Lapin and Bonnie Parkhouse, *Women Who Win: Exercising Your Right in Sport* (Englewood Cliffs, N.J.: Prentice-Hall, 1980), 75.

107. "Girl Pitches 2 Innings for High School on Coast," *New York Times*, 8 March 1978, Sec. B.

108. "Girls Get O.K. to Play H.S. Baseball," Norwalk, Conn., *The Hour*, 12 Oct. 1984.

109. Mariah Burton Nelson, "Are We Winning Yet?" *Glamour*, May 1991, 281.

110. Julie Croteau, interview with author, 26 Oct. 1991.

111. Ibid.

112. Ibid.

113. Ibid.

114. "Girl Cut from H.S. Baseball Team Sues," *Base Woman*, June 1988, 1.

115. Ibid.

116. Tony Kornheiser, "Julie Croteau's Play Deserves to Be Judged on Baseball Field, Not in Court Room," *Washington Post*, 19 March 1988, Sec. D.

117. Ibid.

118. "Girl Cut from H.S. Baseball Team Sues."

119. Kornheiser.

120. Croteau interview.

121. Ibid.

122. "Who's on First?" *New York Times*, 13 March 1989, Sec. C.

123. Edie Gibson, "Who's on First?: Julie Croteau Plays Hardball," *Seventeen*, Sept. 1989, 54.

124. Nelson, 250.

125. "For the Record," *Sports Illustrated*, 17 June 1991, 98.

126. Croteau interview.

7

Women in the Negro Leagues: Effa Manley, Owner, and Toni Stone, Player

Two women should be enshrined in the Baseball Hall of Fame for their contributions to Negro baseball: Effa Manley, co-owner of the Newark Eagles, a Negro National League team from 1935 to 1948; and Toni Stone, who played for the Negro American League's Indianapolis Clowns in 1953 and the Kansas City Monarchs in 1954.

EFFA MANLEY, CO-OWNER OF THE NEWARK EAGLES

Effa Manley, co-owner of the Newark Eagles, a Negro baseball team, was one of the most colorful and influential people in Negro baseball during the 1930s and 1940s. As one writer noted, "No figure cast a larger shadow in Negro baseball in its late period than the amazing Effa Manley."[1] In the 1930s and 1940s women were second-class citizens and blacks had few if any rights. She managed to become a respected force not only in the Negro baseball leagues but also in the black civil rights movement.

Effa Manley's birth like so much of her life, was filled with controversy. Although people assumed she was a light-skinned black, she claimed that she was white. According to her, her mother was white, of German and Asian-Indian descent. Effa claimed that her mother, who did sewing for wealthy white families, became pregnant by her white employer, John Marcus Bishop, a wealthy Philadelphian. Her black stepfather, Mr. Brooks, sued Mr. Bishop for alienation of his wife's affections and in an out-of-court settlement Mr. Bishop paid $10,000. Effa grew up in a black community and culturally always identified with blacks.[2] Within the black community she rarely discussed her heritage. Most friends and acquaintances

19. Effa Manley, second from the left, and Gov. Harold G. Hoffman, second from the right, attend opening day ceremonies, 1942.

assumed she was black. One of her players described her "as a light skinned black woman.[3]

Effa's life became almost totally involved with baseball and civic affairs after she married Abe Manley, a successful numbers racketeer. Both were avid baseball fans and were to become an instrumental force in Negro baseball. Appropriately, they met at the 1932 World Series and were married the next June.[4]

After marrying Abe she became a queen of Negro society and was very active in civic affairs and a crusader for Negro rights. Disturbed that stores in Harlem refused to hire black salesladies, Effa formed the Citizen's League for Fair Play with the Rev. Johnson in 1935. The group picketed stores along 125th Street with the slogan "Don't shop where you can't work."[5] It took six weeks, but in the end the owners relented and a year later approximately 300 Negroes were employed on 125th Street.[6]

As an activist for black rights she often used Newark Eagles baseball games to promote special causes. According to writer Donn Rogosin, "Probably the most remarkable special day in Negro baseball history" was when Effa Manley staged a "Stop Lynching" benefit in Ruppert Stadium. She was treasurer of the National Association for the Advancement of Colored People (NAACP) in New Jersey, at the time, and wanted to raise funds for what she considered one of the most important Negro issues.

Her usherettes wore sashes that read "Stop Lynching" and went through the stadium collecting funds.[7]

During World War II, she did her part to support the war effort. A news photo shows her pinning a NAACP Crusade for Liberty button on the deputy mayor of Newark.[8] Another time she invited the entire 372nd Regiment, a select black military unit, to a game as her guest.[9] She also paid for a bus to bring performers to Fort Dix to entertain the soldiers. As a member of a government gas rationing committee, she heard hardship cases to decide whether or not a person should receive extra gas rations. She was also very proud of the fact that fifty-four Negro baseball players volunteered to serve during World War II.[10]

It is an interesting turn of historical events that provided her husband, Abe Manley, with the opportunity to become a Negro baseball magnate. In 1931 the Negro National League, founded in 1920 by Rube Foster, dissolved. The Depression of 1929 had taken its toll on gate receipts and many teams by 1931 had failed. A few teams continued to barnstorm, but organized black baseball was at an end. Negro baseball was in need of a large infusion of dollars and gambling money soon came to its aid. With most legitimate black businesses either destroyed or weakened by the depression, the only people in the black community with large amounts of capital were the policy kings. To gain respectability and leadership in the black community many became involved in legitimate businesses, charities, or civil rights.[11]

Gus Greenlee, policy king of Pittsburgh's Hill district, saw baseball as his opportunity for gaining legitimacy. He spent $100,000 to build the first completely black-owned stadium in baseball and persuaded his friends in the numbers racket to help him establish the new or second Negro National Baseball League in 1933. Numbers bankers Abe Manley of Newark, Tom Wilson of Nashville, Ed "Soldier Boy" Semler of New York City, and Sonny "Man" Jackson of Homestead, New Jersey, joined him.[12]

Effa Manley's account of how the new league got started is a little different. She said that Greenlee helped to reorganize the Negro National League in 1933, but that this endeavor was unsuccessful. She claimed that it was her husband, Abe, who completely reorganized the league and made it into a professional organization in 1935. "There were twelve Negro baseball teams, operating all over the country dependent entirely on booking agents. . . . [Abe] was interested enough to want to see them organized into a league. And he got five of the teams in the east to go along with him and set up the Negro National League on condition that he would operate a team out of Brooklyn.[13] Gus Greenlee was renamed president of the new organization, and Abe Manley became treasurer.[14]

In an interview in 1977 Effa said that Abe's motive was that he had "retired from his real estate business. . . . So he was no doubt looking for something to do and this was something that just caught his fancy."[15] Effa laughed during the interview when she said that her husband was "retired from the real estate business," but she did not elaborate. In an earlier interview in 1975 with Henry Hecht of the *New York Post*, she was much more direct. Effa said, "Abe was a numbers banker in Camden and he came to New York when the Camden gangsters wanted to take over. They threw a bomb into a club he owned and the D.A., a personal friend of his, told him, 'Abe, you better get out of town.' "[16] Abe took his advice.

Abe was a wealthy, powerful man with an avid interest in Negro baseball, so owning a baseball team appealed to him. He had the money to invest in developing players and could afford the luxury of not always making a profit. As Effa said, "He went into it [baseball] head first with his mind made up to spend any amount of money he had to." Over the years he invested over $100,000 in the team. When he finally sold the team in 1947, according to Effa, he got about 5 percent of his investment back.[17]

Olive Brown, sports editor of the New Jersey *Herald* in 1950, credited the Newark Eagles with having developed more major league Negro stars than any other team.[18] And as Effa said, "Abe died feeling he had made a great contribution to major-league baseball."[19]

Effa always gave credit to Abe for founding the Newark Eagles and for developing so many players. For whatever reason, she also felt it important to stress how honest he was. But honesty may have been a relative term for Effa. Perhaps she considered her husband more honest than many other owners. At any rate, there is evidence that Abe bent the rules in order to have a winning team. In 1942 he signed a talented Paterson, New Jersey, Eastside High School senior, Larry Doby, to the Eagles' roster and paid him $300 a week to play until college started in the fall. Abe was right about Doby's talent; he went on to become the second black in major league baseball when he signed with the Cleveland Indians. The only problem with his signing of Doby was that he listed him on the roster as Larry Walker from Los Angeles. The pseudonym was used to protect Doby's status as an amateur, so that he could play in college. Of course, this was illegal.[20]

When Abe acquired the franchise, Effa immediately assumed an active role as co-owner of the Eagles. She took over the day-to-day business operations of the club, allowing Abe to concentrate on recruitment of players. As business manager Effa made all the hotel and other arrangements for road trips, managed the company payroll, bought the team's equipment, and handled promotions and publicity. Of her role, Effa said, "[I] succeeded in setting up a system of public relations that eventually made the Newark Eagles one of the most talked-about teams in the country."[21] As co-owners the two complemented each other and never had any apparent disagreements.

As Jerry Izenberg, sports columnist for the *New York Post*, said, "She ran an operation far more professional than some of her counterparts in the major leagues."[22] What is amazing is that prior to marrying Abe, Effa had had no financial experience. After graduating from William Penn High School in Philadelphia, she did millinery work.[23] But she was a born business-woman.

She also knew how to get publicity. When Abe acquired the team, she immediately mailed out special invitations for the inaugural game to important officials and other dignitaries. Mayor LaGuardia threw out the first ball. Some of the other people who accepted her invitation were Charles C. Lockwood, justice of the Supreme Court of the State of New York, Lowell Thomas, famous radio commentator, Jimmy Powers, sportswriter for the New York *Daily News*, and George W. Harris, editor of the *Daily News*.[24] All in all there were 185 distinguished guests in the stands.[25]

Unfortunately, only about 2,000 of the projected 10,000 to 15,000 fans showed up for the game, and the Eagles lost to the Homestead Grays 21–7.[26] Effa recalled, "I never saw so many home runs in my life. . . . I went home in the third inning and had my first drink of whiskey."[27]

George Giles, the Eagles' first baseman, remembers that opening day at Ebbetts Field and how mad Effa Manley was when the team lost. "The Homestead Grays near killed us! . . . Mrs. Manley left. When she was displeased, the world came to an end . . . Mrs. Manley didn't like a loser."[28]

When the Eagles had a losing season that first year, she was instrumental in firing the old manager and having Abe appoint George Giles, the new first baseman, as manager. Giles said he was surprised when Abe came up to him and said, "My wife wants you to manage the ball club."[29]

One group she found she had little control over was the white press. She was disappointed when she realized that the white newspapers had a "freeze-out" policy with regard to writing about Negro baseball. Fortunately, the black newspapers gave full coverage and baseball was a major event.[30]

The Brooklyn Eagles' first year of operation was a disappoinment. The Eagles were unable to compete with the Brooklyn Dodgers for fans. The Manleys decided that if they were to survive financially, they had to move the franchise. Abe negotiated with the owner of the Newark Dodgers, a black semi-pro team, and bought the franchise as well as the contract for Raymond Dandridge, a promising third baseman. In 1936 the team officially became the Newark Eagles.[31]

Effa was noted for taking an active part in all league meetings and not being just an appendage to Abe. Believing in her own convictions, at times she gave unsolicited and unappreciated advice to other owners. Dan Burley, sports editor for the *Amsterdam New York Star-News* wrote, "Effa Manley has long been a sore spot in the N.N.L. [Negro National League] setup . . . the rough and tumble gentlemen comprising its inner sanction have complained often and loudly that 'baseball ain't no place for no woman.' "[32] Although the other owners may have complained, they respected her financial judgment. Effa handled all the finances of the Negro National League even though Abe was the official treasurer.[33]

In matters of league policy, business affairs, or issues of civil rights, she was respected. When it came to day-to-day operation of the team, however, she was often considered a nuisance by management. Two Newark managers, Willie Wells and Biz Mackey, said they had difficulty working with her.[34] One favorite story about her meddling ways is the time she supposedly sent a message down to the Eagles' manager to pitch Terris McDuffie, her favorite pitcher. She wanted her girlfriends to see how handsome he was.[35]

Effa Manley believed that she was instrumental in developing players' careers. Most players would have agreed. For example George Giles, who joined the Eagles in 1935, remembered how she told everyone that he was a great first baseman. He said, "I got some pretty good write-ups there—Dan Parker in the *American*, Ed Sullivan . . . in the *News*. Just through her."[36]

In the very first season of play in 1935, Effa was worried about what her players would do for employment in the off-season, and so she arranged for a man in Puerto Rico to sponsor a winter team. With Vic Harris, who managed the Homestead Grays, she assembled a team of about half Eagles and half Grays to play under the Brooklyn Eagles name. As she said, "Puerto Rico accepted them with open arms, put them right in their league."[37] The team members did their part and won the pennant.

As Effa recalled after sending the first team down to Puerto Rico, "From then on a boy that we'd been giving five hundred dollars a month could go down there and get a thousand."[38] In later years this became a mixed blessing. Latin American countries ended up raiding some of the best players from the Negro National League in the regular season.

The Manleys treated their boys as family. Larry Doby, for example, felt so close to the Manleys that he asked them to be the godparents of his first child.[39] Monte Irvin, short of cash for a down payment on a house, borrowed $2,000 or $3,000.[40] Lenny Pearson, who became a Newark tavern owner after leaving the Eagles, recalled: "After I quit playing, she started me out in business. She interceded for me and spoke to people and helped me. She financed the first tavern I ever had. A beautiful, beautiful person in all ways."[41]

But she was also noted for having favorites. Players who weren't on her favored list often feared her. Johnny Davis, an outfielder and pitcher for the Eagles in the 1940s, recalled that he wasn't one of her favorites. "I stayed as far away from that woman as I could. When she had a meeting, I stayed in the back of the room."[42]

He also recalled how she would reprimand a player if he did something she didn't like. As Max Manning, an Eagles pitcher, recalled, "Abe . . .

mostly stayed in the background. . . . Effa . . . ruled the roost."[43] There was no doubt that Mrs. Manley was the boss, and a mixture of fear and team pride probably kept many players in line. Her assertive manner may have been instrumental in averting a threatened player's strike at an East-West game. She proclaimed to the strike committee that "no Newark Eagle was gonna strike, period."[44]

Effa may have kept the players in line, but it was Abe who decided which players to purchase. In 1938 he bought Satchel Paige from Gus Greenlee, owner of the Crawfords. According to Effa, Abe paid $5,000 for Satchel, and to the best of her knowledge this was the only time in the history of the game money was paid for a player.[45] According to Donn Rogosin, the sale price was closer to $2,000 or $3,000, which Rogosin considered a bargain basement price for the most famous personality in Negro baseball.[46] Regardless of what the price was, it was too much because Paige left to play in Mexico and Abe never got his money back. Effa claims that Satchel wrote to say he'd play for the Eagles if she'd be his girlfriend. She never responded.[47]

The 1930s and early 1940s were difficult times for Negro baseball. Most teams were underfinanced, overextended, and operated in the red.[48] World War II changed all this however. During the war years attendance reached all-time highs. In 1944 attendance at Negro baseball's East-West game was 46,247, whereas the major leagues' All-Star Game had only 29,589.[49] By the end of the war, Negro baseball was a $2 million enterprise and represented one of the largest black-dominated businesses in the United States.[50]

There is a sad irony to this period. The combination of Negro baseball's success and the patriotic spirit of black military units led to the integration of the major leagues. But it also sounded the death knell for Negro baseball.

The issue of integration of the major leagues had been raised before the war, but it was a divisive issue. It took the war to change people's minds. Many called for integration after the war, but not everyone. An editorial in *Sporting News*, August 6, 1942, claimed that both blacks and whites preferred separate leagues.[51] American League president Larry MacPhail predicted the failure of Negro leagues if major league baseball was integrated.[52]

Motivated by MacPhail's statement, the Citizens Committee to Get Negroes into the Big Leagues was formed with the aid of the black press. As a member of that committee, Effa Manley responded to MacPhail in the New York *Daily Worker* by saying that "the majors draft dozens of players from the minors every season, but do those leagues fold up? Certainly not. In fact it improves them, because many hundreds of new stars take up the game, and interest generally is heightened by the addition of new talent.[53]

Effa said that rather than Negro baseball owners blocking integration they were all supporting "the fight to end Jim Crow in the majors." The allegation that owners wouldn't sell players to the majors, she said, "is without a doubt the most stupid thing I have ever heard."[54]

After the war, integration of baseball became a major issue. The rallying cry became, "If he's good enough for the navy, he's good enough for the majors."[55] And in 1946 the color line was finally broken when Branch Rickey signed Jackie Robinson to play for Montreal, a Triple "A" International League team.[56]

Although integration of the major leagues was to lead to the demise of the Negro leagues, 1946 was the best year for the Newark Eagles. They beat the Kansas City Monarchs in the seven-game Negro World Series. The team was superb, and two players stood out: Larry Doby and Monte Irvin. They had scored the tying and winning runs, respectively, in the 3–2 victory.[57] Both would later join the major leagues.

The turning point for Negro baseball was near. In 1947 Jackie Robinson became a Brooklyn Dodger. There were sixteen black ball players now in organized baseball. Half of them were on minor league Dodger teams.[58] Black fans in massive numbers began to abandon Negro baseball to see Jackie Robinson and other newly acquired blacks play. Attendance at Newark Eagle games plummeted from 120,000 fans in 1946 to 57,000 in 1947 to 35,000 in 1948, the last year of operation.[59]

After signing Robinson, Branch Rickey continued with his plan to integrate the Dodgers organization by recruiting Don Newcombe and Roy Campanella. Rickey had been criticized for not compensating Tom Baird, co-owner of the Kansas City Monarchs, for Robinson. To avoid further conflict with the Negro leagues, he had his aides ask both Newcombe and Campanella whether they were currently under contract to any Negro team. Don Newcombe wrote, "I am not under contract for my baseball services for any future time," and Roy Campanella denied that he was under contract with the Baltimore Elite Giants for 1946.[60]

But the owners of the Baltimore Elite Giants and the Newark Eagles felt differently. The Baltimore Elite Giants decided to let the issue pass, but Effa Manley acted. She wrote a number of letters to Rickey asking him to meet with her about taking Don Newcombe from the Eagles. Rickey didn't reply.[61]

In 1947 Bill Veeck of the Cleveland Indians called Effa Manley. He said that he was interested in buying Larry Doby from the Eagles and wanted to know what price they wanted for him. Effa replied, "Well, Mr. Veeck, if Larry has a chance to play for your club, I certainly won't stand in his way." Veeck said he'd pay $10,000. Always a negotiator, Effa immediately responded, "Mr. Veeck, you know if Larry Doby were white and a free agent, you'd give him $100,000 to sign with you merely as a bonus." Veeck then made a deal. He said that if Doby stayed with the organization over thirty days that he would give the Manleys another $5,000.[62] Larry Doby became the first black player in the American League.[63]

According to Effa this was the first time that anyone in the major leagues had compensated a team in the Negro National or Negro American League for a player.[64] Effa had established a precedent and after that major league owners paid on average about $5,000 for a player.[65]

With the best players being drafted by the major leagues and black fans deserting the Negro teams, Negro teams could no longer show a profit. In 1947 the Eagles showed a loss of $20,000, and the Manleys sold the team to Dr. Young, a black doctor in Memphis, Tennessee.

Effa Manley defended Negro baseball against any slights or what she believed were injustices. When Jackie Robinson wrote an article in *Ebony* in 1948 entitled "What's Wrong with Negro Baseball?" she was incensed. She immediately sent a letter to Jackie and countered with an article in *Our World.* To challenge the opinions of a black national hero took courage. None of the other owners of Negro baseball teams spoke out, but they appreciated Effa's outspokenness and wrote thanking her for setting Robinson straight.[66]

In her article in *Our World* she blasted both Robinson and major league baseball. She said, "Major league tactics are ruining Negro baseball [and] some people are knifing it in the back. The most outrageous attack came from Jackie Robinson's widely publicized article in a national magazine. No greater ingratitude was ever displayed." After all, according to Effa, Jackie owed his opportunity to play for the Dodgers to Negro baseball.[67]

In his article Jackie attacked every aspect of Negro baseball. He said, "The bad points range all the way from the low salaries paid players and sloppy umpiring to the questionable business connections of many of the team owners."[68] He listed some of the problems as owners' indifference to the welfare of their players and poor road accommodations that ranged from uncomfortable buses to cheap hotels.[69]

Effa suggested in her reply that perhaps Jackie Robinson had been used by the major leagues. She said, "I wonder if he's speaking his own mind or if his statement was for a purpose even he does not understand."[70]

She explained how most of the problems that Jackie cited were due to problems of segregation and discrimination in American society and not the fault of Negro baseball. She challenged the idea that Negro ball players were underpaid when the average player made $100 a week. Further, since most of the teams operated in the red, she felt the owners were particularly generous.[71] The average American worker in 1945 made $44.39 a week.[72]

Effa's appeal to the fans, the press, and major league baseball to keep Negro baseball alive had fallen on deaf ears. The Eagles folded in 1948 and so did two other teams in the Negro National League. The other three teams went to the Western League.[73]

A combination of integration of the major leagues and changing American leisure patterns had taken their toll. Competing forms of entertainment such as movies, travel, and the professional sports of basketball and football had cut into spectatorship. With the invention of television, fans no longer had to travel to games. Major league games were brought into their living rooms. But it wasn't just Negro baseball that suffered; the All American Girls' Professional Baseball League folded in 1954, and many white minor league professional baseball teams also went out of business. After the war attendance at minor league games declined from 42 million to 15.5 million. They were all casualties of changing times.[74]

Although it was sad to see Negro baseball disappear from the American scene, it was a victory for American society. For it meant that black baseball players were no longer going to be second-class athletes but were going to take their rightful place among white players. Integration of major league ball paved the way for integration in other sports.

Effa Manley until her death in 1981 at age eighty-one devoted herself to keeping the history of Negro baseball alive and to gaining recognition for many of its ball players. In 1976 she published her book, *Negro Baseball . . . before Integration*, which she had written with the help of Leon Hartwick, a professional writer. She wrote numerous letters to both the Baseball Hall of Fame and to the *Sporting News*, trying to gain recognition for the Negro baseball leagues and the players. When the Hall of Fame finally recognized eleven players from the Negro leagues she was delighted, but she thought that many more players should have been chosen. She begged the Hall of Fame to admit others. If it were not possible to enshrine others, then, she argued, a plaque listing the names of the great Negro players should be installed and a Negro section established.[75] Her requests were denied.

In 1985, four years after Effa's death, the National Baseball Hall of Fame Museum added an exhibit on black ball. Effa's picture is prominently displayed in that exhibit. But were she alive today, she would be disappointed to learn that her name is not included among the women owners in the women in baseball exhibit that was added in 1988. According to the curator, William Spencer, Jr., the reason for her omission from the women's exhibit is that it would be redundant to list her name in both exhibits.

TONI STONE, FIRST WOMAN TO PLAY NEGRO PROFESSIONAL BASEBALL

Although integration of the major leagues siphoned black fans and players away from Negro baseball, it created a unique opportunity for another black player, Toni Stone. She became the first woman to play Negro professional ball. In 1953 she signed a contract to play second base for the Indianapolis Clowns, a team in the Negro American League.

By the 1950s the few Negro professional baseball teams that were still in existence had managed to survive by relying on showmanship and nov-

20. Toni Stone, second basewoman for the Indianapolis Clowns.

elty. Toni Stone was no doubt hired for the drawing power of a female ball player. The Clowns paid her $12,000 to play second base.[76]

The Clowns were a team with a long history of mixing showmanship and baseball. They were baseball's Harlem Globetrotters. Although they clowned, they were good baseball players. Hank Aaron was a member of the team in 1952.[77] In 1953 when Toni joined, the Clowns were the top-ranked team in the Negro American League.[78]

Toni Stone may have been hired as a novelty, but she was an exceptional player with excellent skills. In first time at bat for the Clowns she batted in two runs.[79] She played second base in 50 of the 175 games the Clowns played that season and had a batting average of .243.[80]

Physically, Toni was a good-sized woman at 5 feet 7 1/2 inches and 148 pounds. Extremely fast, she was clocked at eleven seconds for 100 yards.[81]

When she joined the Clowns, she had tremendous faith in her own ability and didn't want the ball players to treat her any differently than they treated a man. She said, "I know what I am doing and what I am in for. I don't want anyone playing me 'easy' because I am a woman and I don't plan to play easy against them. I am here to play the game."[82]

The only compensation that was made because of her sex was that she used the umpire's dressing room and shower rather than the team dressing room. The rest of the time she stayed with the team. She traveled on the team bus and on the road stayed in the same hotels and rooming houses.[83]

Marcenia "Toni" Stone was no stranger to baseball. Unlike many other women ball players, she hadn't first played softball and then switched to hardball. Toni grew up in St. Paul, Minnesota, playing baseball in her neighborhood with the boys. First she played at the Welcome Playground and then in the Catholic Midget League. It was outsiders who encouraged her to play. Toni said that her parents didn't want her to play baseball, "but there was nothing they could do about it."[84]

She quickly attracted the attention of baseball enthusiasts. Gabby Street, former St. Louis Cardinals manager, saw real potential when he saw her play. He bought her cleats and signed her up for his baseball school.[85] She was extremely fortunate to receive good training at an early age. This was especially unusual considering that girls were prohibited from playing Little League baseball.

In high school she moved up from the parish baseball team to the St. Paul Giants, a semi-professional team that played Sunday ball.[86] She also played with weekend Negro traveling leagues throughout Wisconsin and Minnesota.[87] It was shortly after this that she went out to California to visit her sister who was in the military. It was there that she played with American Legion teams and the San Francisco Sea Lions.[88] Playing for the Sea Lions, a minor league team, she batted .280 and won herself a place on the Negro League's All Star team.[89]

By the time she joined the Clowns she had also played two years with the New Orleans Creoles, a black minor league team, and the House of David.[90] Her career with the Clowns, however, was short-lived. In 1954, when she was twenty-eight, Syd Pollack sold her contract to the Kansas City Monarchs. Pollack then hired two new women to replace Toni. They were Connie Morgan, an infielder, and Mamie "Peanut" Johnson, a pitcher.[91]

After her professional playing days were over, she continued to play recreational ball with the California American Legion champs until she was sixty-two.[92] According to Toni two highlights of her baseball days are the time she got a hit off the legendary pitcher, Satchel Paige, and being honored in the 1960s by the San Francisco Giants. She threw out the first ball to start the season.[93]

Toni Stone's feats have largely been forgotten. Judy Yaeger Jones, president of Her Story Unlimited, a consulting firm in multicultural women's history, says she ran across Toni's name quite by accident. She was glancing through the book *Contributions of Black Women to America* when she came across mention of Toni Stone, who had been a St. Paul resident. She then tried to find out more about her through the traditional library sources, through the local historical societies, and by examining local newspapers. There was nothing. Local sportswriters also said that they had never heard of her.[94]

Eventually Judy Jones was able to contact Toni and the City of St. Paul declared March 6, 1990, Marcenia "Toni" Stone Alberga day. As part of the Minnesota Women's History Month, Toni was invited to St. Paul and to talk at some of the local schools.[95]

Toni, like Effa Manley, was omitted from the women in baseball exhibit at Cooperstown; nor is her name found in the exhibit on black baseball. The oversight should be corrected in the near future. Apparently, the staff did not become aware of Toni Stone until the museum sponsored a reunion for black baseball oldtimers in 1991. The Negro Leagues Baseball Museum which opened January 1991 in Kansas City, Missouri, is also compiling data on Toni Stone.

As the public becomes more aware of Toni Stone and other women who played baseball, opinions about women playing baseball should change and little girls may have the opportunity to dream of being major leaguers and actually play. Toni Stone would love to leave that legacy.

NOTES

1. Donn Rogosin, *Invisible Men: Life in Baseball's Negro Leagues* (New York: Atheneum, 1983), 108.

2. Effa Manley, interview by Bill Marshall, 19 Oct. 1977, A.B. Chandler Oral History Project, University of Kentucky Library, Lexington, Ky.

3. Rogosin, *Invisible Men*, 109.

4. John Holway, *Voices from the Great Black Baseball Leagues* (New York: Dodd Mead, 1975), 319.

5. Donn Rogosin, "Queen of the Negro Leagues," *Sportscape*, Summer 1981, 18.

6. "Prominent Woman," newspaper article, 20 June 1936, NBHFL.

7. Rogosin, "Queen of the Negro Leagues," 94.

8. News photo, NBHFL.

9. Rogosin, *Invisible Men*, 94.

10. Effa Manley interview.

11. Janet Bruce, *The Kansas City Monarchs: Champions of Black Baseball* (Lawrence: University Press of Kansas, 1985), 83.

12. Arthur Ashe, Jr., *A Hard Road to Glory: The History of the African American Athlete, 1919–1945*, vol. 2 (New York: Warner Books, 1988), 33.

13. Effa Manley interview.

14. Effa Manley and Leon Hardwick, *Negro Baseball . . . before Integration* (Chicago: Adam Press, 1976), 42.

15. Effa Manley interview.

16. Henry Hecht, "Women with a Mission," *New York Post*, 15 Sept. 1975.

17. Effa Manley interview.

18. Manley and Hardwick, 97.

19. Holway, *Voices from the Great Black Baseball Leagues*, 325.

20. Joseph Moore, *Pride against Prejudice: The Biography of Larry Doby* (New York: Praeger, 1988), 10–20.

21. Manley and Hardwick, 51.

22. Jerry Izenberg, "Black Baseball Had Its Pride and Pros," *New York Post*, 21 Feb. 1989.

23. Effa Manley interview.

24. Manley and Hardwick, 43–44.

25. Holway, *Voices from the Great Black Baseball Leagues*, 319.

26. Manley and Hardwick, 44.

27. Holway, *Voices from the Great Black Baseball Leagues*, 320.

28. John Holway, *Black Diamonds: Life in the Negro Leagues from the Men Who Lived It* (Westport, Conn.: Meckler Books, 1989), 65–66.

29. Qtd. in ibid., 66.

30. Manley and Hardwick, 44, 46.

31. Ibid, 47.

32. Dan Burley, "Dan Burley's Confidentially Yours," *Amsterdam New York Star-News*, 21 Feb. 1942.

33. Manley and Hardwick, 54.

34. Rogosin, *Invisible Men*, 109.

35. Ibid; Robert Peterson, *Only the Ball Was White*, (New York: McGraw-Hill Paperback, 1984), 137.

36. Holway, *Black Diamonds*, 66.

37. Effa Manley interview.

38. Ibid.

39. Samuel Hoskins, "Abe Manley, Baseball Founder Buried," *New Jersey Afro-American*, 20 Dec. 1952.

40. Holway, *Voices from the Great Black Baseball Leagues*, 326.

41. Ibid., 326.

42. Qtd. in Holway, *Black Diamonds*, 162.

43. Ibid., 124.

44. Rogosin, *Invisible Men*, 110.

45. Effa Manley interview.

46. Rogosin, *Invisible Men*, 137.

47. Effa Manley, "Negro Baseball Isn't Dead! But It Is Pretty Sick," *Our World*, Aug. 1948, 27–29.

48. Jules Tygiel, *Baseball's Great Experiment: Jackie Robinson and His Legacy* (New York: Vintage Books, 1984), 23.

49. Ashe, 39.

50. Tygiel, 24.

51. Ibid., 38–39.

52. Ashe, 38.

53. Nat Low, "Would Negroes in the Majors Hurt Negro Baseball? Certainly Not, It Would Help Says Negro Club Owner," New York *Daily Worker*, 13 Aug. 1942.

54. Ibid.

55. Qtd. in Bruce, 98.

56. Art Rust, Jr., *"Get That Nigger off the Field!"* (New York: Delacorte Press, 1976), 67.

57. Rogosin, *Invisible Men*, 19.

58. Rust, 63.

59. Bruce, 116.

60. Murray Polner, *Branch Rickey: A Biography* (New York: Atheneum, 1982), 175.

61. Tygiel, 87.

62. Manley and Hardwick, 74–76.

63. Edna Rust and Art Rust, Jr., *Art Rust's Illustrated History of the Black Athlete* (Garden City, N.Y.: Doubleday and Co, 1985), 64.

64. Manley and Hardwick, 79.

65. Holway, *Voices from the Great Black Baseball Leagues*, 325.

66. Ibid., 322.

67. Manley, 27.

68. Jackie Robinson, "What's Wrong with Negro Baseball?" *Ebony*, June 1948, 16.

69. Ibid., 17–18.

70. Manley, 27.

71. Ibid.

72. Neil Wynn, *The Afro-American and the Second World War* (London: Paul Elek, 1976), 27.

73. Effa Manley interview.

74. Bruce, *The Kansas City Monarchs*, 118.

75. Allen Richardson, "A Retrospective Look at the Negro Leagues and Professional Negro Baseball Players" (M.A. Thesis, San Jose State University, 1980), 178.

76. Peterson, 204.

77. Rogosin, *Invisible Men*, 149.

78. Diane DuBay, "From St. Paul Playgrounds to Big Leagues, Stone Always Loved Baseball," *Minnesota Women's Press*, 3–16 Feb. 1988.

79. Ibid.

80. Al Marvin, "Clowning Helps Keep Indianapolis Clowns Integrated," *New York Times*, 30 May 1971.

81. "Woman Player Says Could 'Take Care of Self' in Games," *Ebony*, June-July 1953, 50.

82. Ibid.

83. Ibid.

84. Qtd. in DuBay, 5.

85. Ibid.

86. Ibid.

87. Judy Yaeger Jones, "Her Story Unlimited," St. Paul, Minnesota, letter to author, 29 May 1991.

88. DuBay, 5.

89. Tony Blass, "Baseball Pioneer Tells Students to Follow Dreams," *St. Paul Pioneer Press Dispatch*, 7 March 1990.

90. Bruce, 118.

91. Ibid.

92. City of St. Paul Proclamation for Marcenia "Toni" Stone Alberga Day, signed by James Scheibel, Mayor, March 1990.

93. DuBay, 5.

94. "Honoring a Local Hero," *Minnesota Women's Press*, 14–27 March 1990.

95. City of St. Paul Proclamation for Marcenia "Toni" Stone Alberga Day.

8

World War II: The All American Girls' Professional Baseball League

Historical circumstances surrounding World War II led to a novel experiment in professional baseball. Philip Q. Wrigley, the chewing gum magnate and owner of the Chicago Cubs, founded the first and only women's professional baseball league. This league, called the All American Girls' Professional Baseball League, was active in the Midwest from 1943 to 1954. At the peak of its popularity in 1948, nearly 1 million fans came out to see the games. After the league folded in 1954, public knowledge of the league evaporated, and the history of the league lay dormant until 1982 when league members held their first reunion. At their second reunion in 1986 the surviving veterans of the league set a goal of being recognized by the National Baseball Hall of Fame in Cooperstown, New York. In the fall of 1989 the Baseball Hall of Fame dedicated an exhibit to women in baseball. Prior to the publicity surrounding that event, most of the American public was unaware that women's baseball ever existed in the United States. It seems difficult to believe not only that this history was forgotten but that women never again had the opportunity to play professional baseball. What made this period in history unique?

Labor shortages during the war meant that between 1940 and 1942, 4 million women entered the labor market.[1] But it wasn't just the war industries that needed labor; women entered the labor force in all areas. In the sports realm there were women jockeys, umpires, and even football coaches.[2]

Major league baseball was greatly affected by the war. Many players were drafted or volunteered for military service. All the stars went to war. The players who were left were mostly older and 4F players. The pool of young able-bodied men was severely limited. Young high school boys who would never have been able to get a major league tryout were actively recruited. In fact, it was said that the Dodgers' training camp at Bear Mountain took on the appearance of a boys' camp. Jake Pitler, the manager of the Dodgers' Piedmont League farm club in Virginia, described himself as a glorified babysitter and lamented that "when we took off in a bus on a road trip we were loaded with comic books and candy bars, but we carried practically no shaving cream."[3]

The minor leagues were even more severely hurt than the majors. In 1941 there were forty-one minor leagues. By 1943 their number had dwindled to nine.[4] Many had been forced to suspend operations. Although the majors could operate with older and 4F men, Philip Wrigley feared that even these men might be recruited for the war industries.

Wrigley worried that major league stadiums, especially Wrigley Field, would lie vacant. He came up with the idea of a women's softball league as a way to fill the stadiums and to maintain public interest in baseball. Amazingly enough, this was not such a novel idea, since women's softball was a well-established sport by the 1940s. In the 1920s, as part of an effort to improve employee morale, many companies had organized basketball, baseball, softball, and bowling teams. Some of these companies sponsored their own highly competitive women's softball teams as promotional gimmicks. New Deal public works programs of the 1930s built recreational parks, and many cities and towns had their own softball leagues. The Amateur Softball Association was established in 1934. By the mid–1940s, the *New York Times* estimated there were 600,000 teams. These teams were sponsored by parks, churches, companies, YMCAs, and other groups.[5] Women's softball games actually were better attended than men's. In fact, softball in general had more spectators than baseball. In 1939 it was estimated that 60 million people watched softball games. That was about 10 million more than watched baseball.[6] Softball was especially popular in the Midwest, and the first national softball tournament was held at the World's Fair in Chicago.[7]

In 1942 the newly formed International Girls' Major League made up of thirty-two of the stronger women's softball teams was featured in the *Saturday Evening Post.* The writer stressed the masculine characteristics of the players and especially of the Savona sisters when he wrote, "The frailest creature on the diamond is frequently the male umpire. . . . Miss Olympia, although built like a football halfback, looks frail compared to Miss Freda. . . . Olympia runs the bases, slides like a man and catches like a man. If she could spit, she could go with Brooklyn.[8]

Softball had an image problem. Players were frequently pictured as being masculine, physical freaks or lesbians. Teams tended to have burlesque-type names such as Slapsie Maxie's Curvaceous Cuties, Barney Ross's Adorables, and the Dr. Pepper Girls of Miami Beach.[9] The image portrayed was not that of the wholesome all-American girl. Mothers and fathers did not want their daughters to emulate softball stars. Because of this, player image became an important factor to Wrigley. He wanted to establish a professional high-class women's softball league that would be seen as good, clean, all-American family entertainment. He hoped to capitalize on the popularity of women's softball, but at the same time to create something new and better. In this new league, femininity would be stressed. The players would look and behave like ladies. They would wear makeup and skirts, not male uniforms or skin-tight shorts. And the teams would have dignified, regular baseball names. He envisioned that the women would play in major league parks when the men's games were not scheduled. He approached the other National League owners with this idea. No one but Branch Rickey, president of the Dodgers, showed any interest. Like Wrigley, Rickey was noted for being an innovator.

In 1943 the All American Girls' Softball League (AAGSBL) was formed as a non-profit organization with three trustees: Philip Wrigley; Paul Harper, Cubs attorney and member of the board of directors; and Branch Rickey. Wrigley was the major force behind the idea and provided the financial backing. Branch Rickey primarily lent his name and served as an advisor to the operation. Wrigley used his Cubs organization to run the AAGSBL. He appointed Jim Gallagher to formulate rules and regulations governing play and players. Arthur Meyerhoff, head of the major advertising agency used by the Cubs organization, was put in charge of promotion and advertising.[10] Ken Sells, former assistant general manager of the Cubs, became the president of the league and was responsible for the operation of all league and team affairs.[11]

Patriotism rather than profit was the official reason that Wrigley gave for establishing the All American Girls' Softball League. He wanted to provide wholesome entertainment to boost the morale of factory workers.[12]

The league was formed as a non-profit patriotic endeavor.[13] To this end, the women would also play United Service Organizations (USO) show games on military bases,[14] visit hospitals, raise money for war bonds, and help to develop youth programs.[15] And the league fulfilled its patriotic role of building national morale. As a patriotic gesture, before every game the teams lined up in V formation on the field. The women were also active in buying war bonds and in encouraging the public to purchase them.

The war effort also resulted in a historical first at Wrigley Field. On July 1, 1943, the Racine Belles, Kenosha Comets, and the Rockford Peaches participated in a nighttime double-header under the lights. The games were to benefit the Women's Army Corp recruiting unit. In 1944 the field was illuminated again for a night game to benefit the Red Cross. The teams played under portable lights that used about 38,600 watts. To properly light the field at least 30,000 watts are needed, so they were dimly lit games. The next time Wrigley Field was illuminated was on August 8, 1988, amid much publicity announcing the event as the first time a game had ever been played under lights. Much as the history of the AAGBL had been forgotten,

21. **Betty Weaver at bat during a night game.** *From the Collection of the Northern Indiana Historical Society.*

so apparently was the lighting of the field in 1943 and 1944. Although the Wrigley Field front office was informed of its mistake, there was no correction. Its official comment was that it could neither confirm nor deny the previous incidents.[16]

Wrigley was a firm believer that money bred money, and therefore he was willing to invest in start-up costs for the league. In order to sponsor a team, a city was required to raise $22,500. This amount was then matched by Wrigley.[17] Wrigley not only paid half of the team operating costs but also provided the starting costs for the league.[18] It is estimated that it cost between $200,000 and $250,000 to establish the league.

The league started with four teams that played a 108-game schedule.[19] The teams were the Rockford (Illinois) Peaches, the South Bend (Indiana) Blue Sox, the Kenosha (Wisconsin) Comets, and the Racine (Wisconsin) Belles.[20] The teams were located in mid-sized war production cities within 100 miles of Chicago. In each locale, softball had been popular since the 1930s.[21]

The distances between teams was kept to a minimum for two reasons: First, wartime gas rationing put a limit on team travel. Second, in the 1940s the decorum of travel for unaccompanied ladies was problematic. This was true even if they had female chaperons. Consequently, overnight travel was frowned upon and games were scheduled within a day's train ride. The 1943 souvenir booklet for the Rockford Peaches stressed the propriety of the girls' travel. "Girls travel by train, stop at best hotels in each town . . . while traveling. In home city, girls stay in private homes. All girls are feminine—no so-called Tomboys. They visit beauty salons regularly."[22] There was to be no doubt in the public's mind that these were "proper" girls.

When not on the road, the girls lived in private homes in their hometown cities. They became part of the community. These small cities embraced these players as their own. They became local celebrities. There were fan clubs and people were constantly asking them for their autographs. Rallies before games and parades for winning the playoffs were common. The communities provided a strong support system. Town sponsors often aided the girls in getting employment when the season was over. For example, in Racine in the off-season girls worked for Western Publishing, Hamilton Beach, or S.C. Johnson.[23]

Although Wrigley had originally hoped to establish teams in large cities such as Chicago and Detroit, it was the smaller cities that provided the essential ingredients for successful franchises and fan loyalty (see AAGBL Franchise List). Probably because of their size, there were fewer competing forms of entertainment and a greater sense of community bonding. Interestingly enough, when the Milwaukee and Minneapolis franchises were added to the league in 1944, they could not compete with major league baseball in those cities and quickly folded.[24]

AAGBL League Franchises

Team	*Years*
Rockford (Illinois) Peaches	1943–1954
South Bend (Indiana) Blue Sox	1943–1954
Racine (Wisconsin) Belles	1943–1950
Kenosha (Wisconsin) Comets	1943–1951
Milwaukee (Wisconsin) Chicks	1944
Minneapolis (Minnesota) Millerettes	1944
Grand Rapids (Michigan) Chicks	1945–1951
Fort Wayne (Indiana) Daisies	1945–1954
Muskegon (Michigan) Lassies/Belles	1945–1950 and 1953
Peoria (Illinois) Redwings	1946–1951
Chicago (Illinois) Colleens	1948
Springfield (Illinois) Sallies	1948
Kalamazoo (Michigan) Lassies	1950–1954
Battle Creek (Michigan) Belles	1951–1952

Adapted from AAGBL Cards, 1984.

Wrigley believed that women's teams drew a different crowd than men's teams and did not worry so much about minor league competition. Of greater concern to him was the resistance and competition from other established professional women's softball leagues, especially those in the Chicago area. Wrigley became determined to set his women's league apart from these leagues in order to eliminate some of the problems of competition. His approach was two-pronged: one, he changed the game the girls played from softball to a hybrid of fast-pitch softball and baseball; two, he changed the image of the softball player from that of a physical anomaly to that of an attractive, feminine lady who just happened to possess masculine athletic skills.

The league began by playing with a 12-inch ball that was slightly harder than a softball, a distance between bases of 65 feet, with 40 feet from plate to mound, and with the pitcher using a windmill underarm. Changes occurred over the years, until by 1954 they were playing regulation major league baseball.[25] By 1945 the league officially changed its name from AAGSBL to All American Girls' Baseball League (AAGBL).[26] Even from the beginning, reference was made to the girls playing baseball. In fact, midway through the 1943 season, Wrigley appealed to the press to refer to the game as "Girls Baseball."[27] Although the press obliged, there may have been some debate over the name change by others. The game, a hybrid of baseball and softball, was officially neither. Consequently, for some time the group was referred to as the All American Girls' Ball League. It was not until 1945 that it was officially called "Base Ball League."[28]

Femininity of the players became a key factor. There was to be no doubt left in the public's mind that in physical appearance, manner, and dress these girls were not physical freaks, Amazons, or in any way masculine. First and foremost the players were ladies who just happened to have incredible baseball talent. Rather than wearing pants, Wrigley's ladies wore short skirts with satin underpants. The uniform was designed by famed poster artist Otis Shepard, who created the Wrigley pixies.[29] The uniforms were very similar to tennis, field hockey, or skating costumes of the times. To assure that girls had an air of good breeding about them, Wrigley hired Helena Rubenstein, the world-renowned beauty expert, to set up a charm school for the players. Instructors were to teach the recruits proper etiquette and use of makeup.

The opening night double-header of the inaugural season went as planned. The players looked cute in their short skirts and they played well. The second night the training broke down and two of the ladies got into a heated argument that almost ended in a brawl.[30] It was obvious that the chaperons were going to have to be more vigilant in enforcing proper decorum. To reinforce the chaperons in disciplining the girls, $10 fines were levied against players for being ejected from a game for arguing and $50 fines for appearing in public in sloppy attire.[31]

The idea of charm school was more than merely a publicity gimmick to Wrigley. He was serious about having polite, ladylike players. The press loved the idea, and articles about lady ball players going to charm school appeared in most popular magazines. Needless to say, charm school met with mixed reactions among players. Some found it ludicrous, but others saw it as helpful. After all, elite women's colleges such as Smith, Wellesley, and Vassar also stressed proper dress and decorum. At such colleges this was called "gracious living." So Wrigley's attitudes were in keeping with the times.

Branch Rickey was likewise very image-oriented. He believed in a clean-cut collegiate image for male professional baseball players, and consequently thought women players should have a similar image.[32] In order to promote this image of feminine purity and respectability, it was necessary to control the girls' public lives and to a large extent their private lives as well. Signing with the All American Girls' Professional Softball League was almost like attending a finishing school or an elite women's college such as Smith or Vassar. But the girls had chaperons rather than house-mothers. Each team had a male manager and a female chaperon. The players' parietal hours were well-supervised. Players had to get permission to go out with men, and their dates were carefully screened.

22. Catcher Ann O'Dowd holds a compact while Beverly Hatzell puts the final touches on her makeup. *From the Collection of the Northern Indiana Historical Society.*

Chaperons served as surrogate parents. They functioned (1) to protect the girl's public images (2) to provide needed services such as taking care of hotel reservations and bus arrangements and (3) to assure the parents of girls under the age of eighteen that they were being well cared for and supervised.

Although the actual duties of a chaperon varied somewhat depending upon the team, all chaperons were responsible for monitoring curfews, making sure that the girls conducted themselves as ladies, and acting as trainers and often managers. Some of the rules of conduct that chaperons were responsible for enforcing were to make sure that girls did not drink, smoke, or appear in slacks in public; that whenever they were in public, they wore lipstick (see photo 22); that they were seen only in proper company and "not with the wrong kind of man"; that they were in the hotel at least two hours before a game; and that they obeyed the 12:30 A.M. curfew. Since many of the girls who played on these teams were under eighteen, not only did they need someone to supervise them but, in many instances, their parents would not have let them sign with the league if they weren't supervised. As Betty Trezza recalls, "My mother wouldn't let me play until I convinced her we'd be chaperoned."[33]

A 1990 survey of retired players revealed that the majority of the women accepted the idea of charm school, chaperons, rules, and regulations. Seventy percent felt that these restrictions were necessary in order "to have a good image for the public."

Chaperons too were carefully monitored and had to present a proper image. They were required to wear military-type uniforms that resembled the uniforms of airline stewardesses.[34] A June 15, 1946, Chicago Board Meeting, for example, debated the issue of whether or not chaperons should be allowed to take off their jackets on hot nights while at games. The final decision was that they would be allowed to take off their coats while sitting on the bench but had to put them on if they went onto the field. Image was paramount. Most of the chaperons were physical education teachers, former softball players, or in later years former AAGBL players. But some had no athletic background at all.[35]

Newspaper and magazine headlines read, "Belles of the Ball Game," "World's Prettiest Ballplayers," and "Darlings of the Diamond." For the most part the players enjoyed their public image. As Pepper Paire, a veteran catcher, said in an interview in 1987, "You'll think it sounds corny now, but back then we were pleased to be All-American girls and we considered ourselves just that."[36] "We thought it was our job to do our best, because we were the All-American girls. We felt we were keeping up our country's morale."[37]

But that's not to say the girls were always perfect little angels. Most of the girls were young, immature, and high spirited. Comradeship revolved around singing team songs, playing cards, gossiping, and playing pranks.[38] Lillian "Tennessee" Jackson recalled the fun they had on the bus. "The nights traveling on the team bus, singing, playing cards. Sometimes we shot craps. We'd get down in the aisle of the bus. The chaperon would watch us, and not say a word. Somebody would have a mouth organ and another a guitar, and we'd harmonize for hours."[39]

The public was unaware of any errant behavior. The league had complete control over the girls' behavior, and publicity was controlled by Meyerhoff. The women were in a separate league and they weren't competing with men. Therefore, the male macho image of baseball was unaffected. And yet the women were true professionals and were far from weak. They often played every night of the week with a double-header on the weekend. Helen Callagan described the rugged routine. "After a double-header, we'd shower, get dressed, travel all night in the bus, get to our hotel at 8 or 9 in the morning, shower, play two games of baseball in 110 degrees of heat, then do it all over again the next day."[40]

The games were strenuous, and as in the major leagues there were injuries—from pulled muscles to broken bones. But the women had an

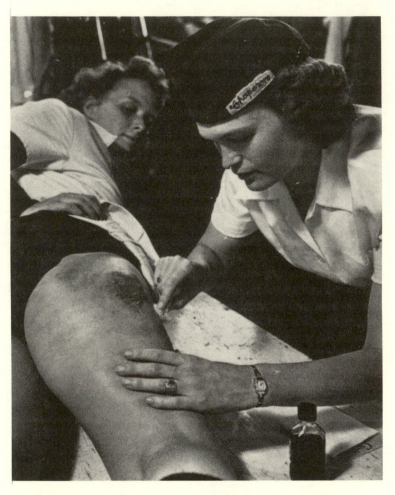

**23. Chaperon Dorothy Green tends to the "strawberry" on
Louise Fletcher's leg.**

added danger—bare legs. "Strawberries" (abrasions) were a common oc-
currence. (See photo 23.) As Helen Callagan said, "We played tough, even
when we were hurt. Not like today when these big-money ballplayers . . .
[have] a little pulled muscle [and don't] play. . . . We'd have strawberries
on our legs from sliding in skirts, . . . and the chaperones would just tape
us up and out we'd go."[41]

The quality of play was as important as appearance to Wrigley. He knew
that fans enjoyed close games with lots of excitement. He wanted the teams
to be as equally matched as possible. For a long time he had been an
opponent of the reserve clause in professional baseball. Now was his chance
to try something different. Rather than individual clubs owning the girls'

contracts as in the major leagues, he proposed that the league issue all contracts. In this way girls could be assigned to the different teams based on skills and the teams could be kept fairly even. Wrigley's motivation for eliminating the reserve clause was not designed to protect the player but, rather, to protect the game. The idea of free agency had nothing to do with it. Players were the property of the league, and therefore individual players couldn't negotiate salary by saying they would play for another team. This eliminated the possibility of salary wars between teams. Since there was only one baseball league, the league had absolute control over the players.

Wrigley not only wanted the teams to be evenly matched; he also wanted the level of play to be high. After all, he was billing the new league as the third major league. Therefore, he made every effort to recruit highly skilled players. But he drew the line at hiring masculine-appearing players. Thirty baseball scouts searched amateur and semi-professional baseball and soft-ball teams throughout the United States and Canada.[42] Regional tryouts were held in both countries. In April 1943 seventy-five women attended the final tryout at Wrigley Field.[43] From this group the four team managers were told to select seventeen players for each club. By the time the season started, the teams would be reduced to fifteen players.

Since no manager knew which group he would eventually have, each was interested in making sure that the teams were equal. Once selected, the four teams were then assigned at random to the various cities. This should have assured that the teams were competitive. As is often true, teams play differently as a whole than as individual players. Mid-season adjustments were needed. The league office switched two girls on three of the teams and left the Racine team as it was.[44] In future years, to promote community loyalty to the team, star players and hometown favorites were rarely traded.

Most of the girls signed were young, single, and very provincial. There were a few married women with children. Players' ages ranged from about fifteen to twenty-eight.[45] For example, Dolly Pearson was only fourteen when she tried out.[46] Dottie Kamenshek was seventeen and had been playing industrial softball; but because she was underage, she still had to have her mother's signed permission to try out.

For the girls playing not only was fun but also offered opportunities to travel. Many of these girls had never been outside their hometowns. Dorothy Green remembers how exciting it was. "We traveled in big-league style. . . . We had a private bus. Every Sunday somebody would throw a party for us. We went to spring training in Havana, Cuba, Florida, Chicago."[47]

Playing was also profitable. Because Wrigley had to compete with war industry salaries, wages were high. Salaries ranged from $55 to $150 plus expenses, although some stars were paid more.[48] The women actually earned more money than most men in the minor leagues.[49] Sophie Kurys, one of the earliest players to sign, recalled, "I started out at eighty-five dollars a week, but got as high as $375. Also I received bonuses for signing—sometimes $1,000."[50] In those days $85 was considered a lot of money, since the average wage was only about $40 a week.[51]

To further enhance the image of these women playing professional baseball, managers for the teams were recruited primarily from the ranks of major league baseball. Over the first six years, approximately seventeen former major league stars served as managers.[52] Some of the managers were Hall of Famers such as Jimmie Foxx, Max Carey, and Dave Bancroft.[53] Bill Wambagass, the only person to ever make an unassisted triple play in a World Series game, also coached a team for awhile.[54] Nineteen professional ball players served over the history of the league.[55]

The original four teams were managed by three former major league players—Bert Niehoff, Eddie Stumpf, and Josh Billings—and a major league hockey player, Johnny Gottselig of the Chicago Black Hawks. Gottselig was the only manager with actual experience coaching women's softball.[56] Two of the four umpires for the new league also were drawn directly from major league baseball—Knotty Porter from the Southern Association and Bill Green from the Virginia League. Both were experienced minor league umpires.[57]

The organization as well as the rules were drawn from baseball. The AAGBL played with nine players rather than ten, which was standard in the softball leagues. Runners were allowed to lead off and to steal bases. The pitching mound was lengthened to 40 feet instead of 35 feet in the hopes of cutting down the number of strikeouts and with the intent of livening up play. Players used regulation baseball bats and wore baseball gloves. In the first season, mention was made of reducing the size of the ball from twelve to ten inches.[58]

The first season of play the AAGBL drew a crowd of 200,000. Although it grossed $125,000 in gate receipts, it ended up $75,000 in the red.[59]

An article in *Baseball Magazine* stated that "the league was little more than a C or D circuit under Organized Baseball's set-up."[60] But President Kenneth Sells commented that although the AAGBL had started out on a small scale, "it is inevitable that we will be in the big league parks. . . . It may be in 1945—and it may be in five years—but it won't take as long as it did for other major league sports to become established."[61]

Early on Wrigley had recruited top amateur softball players for his teams. In the Chicago area this had caused some friction among the local managers, who claimed that Wrigley was raiding their teams. In an attempt to stop this practice, they hired an attorney. Unfortunately, they discovered that they had no recourse because they were an amateur league and their girls were not under contract.[62] Incensed, they decided to fight Wrigley head on, and in 1944 they formed the National Girls Baseball League.

The National Girls Baseball League (NGBL) was formed with four semi-pro softball teams from the Chicago area. The NGBL was designed to challenge the unique baseball status of the AAGBL and to provide direct competition. Although it never received the financial backing or the publicity of Wrigley's league, it operated successfully until the 1950s. Competition between the two leagues for players and publicity was constant, and this eventually led to raids on players and salary wars.[63]

The NGBL served as a ongoing catalyst for the AAGBL to strive to remain unique. This competition served to continually make AAGBL rules more like major league baseball's, so that by the last season of play in 1954, AAGBL teams were playing by official baseball rules. Because of this, the AAGBL became the only women's league ever to have professional baseball status. The NGBL remained more closely tied to softball, continuing to use underhand pitching and an official-sized softball.

It is important to remember that softball rules and regulations in the 1940s also were undergoing change. As a result, experimenting with pitching distances and base path differences was not unusual. In 1943 AAGBL rules were a hybrid between baseball and softball. Leading off the base, stealing bases, and sliding were permitted, as in baseball. All these were forbidden in softball. The pitching mound distance was 40 feet, which was slightly shorter than the regulation softball distance in 1940 and considerably shorter than for baseball. The ball was 12 inches, which was regulation softball size as compared to a 9-inch baseball. The base paths were 65 feet apart. (See AAGBL Regulations, 1943–1954.)

AAGBL Regulations, 1943–1954

Year	Ball Size	Basepaths	Pitching Mound	Style
1943	12″	65	40	Underhand
1944	11 1/2″	68	40	Underhand
1945	11 1/2″	68	42	Underhand
1946	11″	72	43	Underhand/side arm
1947	11″	72	43	Underhand/side arm
1948	10 3/8″	72	50	Overhand/side arm
1949	10″	72	55	Overhand/side arm
1950	10″	72	55	Overhand/side arm
1951	10″	72	55	Overhand/side arm
1952	10″	72	55	Overhand/side arm
1953	10″	75	56	Overhand/side arm
1954	9 1/4″	85	60	Overhand/side arm
July 1954	9″	90	60	Overhand/side arm

Data compiled by National Baseball Hall of Fame.

By the end of the 1944 season Wrigley's worry that major league baseball would be suspended was over and his thoughts again focused on his beloved Cubs. Losing interest in the AAGBL, he sold the league to Arthur Meyerhoff, who was head of advertising, for $10,000 with the understanding that the league would continue in its original form.[64]

The period from 1943 to 1944 has been called the league's "trusteeship period." During this time the league was under the control of the three trustees and the day-to-day operations were handled by the league president, Ken Sells.[65] Wrigley continued to provide almost unlimited seed money, experts in baseball management, advertising, and business by way of his connections in baseball and with the Cubs organization, as well as a carefully orchestrated press coverage. With his many resources he had successfully launched the league.

Meyerhoff changed the organizational structure when he took ownership in the fall of 1944. He created a profit-making corporation to run the non-profit league. The management corporation was responsible for overall league operations, which included hiring personnel, drawing up league schedules, handling publicity, recruitment, and spring training for all players. In return for handling administrative services and promotion, the management corporation received a percentage of the gate receipts.[66] Day-to-day operations of the individual teams were placed under the control of local team directors, who were often the businessmen who sponsored or financially backed the local teams.[67] The third season opened with the expectation that by September 5, more than 540,000 people would have come out to see the games.[68]

An article in *American Magazine* proclaimed, "Not so long ago girls' baseball rated along with checkers for spectator interest. Now there are nights when you have to stand up in back to see what is going on at the plate."[69]

Women's baseball became so popular that in 1945, the first season that the Fort Wayne Daisies played, they outdrew the men's semi-pro team. They averaged 1,300 spectators to 500 for the men. And they charged more, seventy-five cents compared to fifty cents. They also received more newspaper coverage than the men's semi-pro team or the local men's world champion softball club.[70]

E.V. Moss, in *Baseball's Bluebook*, speculated that the reason for its popularity was the excitement the girls' playing generated. "The girls game kept the spectator on edge with a greater number of spotlight episodes, such as base stealing, home runs inside the park and a continual pressure and movement toward the plate and around the diamond threat that is often lacking in low grade baseball."

An article in *Forbes* magazine extolled the virtues of the AAGBL. It credited the league with increasing factory worker morale, and community spirit, creating new town pride and all-around friendliness, and substantially decreasing juvenile delinquency.[71]

The management corporation period that lasted from fall 1944 to fall 1950 proved to be the most successful period both financially and in terms of spectators. During this time the league grew to ten teams. Like his predecessor, Wrigley, Meyerhoff believed that promotion and publicity were essential in order to attract the public. Meyerhoff was willing to spend large amounts of money because he believed that one's profit was directly related to one's financial investment.[72]

Meyerhoff used spring training as a way of publicizing the league. Players from all the teams trained together, so that camp became a showplace for the league. Camps were held in various places such as Florida and Mississippi. The most widely publicized camp was held in Havana, Cuba, in 1947. It received widespread international and national press coverage.[73] One hundred fifty girls participated in the camp's ten days of spring training, and during that time they were treated as celebrities by the Cuban government. The public loved them, and more than 30,000 people attended the four exhibition games.[74] In fact, the girls' games outdrew the Brooklyn Dodgers, who were also training there.[75] The girls' tour gave birth to the Latin American Feminine Baseball League, a number of whose players eventually played for the AAGBL.[76]

Movietone News made a newsreel of one of the exhibition games. The newsreel, called *Diamond Girls,* was seen in theaters throughout the United States. Popular magazines such as *Holiday, Collier's,* and the *Saturday Evening Post* also ran feature articles about the league.[77] In fact, the league was so popular that the 1947 *Major League Baseball Yearbook* published by Dell featured Stan Musial on the front cover and Sophie Kurys on the back cover.[78]

Attendance and league popularity peaked in 1948. For the ten teams attendance was estimated at about 1 million.[79] As one ex-manager remarked, "Talk about crowds—why, some towns draw four times their population every season. If the New York Yankees stirred up that kind of excitement, they'd draw 32,000,000 fans."[80]

Things were looking good. There was a strong junior network of teenage girls' baseball teams in most of the affiliated cities. These had developed as part of Wrigley's policy that as a non-profit organization the league would put funds back into worthwhile community projects. These junior teams also provided new recruits and continuing community interest in the franchise team. In 1948 Muskegon had eight Junior Lassies teams. In Racine four teams played a regular schedule. They were a mirror image of the women's professional team, using regulation equipment and uniforms. Former local men's baseball players and sports stars managed the teams.[81]

24. **The Racine Belles at Sloppy Joe's Bar, Havana, Cuba. (L-R) Maddy English, Sophy Kurys, Eleanor Dapkus, Irene Hickson, Marnie Danhauser, Pepper Paire, and Dorothy McGuire.** *From the Collection of the Northern Indiana Historical Society.*

Recruitment of new players did not seem to be a problem in 1948. The media had awarded celebrity status to many of the players, and to be a female ballplayer was prestige conferring. Rosters contained names of players from twenty-seven states, as well as Cuba and Canada.[82] But there were also many veterans in the league. In 1948 twenty-one players had played for six years, and another thirty-four for five years. The Racine Belles had the most veterans, with twelve players having played five or six years.[83] Although this was not considered a problem, it was to plague the league a few years later. As players got older, some wanted to retire, get married, and have families. Thus it was necessary to have a full complement of highly skilled recruits.

There were also manager problems. A *Collier's* magazine article called the All American League the "Little Big Horn of the management profession," citing that twenty-eight managers, seventeen of whom were former major league stars, had resigned or been fired since the league started.[84]

By 1950 the rosy picture had changed. Attendance and gate receipts were falling. Several teams were on the brink of financial disaster. The Rockford Peaches were saved from bankruptcy by loyal fans who raised the necessary money to keep the team solvent.[85]

Because many local team owners felt financially squeezed, they objected to the management corporation's high-budget costs for administration and publicity. They felt that the individual owners could handle their own affairs more inexpensively. Consequently, there was a falling out and Meyerhoff agreed to transfer ownership and operation of the league to the individual owners. The autonomous team ownership period lasted from 1951 to 1954.[86] After the Championship Series in September 1954, the team owners voted to suspend the 1955 season.[87]

It was the end of an era. For the women who played, it was the end of a dream. Parting was difficult. As Lil Jackson said, "When I realized I couldn't play anymore, my heart was broken.... For a time I couldn't watch a game from the stands; it hurt too much."[88] As Sophie Kurys remembered, "The League was the best thing that ever happened to me."[89] And as Dottie Collins recalled, the women who played weren't feminists. In fact, they were totally unaware of the historical significance of their play. "We didn't realize what we had. We were just a bunch of young kids doing what we liked best. But most of us recognize now that those were the most meaningful days of our lives. Times have changed; I don't think we could ever have a league like that again."[90]

Although the end came in 1954, the decline had begun in 1951. In part this was due to structural changes in the league. The major reasons, however, were changing social conditions in society. Decentralization of the league and the emphasis on individual ownership resulted in localizing the league. Owners became more interested in promoting their own teams than in promoting the league as a whole. National publicity expenditures went from a 1948 budget of $8,445 to a 1952 budget of $200.[91] There was virtually no money allotted for national publicity of the league and little money for recruitment of players outside local franchise areas. Consequently, the caliber of new players declined.

Without a central body, self-interest reigned. Owners lost sight of the original philosophy of having a balanced league and thought only of having a winning team. As opposed to earlier years, when several teams (the Peaches, the Blue Sox, the Belles, and the Chicks) competed for the pennant or league championship, one team came to dominate. This team, the Fort Wayne Daisies, became similar to the legendary Yankees. It recruited the most talent and dominated the league. Although the team never won the Championship Series playoffs, it was the league champion or pennant winner from 1952 to 1954 (see listing of AAGBL Pennant and Championship Winners).[92] This imbalance hurt overall league attendance.

AAGBL Pennant and Championship Winners

Team	Pennants	Championships
Rockford Peaches	1945, 1950	1945, 1948, 1949, 1950
South Bend Blue Sox	1943, 1951	1951, 1952
Racine Belles	1943 (1/2), 1946, 1948	1943, 1946
Kenosha Comets	1943 (1/2)	
Milwaukee Chicks	1944	1944
Minneapolis Millerettes		
Grand Rapids Chicks	1948	1947, 1953
Fort Wayne Daisies	1952, 1953, 1954	
Muskegon Lassies/Belles	1947	
Peoria Redwings		
Chicago Colleens		
Springfield Sallies		
Kalamazoo Lassies		1954
Battle Creek Belles		

Adapted from AAGBL Cards, 1984

As the pool of spectators decreased for baseball in general, competition between the AAGBL and the NGBL became more intense. In an attempt to attract fans, competition for star players gave rise to player raids. This served to inflate salaries and exacerbate financial problems. Both leagues ended up failing in the 1950s.

The AAGBL had an additional problem that the NGBL did not have. It was easier to find women who could play softball than it was to find women who could play baseball. The AAGBL game now was distinctly different from softball. Most of the early softball players who had been recruited accommodated their game to baseball over a period of time as

25. The Fort Wayne Daisies in their locker room. (L-R) Kay Blumetta, Jean Smith, Marge Pieper, Wilma Briggs, Dottie Schroeder, and Ruby Heafner. *Courtesy of Ruby Heafner.*

26. **A postcard of the Racine Belles from 1947.** *Courtesy of Ruby Heafner.*

the AAGBL game changed from softball to baseball. Now the players had to be skilled baseball players from the beginning. Some of the glamour of playing baseball was also lost after the war. It was no longer seen as a patriotic endeavor for the women to entertain the public. As Snooky Doyle, a shortstop who played eight seasons, recalled, after the war "there was a stigma attached to being a woman and playing baseball."[93]

Furthermore, many of the AAGBL players were getting older and wanted to retire. Family life became an important factor. Of twenty-five players who quit the league in 1950, almost half cited family reasons. Four retired because of marriage, three for pregnancy, three to take care of ill family members, and one for reasons of childcare. Another nine retired because of advanced age or injuries.[94] When the women retired, they left a void. The league may also have suffered from a change in game policy. Originally the league had been conceived as a separate women's league. As individual franchise owners looked for promotional gimmicks to increase revenue, some resorted to having their teams play exhibition games against males. Usually the teams exchanged batteries (pitcher and catcher).[95] This put the women in direct competition with men and thereby altered the image of the women's league from that of a separate and distinct third major league.

The AAGBL was also a casualty of the times. Attendance at AAGBL games was affected by competing forms of entertainment, and television, as were minor and major league men's teams The 1950s also brought major changes in the social definition of women's roles. Again there was strict sex-role segregation. The war was over, and women were expected to relinquish their jobs to the men. The ideal female role became that of full-time housewife and mother. Women's magazines such as *Good Housekeeping* glorified that role, and Americans seemed happy to embrace traditional roles once again. After the war's disruptions, family togetherness and stability were particularly appealing.

Historical and social events had changed and women's baseball was an aberration. Little girls were no longer encouraged to play baseball with their brothers. Little League baseball came to replace sandlot baseball and had a no-girls-allowed policy. The fact that women had played baseball during the war years was forgotten. Years later, that role was so antithetical to the "feminine" role that even if someone mentioned it, the natural assumption was that they had played softball.

A certain irony is obvious when one looks back on this era—an era of unprecedented opportunity for women to participate in baseball. After all, women today are barred from playing baseball, which remains a male preserve. Yet the women who played baseball during World War II were treated as children and depicted as the weaker sex. There was still strict sex-role segregation. Women could be "feminine" players and chaperons, but they were not allowed to be managers or coaches. The teams were

forbidden to play even exhibition games against male teams. Yet the league
was billed as the third major league and the women were expected to
possess all the skills of professional baseball players. But femininity and
athletic prowess were seen as two separate domains. As Susan Cahn has
stated, "By continuing to see athletic ability as masculine skill rather than
incorporating athleticism within the range of feminine qualities, the
league's ideology posed no challenge to the fundamental precepts of gender
in American society."[96] After World War II the realms of work and sports
were again seen as proper masculine endeavors, while proper feminine
endeavors were raising children and keeping house.

NOTES

1. Mary Pidgeon, *Women's Work and the War*, American Job Series Occupational Monograph No. 36 (Chicago: Science Research Assoc., 1943), 5.
2. Merrie Fidler, "The Development and Decline of the All-American Girls Baseball League, 1943–1954" (M.S. thesis, University of Massachusetts, Amherst, 1976), 45.
3. Richard Goldstein, *Spartan Seasons: How Baseball Survived the Second World War* (New York:Macmillan, 1980), 160.
4. Ibid., 155.
5. Susan Cahn, "No Freaks, No Amazons, No Boyish Babes," *Chicago History Magazine*, Spring 1989, 30.
6. Merrie Fidler, "The All-American Girls' Baseball League, 1943–1954," in *Her Story in Sport: A Historical Anthology of Women in Sports*, ed. Reet Howell (West Point, N.Y.: Leisure Press, 1982), 591.
7. Felucia Halpert, "How the Game Was Invented," *Women's Sports and Fitness* 9 (July 1987): 50.
8. Robert Yoder, "Miss Casey at the Bat," *Saturday Evening Post,* 22 Aug. 1942, 16, 48.
9. "Ladies of Little Diamond," *Time*, 14 July 1943, 74.
10. Paul Angle, *Philip K. Wrigley: A Memoir of a Modest Man* (Chicago: Rand McNally, 1975), 105–106.
11. "Ladies of Little Diamond," 74.
12. Eric Zorn, "The Girls of Summer," *Chicago Tribune*, 12 Dec. 1982.
13. Anne Graham, "Yes, Virgina, Women Really Did Play Baseball," *Tuff Stuff*, 8 Aug. 1987.
14. Zorn, 4.
15. Sharon Roepke, *Diamond Gals: The Story of the All American Girls Professional Baseball League*, 2nd ed. (Flint, Mich.: AAGBL Cards, 1988), 5.
16. Diana Helmer, "The Night the Lights Went on at Wrigley," *Sports Collectors Digest*, 2 Sept. 1988.
17. Diana Helmer, "Belles of the Ballpark," *Sports Collectors Digest* 2 Sept. 1988, 119.
18. Jack Fincher, "The 'Belles of the Ball Game' Were a Hit with Their Fans," *Smithsonian* 20 (July 1989): 91.

19. Ron Berler, " 'Man, We Could Playball': The Girls of Summer Shine Again," *Chicago Sun-Times*, 27 Sept. 1987.

20. Jay Feldman, "Glamour Ball," *Sports Heritage* (May/June 1987):60.

21. Fidler, "Development and Decline," 54.

22. *Rockford Peaches Souvenir Book*, 1943, 9.

23. Helmer, "Belles of the Ballpark," 119.

24. Angle, 111.

25. Helmer, "Belles of the Ballpark," 119.

26. Fidler, "The All-American Girls' Baseball League, 1943–1954," 595.

27. Roepke, 6.

28. Fidler, "Development and Decline," 52.

29. "Ladies of Little Diamond," 74.

30. Ibid.

31. Zorn, 4.

32. Fidler, "The All-American Girls' Baseball League, 1943–1954," 599.

33. Fincher, 93.

34. David Young, "Seasons in the Sun," *Women's Sports*, Oct. 1982, 51.

35. Fidler, "The All-American Girls' Baseball League, 1943–1954," 598.

36. Qtd. in Larry LaRue, "Belles of the Ball," *Press-Telegram*, 17 May 1987.

37. Ron Berler, "Mama Was a Major-Leaguer," *Arizona Republic*, 4 Oct. 1987.

38. Fincher, 97.

39. Qtd. in Berler, " 'Man, We Could Play Ball.' "

40. Qtd. in Todd Gold, "This Mother Could Hit," *Visages*, no date, NBHFL, 81.

41. Ibid.

42. Graham, 8.

43. Roepke, 7.

44. Herbert Simons, "Cherchez La Femme," *Baseball Magazine*, March 1944, 336.

45. Helmer, "Belles of the Ballpark," 119.

46. Young, 51.

47. Robert Doolan, "Greene Enters Hall of Fame," *Middlesex News*, 22 July 1988.

48. Roepke, 7.

49. AAGBL Card 2.

50. Qtd. in Ron Coons, "Short-Pants Star? Sophie Wins the Trophy!" *Courier Journal and Times*, Sept. 1976.

51. Roepke, 7.

52. Bill Fay, "Belles of the Ball Game," *Collier's*, 13 Aug. 1949, 44.

53. Graham, 8.

54. Doolan.

55. Roepke, 7.

56. Ibid.

57. Simons, 358.

58. Ibid.

59. "Baseball, Maestro, Please," *Time*, 31 July 1944, 40.

60. Simons, 336.

61. Ibid., 358.

62. Fidler, "Development and Decline," 58.

63. Cahn, 33.

64. Young, 50.

65. Fidler, "The All-American Girls' Baseball League, 1943–1954," 592; Roepke, 12.

66. Fidler, "The All-American Girls' Baseball League, 1943–1954," 592.

67. "Girls' Baseball," *Life*, 4 June 1945, 63.

68. James Gordon, "Beauty at the Bat," *American Magazine*, June 1945, 24.

69. Fidler, "The All-American Girls' Baseball League, 1943–1954," 73.

70. Qtd. in "Joanne Winter, Pitcher, Racine Belles, 1943–1950: The History of the All-American Girls Professional Baseball League, 1943–1946," NBHFL, 5.

71. Norman Klein, "Baseball-Business Booster," *Forbes*, 1 April 1947, 21.

72. Young, 50.

73. *All-American Girls Professional Baseball League 1943–1954 Souvenir Program*, 1986, 3.

74. Sharon Roepke, "Females Have Been Playing Ball Thousands of Years: Professional Women's Baseball League Existed from 1943–1954," *Collegiate Baseball*, 26 Feb. 1988, 3.

75. Fidler, "The All-American Girls' Baseball League, 1943–1954," 600.

76. Cahn, 36.

77. LaRue.

78. *All-American Girls Baseball League Souvenir Program*, 1949, 6.

79. Fay, 44.

80. *All-American Girls Baseball League Souvenir Program*, 1949, 6.

81. Ibid., 5.

82. Ibid., 6.

83. Fay, 44.

84. *All-American Girls Professional Baseball League 1943–1954 Souvenir Program*, 1986, 2.

85. Roepke, *Diamond Gals*, 12.

86. *All-American Girls Professional Baseball League 1943–1954 Souvenir Program*, 1986, 2.

87. Qtd. in Berler, "Mama Was a Major-Leaguer."

88. Qtd. in "Girls' Ball Club Reunites," *MJA*, 18 Sept. 1986.

89. Reyn Davis, "The Girls of Summer," *Winnepeg Free Press*, 19 Aug. 1988.

90. Helmer, "Belles of the Ballpark," 121.

91. *All-American Girls Professional Baseball League 1943–1954 Souvenir Program*, 1986.

92. Qtd. in LaRue.

93. Qtd. in ibid.

94. Fidler, "Development and Decline," 279.

95. "Joanne Winter," 11.

96. Cahn, 41.

9

Profiles of Some All American Girls' Professional Baseball Players

If baseball was an exclusive male domain in the 1940s, how did Wrigley find these women players? Who were they? Where did they come from? How did they learn to play baseball?

From 1943 to 1954 approximately 538 women played AAGBL ball. Although many of the women as children may have played baseball with their brothers or the boys in the neighborhood, most of their experience was playing softball. After all, there were no women's baseball teams.

Scouts scoured the United States and Canada for athletic young women who could play a hybrid brand of softball-baseball. The women were mostly young and of high school or college age. The majority were between the ages of eighteen and twenty-two, although the ages ranged from fourteen to twenty-eight. Most were single. For example, in 1946 of 144 players only 12 were married and 3 of those had children.[1] Since the season ran from May to September, many of the younger girls could play in the summer and still attend school in the winter. From 1943 to 1947 all the players were white. This was also true of major league baseball and reflected the segregation in American society. Jackie Robinson didn't break the color line until 1947.

The composition of the AAGBL also changed in 1947, when it held its spring training camps in Havana, as did the Brooklyn Dodgers. The Cuban response to the women's games was overwhelming. In fact, the Cubans were so enthralled with the idea of women's baseball that they started their own league, the Latin American Feminine Baseball League. The AAGBL now had a new untapped source of female players.

In 1948 the first group of Cuban players were recruited to attend spring training. Four made the cuts and played throughout the regular season. The four regular-season players all came from Havana. Mirtha Marrero and Migdalia Perez played for Chicago, Gloria Ruiz played for Peoria, and Luisa Gallegos played for Peoria and South Bend.[2] Gloria Ruiz played only one season, and Luisa Gallegos two. However, both Migdalia Perez, 1948–1954, and Mirtha Marrero, 1948–1953, had long successful careers.[3] Neither ever made All Star status. In 1949 another Havana player, Isabel Álvarez, joined the Daisy pitching staff and played from 1949 to 1954.[4]

By 1948 the player makeup was diversified both ethnically and geographically. At the start of the season players hailed from twenty-seven states, Canada, and Cuba. States with the largest number of players were Michigan (thirty), Illinois (seventeen), California (fifteen), Pennsylvania (twelve), and Ohio, Indiana, and Wisconsin (ten each). Canada had sixteen.[5] But there were still no black players.

By 1950 the league was in financial trouble and player recruitment was a definite problem. Many of the older players were retiring, the budget for national recruitment was severely cut, and it was difficult to find recruits who played baseball rather than softball. At this time, some of the teams considered hiring black players. A newspaper article dated May 10, 1951, mentions that "two Negro girls, the first in the American Girls Baseball League worked out with the Sox at Playland Park yesterday. The two are Elizabeth Jackson, an infielder, and Marie Maxier, an outfielder, both from South Bend."[6] Apparently they didn't make the team because the May 21, 1951, South Bend Blue Sox team roster doesn't list their names.[7]

But for the first time, black players became an issue. At the November 14, 1951, board of directors meeting for the league the question of hiring black players was discussed "at length, with various views from different cities. The consensus of the group seemed to be against the idea of colored players, unless they would show promise of exceptional ability, that in event a club did hire one of them that none of the clubs would make her feel unwelcome."[8]

Apparently no female Jackie Robinsons tried out. In fact, the league records make no further mention of black players trying out. An attempt was made to recruit a black player in 1952, but there is no mention of whether the player was interested in playing AAGBL ball. A league memo dated Tuesday, June 3, 1952, states: "Sheehan got in touch with a colored player, shortstop, in Cincinnati and she will report Monday. She is sponsored by Mueller." Apparently she never played for the league, nor did any other blacks.

When the league administration changed from the management corporation to that of the individual team ownerships in 1951, team owners began to explore all kinds of ways to recruit top players for their teams. The old rules against not recruiting masculine-looking women or women who had left the AAGBL to join another league were dropped. An example of the changing policy could be seen in 1951 when the AAGBL tried to sign the Savona sisters, both masculine-looking players from the National

Baseball League, a Chicago softball league. The two leagues, both struggling to survive because of reduced attendance, became locked in a competitive bidding war for highly skilled players. An AAGBL memo of April 30, 1951, states: "Several girls have jumped to the Chicago League and are listed in the *Chicago Tribune* today."[9]

At the November 14, 1951, board meeting, it was decided to try to re-recruit players who had been lost to the National Baseball League. This was a complete reversal of policy in that the rules stated that if a player left the league for another league, she could never be reinstated. In the minutes it was suggested that a list of players who had gone to the Chicago League be given to the business office by each club. Then a letter was to be prepared and sent to these players "informing them of their eligibility for the newly organized league, that all previous penalties were waived under the new management, but that any girl deviating from the policy from this time on would be barred with positively no alternative."[10]

Recruitment of players continued to be a problem right up to the end of the league in 1954. Under the autonomous team management period, recruitment of players became more localized, since there was no national recruiting effort by a central administrative body. Some believe that the caliber of recruited players declined. But a substantial number of players had long careers, and many of the stars of the early years were still playing in the 1950s. So the level of play probably didn't decline very much.

Profiles of some of the All Stars from 1943–1954, one league fan favorite, and the Players of the Year from 1945 to 1954, are included here to indicate the high skill level of the players. There were no official All Star or Player of the Year selections during the first few years. The selection of a Player of the Year began in 1945. The selection of an All Star team became an official league practice in 1946, but there was an unofficial All Star team in 1943. The Player of the Year was selected by the managers, and the All Star team was selected by the league sportswriters. This practice continued until 1954.

ALL STARS

The All Star players profiled are Ann Harnett, third base, 1943; Shirley Jameson, outfielder, 1943; Bonnie Baker, catcher, 1943, 1946; Dorothy Schroeder, shortstop, 1952, 1953, and 1954; Dottie Kamenshek, first base, 1943, 1946 through 1951; and Ruth Richard, catcher, 1949 through 1954.

Ann Harnett

A twenty-three-year-old Chicagoan, Ann Harnett, was the first player signed by Wrigley. From 1942 to 1943 Ann Harnett was the softball organizer for the Chicago playgrounds.[11] Some believe that she was instrumental in helping Wrigley design the league. According to Meyerhoff, she was a consultant to Wrigley, who took her ideas into account. Harnett was a regular at the 1942–1943 winter meetings at the Wrigley Building, which laid the foundation for the league. Wrigley probably wanted a woman's opinion as well as someone who was knowledgeable about women's softball. From Wrigley's standpoint Ann was the ideal woman; she was an excellent player and administrator, as well as being attractive. Otis Shephard, Wrigley's Art Director, used her as a model when he designed the league uniform. Sportswriters often described her as "a statuesque redhead with a winning personality."[12] She was 5 feet 6 1/2 inches tall and weighed 130.[13]

Ann was an outstanding and versatile player. During her career, which lasted from 1943 to 1947, she played catcher, third base, and outfield. From 1943 to 1946 she played for the Kenosha Comets. In her last year she played for the Peoria Redwings. In 1943 she had been one of the top batters, and led the league in extra base hits (twenty-six) and runs batted in (RBIs) (sixty-nine).[14] The league city newspaper sportswriters selected her as the best third basewoman. This was an unofficial league All Star team.[15]

When her mother died Ann promised her she would become a nun, and true to her words, when her playing days were over, she entered the convent. But her baseball skills were put to good use because she coached a Catholic high school boys' baseball team. She died in the 1960s.[16]

Shirley Jameson

Of the original four players signed by Wrigley, Shirley Jameson was the second. The other two, besides Harnett and Jameson, were Clara Schillace and Edie Perlick. (See photo 27.) These players were carefully selected from the Chicago amateur softball association league to be the models for the All American Girls' Professional Softball League. They epitomized the carefully constructed image of feminine, attractive, well-mannered ballplayers. Press releases and publicity photos showcased them. Shirley Jameson was an attractive, petite 4 feet 10 3/4 inches, 104 pounds. A college graduate from a middle-class background, she was a physical education teacher in Chicago. At twenty-three she had the maturity to handle the publicity that was to be created around her.[17]

She was recruited directly by P.K. Wrigley, although he had first discussed the idea with her father. Wrigley arranged for her to have lunch with Ken Sells and Arthur Meyerhoff so that they could tell her about the plans for the new league. There were no tryouts. She signed a contract for $75 a week with the understanding that she could miss spring training due to her teaching commitments. She was paid about $25 more a week than

**27. The first four players signed for AAGBL. Seated: Shirley Jameson.
Standing (L-R): Clara Schillace, Ann Harnett, and Edie Perlick.**
From the Collection of the Northern Indiana Historical Society.

the regular starting salary. Jameson and Harnett were assigned to the
Comets, the Kenosha, Wisconsin, team, and were roommates.

The four original signers attended many meetings with Wrigley, Meyerhoff, Sells, and others who were instrumental in launching the league.

They were asked their opinions, tried out versions of the proposed uniform, and posed for numerous publicity pictures.

Shirley played center field for four years, 1943–1946, for Kenosha. A left-handed thrower who batted right, she was known for her speed. In 1943 she batted .271, set a record for most stolen bases, and was selected for the All Star team. She was also part of the team that played under the lights at Wrigley Field that year. Her record for most runs scored, 111, stood until 1946, when it was broken by Sophie Kurys.[18]

Shirley claims that she quit at the end of the 1946 season because she had been injured and didn't feel that she could give the league $125 a week worth of effort. A year later, in 1947, Wrigley contacted her to scout for the league, and this she did for two years. She was paid $100 a week plus all expenses.

According to Shirley the Wrigley organization received thousands of letters from girls all over the country who wanted to try out for the AAGBL. It was her job to review the applications and then to conduct tryouts. She said that it was difficult to recruit girls from the Chicago area because if they weren't students, most of them had full-time jobs with companies such as Western Electric or Illinois Bell. These girls were not about to give up a good job to play baseball. But she could occasionally recruit them for Kenosha because there were many companies there such as Nash Rambler, Jockey men's underwear, and Simmons mattress company. The local businessmen in these companies were very supportive of the team and often hired the girls in the off-season. Jockey even made special ladies' underwear for the Kenosha team. Shirley believes it was because of the AAGBL that Jockey learned how to fit women.

Bonnie Baker

Bonnie Baker, a Canadian from Regina, Saskatchewan, was another of the first players. She was born in 1918 and began her baseball career at twenty-five. She was 5 feet 5 1/2 inches tall, weighed 133, and had been a fashion model.[19] She came to symbolize the league image of the "feminine baseball player" and was the most publicized player in the league.

But she was more than window dressing for the league. She was an outstanding player and all-around athlete. One of nine children in a ball-playing family,[20] she was a basketball, softball, and track star in high school.[21] In the AAGBL she was selected All Star catcher in 1943 and 1946. Described as a "money hitter," Bonnie was at her best with runners on base.[22] She played nine seasons from 1943 to 1949 as a catcher and infielder for the South Bend Blue Sox; 1950 for South Bend and Kalamazoo; and 1952 for Kalamazoo alone. In 1950 she left South Bend mid-season to play and manage the new Kalamazoo team—the first and only woman manager in the league. Her managerial role didn't sit well with many of the owners, however. They felt that women shouldn't be managers. Baker attributed their fury to the fact that she "took over a last-place team and moved them up three rungs in the standings. . . . But the league didn't like it. You can't have a woman like me beating Jimmie Foxx."[23] Bonnie finally moved into an executive league position, but the ban on women managers remained. After leaving the league she became a sportscaster for a while and in 1986 was managing a curling rink in Regina.[24]

Dorothy "Dottie" Schroeder

Dottie Schroeder is the only player to have played all twelve seasons. At a time when the average size of a woman baseball player was 5 feet 4 inches, she was considered big at 5 feet 8 inches and 150 pounds. She came from Sadorus, a small town in Illinois.[25]

A 1946 newspaper article compared her to the immortal Honus Wagner and called her the "Honey Wagner" of the AAGBL. It quoted Charlie Grimm, manager of the Chicago Cubs, as saying, "If she was a boy I'd give $50,000 for her."[26]

Selected the All Star team shortstop for 1952, 1953, and 1954, she holds longevity records for most at bats, games, putouts. Her overall career fielding percentage was .913. In 1951 she was the home run leader for the league, and in 1953 for the Lassies. Her batting improved as she got older. In 1943, when she was fifteen and started playing shortstop for the South Bend Blue Sox, she batted .188 and hit one home run. In 1954, her last year, she batted .304 and hit seventeen home runs.[27]

In 1954 she got a taste of men's baseball when she played for the Kalamazoo All City's men's squad against the Grand Rapids Black Sox. But her baseball career didn't end in 1954; she continued to play for Allington's All Americans. Bill Allington, who had managed the Rockford Peaches for eight years and the Fort Wayne Daisies for two, started the All Americans when the AAGBL folded. The All Americans barnstormed across the country playing local men's teams from 1954 to 1957.

Dottie Schroeder now lives in her hometown and has been employed by Collegiate Cap and Gown of Champaign, Illinois, for thirty-four years.[28]

Dottie "Kammie" Kamenshek

Dottie Kamenshek, a Cincinnatian, was another longtime career player. She played for the Rockford Peaches for ten years from 1943 to 1951 and then again in 1953. She retired in 1951 to become a physical therapist. In 1953 the financially desperate Peaches convinced her to make a comeback in an effort to revive gate receipts.[29]

She was considered the best first basewoman in the AAGBL. In fact, former Yankee first baseman Wally Pipp thought she was so good that he predicted she would be the first woman in the majors. He said that she was the best first baseman he had ever seen—man or woman.[30]

She almost got her chance to play with the men when the Fort Lauderdale Club of the Florida International League tried to buy her contract from the AAGBL in 1950. The AAGBL turned down the offer, citing that she was indispensable to Rockford and that women were not meant to play in men's leagues. It said that women "could not help but appear inferior in athletic competition with men."[31] Amazingly enough, Kammie agreed with them. "I thought it was a publicity stunt. . . . I was 5 foot 6, 140 pounds. How many men can play first base at that size?"[32]

She was one incredible player. Selected for the 1943, 1946, 1947, 1948, 1949, 1950, and 1951 All Star teams, she was consistently one of the top ten batters and won the batting crown in 1946 and 1947 with batting averages of .316 and .306. In 1950 she batted .334, and in 1951 .345. She had an amazing record of only eighty-one strikeouts in 3,736 times at bat.[33]

But her baseball days took a physical toll. She suffered from back problems during her last two years of play and wore a brace.[34] This may have influenced her choice of career after she retired from baseball. In 1952 she graduated from Marquette University with a degree in physical therapy and eventually became the chief of the Los Angeles Crippled Children's Services Department.[35]

Kammie had been discovered by an AAGBL scout when she was seventeen and playing industrial league softball in Cincinnati.[36] Her mother had allowed her to sign with the league if she promised to return in September to complete her high school education.[37]

Ruth "Ritchie" Richard

Ruth Richard began her baseball career when she was nineteen. She was 5 feet 4 inches and 134 pounds. Although she is best remembered as a star catcher, she also played outfield.[38]

In six of the eight seasons that she played, Ruth Richard was selected as the best catcher in the league—an outstanding accomplishment. She was the All Star catcher from 1949 to 1954. Although she toured Central America with the AAGBL All Stars in 1949, her career actually began in 1947 with the Grand Rapids Chicks. In 1948 she was traded to the Rockford Peaches and became a mainstay of the team.[39] The 1948 *Rockford Yearbook* proclaimed that she was "among the best finds of year. . . . Ruth Richard . . . had a sparkling year behind the mask in her first season as a regular with Rockford.[40] When she broke her leg in the second year of play, loyal fans raised $600 to help her out while she recuperated. This was a considerable amount of money back then.[41] By 1952 her salary was $430 a month.[42] She remained loyal to Rockford and stayed with them until 1954 when the league folded. Her career continued as a member of Bill Allington's All Americans.

When her playing days were over, she returned to eastern Pennsylvania and took a job with AMETEK, U.S. Gauge Division, a company that manufactures pressure gauges and automotive and aircraft instruments. In 1991 she was a lighting specialist for cockpit instruments.[43]

When asked what effect playing on the AAGBL and Allington's All Americans had on her life, she responded: "I live in a very small rural community in eastern Pennsylvania and probably would have been here all my life. I had the opportunity to travel all over the USA, Canada, Mexico, Venezuela, Costa Rica, Panama, Cuba, Puerto Rico, and others. I am certain this would not have happened otherwise. Secondly, and even more important, I met some people who remain my friends to this day."[44]

Faye Dancer

Although Faye Dancer never made an All Star team, her profile is included here because of her star status with the fans. A true character and exhibitionist, she was one of the most colorful and fun-loving players in the league. The fans loved her, and she thrived on their attention. As she said, "I'll probably be remembered as a crowd favorite, a little crazy. . . . I always had fun."[45] Some of the funny incidents for which she is remembered include catching fireflies during a game and pinning them to her hat, turning somersaults in the field, and calling an unofficial timeout so that she could get a drink of water.[46] Indeed, she received the nickname "Tiger" prior to joining the AAGBL, a nickname reflective of her enthusiastic antics meant to make games fun for the fans.[47]

Faye was superstitious, or at least she led fans to believe she was. She claimed that having a fan rub a glass eye during a game brought the team luck. Consequently, she collected glass eyes wherever she went. Stuffed animals, mounted fish, all were fair game. One of the hardest eyes she ever collected came from a carousel. She said, "I had to go on a carousel horse 18 times before I got the glass eye out."[48]

But Faye was not just a clown, she also played her heart out. She retired in 1950 with a ruptured disc from a sliding injury. The injury was compounded by chipped vertebrae, an injury that she sustained when making a diving catch.[49]

Faye Dancer was 5 feet 6 inches and 149 pounds.[50] She played six seasons for three different teams—the Minneapolis Millerettes in 1944, the Fort Wayne Daisies from 1945 to mid–1947, and the Peoria Redwings, with whom she played part of 1947, and 1948 and 1950. Over the course of her career she played outfield, infield, and pitcher. Noted for stealing bases and being a power hitter, in 1948 she was second behind Sophie Kurys in stolen bases.[51]

She retired to her hometown of Santa Monica, California, where she worked as an electronics technician.[52]

PLAYERS OF THE YEAR

The Players of the Year from 1945 to 1954 were as follows:

1945—Connie Wisniewski, Grand Rapids Chicks, pitcher

1946—Sophie Kurys, Racine Belles, second base

1947—Doris Sams, Muskegon Lassies, utility infielder

1948—Audrey Wagner, Kenosha Comets, outfielder

1949—Doris Sams, Muskegon Lassies, outfield

1950—Alma Ziegler, Grand Rapids Chicks, pitcher, second base

1951—Jean Faut, South Bend Blue Sox, pitcher

1952—Betty Foss, Fort Wayne Daisies, first base

1953—Jean Faut, South Bend Blue Sox, pitcher

1954—Joanne Weaver, Fort Wayne Daisies, outfield

Connie "Iron Woman" Wisniewski, 1945

One sportswriter described Connie Wisniewski's pitching as "hotter than a three-alarm fire."[53] Another called her the "Christine Mathewson" of women's baseball.[54] Her incredible pitching for the Grand Rapids Chicks earned her the Player of the Year award in 1945, the first year it was offered. It also earned her the nickname "Iron Woman" for performing the "iron man" feat of pitching both ends of a double-header. She managed to accomplish this three times and two of those times to win both games of the double-header.[55] Her season record was thirty-two wins and eleven losses in forty-six trips to the mound. Her earned runs per game average was .81—that year's league record. Her accomplishments were even recognized by major league baseball when her picture appeared on the back of *Major League Baseball*.[56]

Another sportswriter marveled at her endurance and stamina. He said, "While major league pitchers go to the mound once every four or five days, this frail pitcher of the weaker sex . . . piled up her record with only a single day's rest between games."[57] In 1945 she pitched 391 innings, threw to 1,367 batters in forty-six games for an AAGBL record.[58] Obviously, she was neither frail nor weak. But this was the feminine image that writers liked to portray and that the AAGBL management encouraged. Connie was actually one of the bigger women in the league at 5 feet 8 inches, 150 pounds.[59]

Her 1945 pitching won her the Player of the Year award, but her 1946 pitching record was even better than 1945. In 1946 she pitched in 48 games and won thirty-three and lost nine for a win-loss percentage of .786. Again she was recognized as the best pitcher in the league and was the pitcher chosen for the All Star team.[60] In 1947 the distance from mound to home-plate was lengthened from 68 feet to 70 feet and her pitching became less effective. In thirty-two games her win-loss record was 16–14 with an ERA of 2.15. She still managed to be one of the best pitchers. In 1948 her pitching career came to an end when overhand pitching became official and the pitching distance was increased to seventy-two feet. She pitched only eight games, winning three and losing four. She simply wasn't able to adjust to pitching overhand. But her playing days were far from over. During the 1948 season she switched to outfield and became a star at that position. It was as an outfielder that she was selected for the All Star teams of 1948, 1949, 1951, and 1952.[61]

Connie Wisniewski was also an excellent hitter with a batting average over .250 from 1946 through 1952. She had a .326 batting average in 1951, which placed her third among batters in the league.[62]

Her career lasted eight seasons. Joining the league in 1944 at age twenty-two, she began her career with the Milwaukee Chicks. The franchise moved to Grand Rapids the following year, and there she played for the Grand Rapids Chicks from 1945 to 1949.[63] In 1950 she jumped to the Chicago National Girls Baseball League, a fast-pitch softball league, and by doing so upped her salary from $100 a week to $250.[64] Then in 1951 she returned to the AAGBL, where she stayed until she retired in 1952.

Connie holds an incredible number of AAGBL records for the years 1943 through 1948: most home runs, 1948, 7; most advanced bases, 1948, 127; champion batter, 1948, .289; most completed games, season, 1946, 40; most games pitched season, 1945, 46; most innings pitched season, 1945, 391; 1946, 366; lowest earned run average, season, 1945, .81; 1946, .96; highest percentage of games won, season, 1944, .697; 1945, .744; 1946, .786; most games won, 1945, 32, 1946, 33; most at bats off pitcher, season, 1,367.[65]

A Detroit, Michigan, native, Connie Wisniewski retired to Gladwin, Michigan, after her playing days ended.

Sophie Kurys, 1946

Sophie Kurys was nicknamed the "Flint Flash" for her swiftness in stealing bases. Once she got on base, she was virtually unstoppable. Eighty percent of the time she stole at least one base. She averaged more than 100 stolen bases per season, and her professional seasonal record was 201 stolen bases in 1946. That year in 203 attempts she was tagged out only twice for an incredible success rate of 99 percent. No wonder she was named Player of the Year in 1946. Sportswriters referred to her as the Tina Cobb of the league, after Ty Cobb, the legendary Detroit Tigers base stealer. But Sophie's career record of more than 1,000 stolen bases beats Ty Cobb's record of 892. Sophie was in a category all her own.[66] Sophie's record still stood as of 1991. At the beginning of the 1991 major league season Rickey Henderson was three bases short of Lou Brock's record of 938, but he was off Sophie's official record of 1,114.[67]

What is even more phenomenal is that she slid into base with bare legs. Strawberries (abrasions) were an occupational hazard that one lived with. As Sophie recalled, "I rarely wore sliding pads. . . . I didn't like them. It would be strapped around my waist and taped to my thigh. It was too bulky and I felt it contained me. Besides, it would protrude a little bit under the skirt. It looked like your slip was showing—and that's murder for a woman."[68]

Sophie wasn't unusual in refusing to wear sliding pads. In the interest of femininity most players just toughed it out. After all, they weren't allowed to wear pants. Sophie, however, developed a unique hook slide in order to save some wear and tear on her body. She dove head first like Pete Rose.[69]

In her outstanding 1946 season, "Sophie set no less than five all-time league records: Most Runs Scored in One Season 117, Most Stolen Bases One Season 201, Most Bases on Balls in One Season 93, Most Runs Scored One Game 5, Highest Fielding Percentage One Season at Second Base .973."[70] She also had a batting average of .286.[71] Her picture was featured on the back cover of the 1947 annual *Major League Baseball: Facts, Figures and Official Rules*.

Her batting average was in the top twenty every year but 1947.[72] She was selected as the best second basewoman for the All Star teams of 1946, 1947, 1948, and 1949. In 1948 she was the top hitter for the Belles, the sectional championship team. Three years in a row she led the league for most runs scored and for five years had the most stolen bases.[73] In 1950 she captured the league home run record with seven.[74] She then toured South America with an AAGBL All Star team.[75]

Sophie was one of the earliest players signed by the AAGBL and played eight seasons for the Racine Belles, 1943–1950, and one season for the Battle Creek Belles in 1952.[76] A star player, she was paid as much as $375 a week plus a bonus of $1,000 for signing.[77] Even at this salary, the AAGBL could not compete with the National Girls Baseball League of Chicago, which lured her away in 1951. In a bidding war the AAGBL reclaimed her in 1952, only to lose her again to the NGBL after the season started.[78] After leaving the AAGBL Sophie played softball for four years in Chicago and one year in Phoenix.[79]

Her career ended, as it had started, with softball. When her parents gave her permission to sign with the AAGBL in 1943, Sophie was seventeen and already a seasoned softball player. She had played on the 1939 Michigan State Championship softball team. In fact, she was the Most Valuable Player of the state tournament at age fourteen.[80]

Sophie Kurys was 5 feet 5 1/2 inches and weighed 125 pounds. A Flint, Michigan, native, she settled in Scottsdale, Arizona, after her playing days were over. However, her sporting days continued with a golf scholarship to Scottsdale Community College.[81]

Doris "Sammy" Sams, 1947, 1949

An outstanding player, Doris Sams played eight seasons, 1946 to 1953, for the Muskegon and Kalamazoo Lassies. Twice she was elected Player of the Year, 1947 and 1949.[82] When she was elected Player of the Year for the AAGBL, in 1947, Ted Williams of the Boston Red Sox was chosen Most Valuable Player in the American League. Ted and Sammy shared the cover page of the 1948 *Major League Baseball Yearbook*.[83]

Every season except her first and last she was elected to the All Star team. In 1947, 1948, 1949, and 1950 she made the All Star team both as a pitcher and outfielder, and in 1951 and 1952 she was an All Star outfielder. But if that record isn't impressive enough, she took the league batting crown in 1949 and set a league home run record in 1952. She was one of the top batters in the league every season from 1947 to 1952. On August 18, 1947, she pitched a perfect game against the Fort Wayne Daisies.[84]

In her last season of play, 1953, she missed the first half of the season because of illness. When she came back, though, she was spectacular. She batted .312 and had a perfect fielding average of 1.000.[85]

The 1948 *Major League Baseball Facts, Figures, and Official Rules* described her as a true champion. "Sammy . . . is possessed of the cool, calm and self-possessed manner that is known to sports as competitive poise—the true attribute of the great performer—and the stuff of which champions are made."[86]

By age nine she had already come to the attention of the press when she won the 1938 Southern Appalachian Marbles Tournament and became the first girl to qualify for the National Marbles Tournament in Chicago.[87] At nine she was also a superb softball pitcher and was already pitching against adult women. By age eleven she was the leading pitcher for Knoxville's State and Regional Pepsi Cola Softball team and at fourteen she pitched in the National Softball Championship. By the time she joined the AAGBL in 1946, she had played for eight straight years on Knoxville softball teams that qualified for the State Softball Tournament.[88]

In 1969 Doris was elected to the Tennessee Hall of Fame. The *Knoxville Journal* stated, "Miss Sams, probably the most versatile distaff athlete in the state's history."[89] Tennessee honored her twice for her athletic feats.

In 1970 she was inducted into the Tennessee Sports Hall of Fame and in 1982 into the Knoxville Sports Hall of Fame.[90]

In 1954, after her playing days ended, she went to work for the Knoxville Utility Board as a computer operator.[91] She still managed to be active in sports and to excel, becoming a multi-sport champion.[92]

Looking back on her playing days Doris Sams says, "We were a large group of women, who came together from all parts of the country. We loved the game we played, never dreaming that fifty (50) years later to find that we had made history."[93]

Audrey Wagner, 1948

Audrey Wagner, 5 feet 7 inches, 157 pounds, was one of the first AAGBL players. Hailing from Bensonville, Illinois, she joined the Kenosha Comets in 1943 at age fifteen. For seven seasons she was a standout player for the Comets. She was an excellent outfielder with a hot bat and was one of the league's top power hitters. In 1947 she set the league record for extra base hits and missed winning the league batting crown by one point. She won it in 1948 with a .312 batting average. That year her fielding percentage was 1.000. Her exceptional performance earned her Player of the Year for 1948.[94] *Major League Baseball 1949* proclaimed that Audrey "has been chosen as the Player of the Year in 1948 on the strength of her fine all-around season and her clear-cut batting championship."[95]

What is more amazing is that she accomplished all this after missing the first ten games of the season because she was finishing up her pre-med courses at Elmhurst College. Her AAGBL earnings helped to finance medical school.[96] Both years, 1947 and 1948, she was elected to the All Star team as an outfielder.[97]

Then in 1950 she jumped to the Chicago National League. Her motive for jumping leagues was apparently not for more money—the usual motive—but for the opportunity to attend medical school and still play ball.[98] After graduating she left her baseball career to set up a pediatric practice in California.[99]

Alma "Ziggy" Ziegler, 1950

Petite, 5 foot 3 inch Alma Ziegler, captain of the Chicks, was noted for her enthusiastic, high-spirited, aggressive play. The 1947 Grand Rapids Chicks yearbook described her as the "spark plug of the team."[100] Her winning spirit and drive to excel inspired her teammates and caught the imagination of sportswriters. In 1950 she was the sportswriters' unofficial choice for Player of the Year and the official choice of the AAGBL managers.[101] She was elected to the All Star teams of 1950 and 1953. She was an outstanding overhand pitcher from 1948 to 1954. In 1950, her best year, her win-loss record was 19–7 for a .731 win percentage. She pitched 126 games in her career, winning 60 and losing 34 for a lifetime average of .640. A versatile player, she began her career as a second basewoman and was outstanding at that position in all eleven seasons. Her eleven-season fielding average was .950. Her only weakness was her batting; her lifetime batting average was .173. Indeed, she once described herself as "the hitless wonder."[102]

Her intensity sometimes got the better of her. Dolly Tesseine recalled an incident when she was playing shortstop and Alma spiked her coming into second. "Ziggy was about as aggressive a player as there was in the league. I said to her, 'Next time you do that, I'm going to jam the ball down your throat.' When I came to bat, she threw for my head. . . . She put me on the ground. When she came up, our pitcher fired at her head. Nobody got hurt and that was that."[103]

Alma, or Ziggy as she was called by her friends, was one of the stalwarts of the league. She played eleven of the twelve seasons that the league operated, and all of those with the Chicks. Her playing days began at age twenty-three with the Milwaukee Chicks. When the franchise moved to Grand Rapids in 1945, she moved with it and continued to play for the team until 1954.[104] After retiring from the AAGBL she became a court reporter.[105]

Jean Faut, 1951, 1953

Jean Faut, 5 feet 4 inches, 137 pounds, was an extraordinary overhand pitcher. Unlike most pitchers who started out pitching underhand in softball and learned to pitch overhand in the AAGBL, Jean was an experienced overhand pitcher when she joined the South Bend Blue Sox in 1946.[106] She grew up in East Greenville, Pennsylvania, playing baseball with the boys. At age fourteen she pitched batting practice five days a week for a men's semi-pro team and also played in some of their exhibition games.[107]

As Jean said, "I had more experience than most of the girls in the AAGBL. I came into the league with a fastball, a sharp curve, screwball, drop and change—and a lot of deviations from these basic pitches. The AAGBL umpires, who were men, always insisted they could hit me. They watched me pitch all the time, but they could never hit me when they tried."[108]

She had further help from her husband, Karl Winsch, whom she married in 1947. He had had a brief major league pitching career with the Philadelphia Phillies and was able to give her pointers and offer her support. He became the manager of her team, the Blue Sox, in 1951, and continued as manager until 1954.[109]

For every season Jean played from 1946 to 1953, she had a winning pitching percentage. Her lifetime overall AAGBL percentage was .686.[110]

Her Earned Run Average (ERA) for six of the seven seasons was an impressive 1.24. In fact, in 1950, 1952, and 1953 she had the best ERA in the AAGBL.[111] During her career she pitched two perfect games, one on July 21, 1951, and the other on September 3, 1953. And in 1949 she set a league record for most shutouts. She was elected to the All Star teams of 1949, 1950, 1951, and 1953. Twice Player of the Year, in 1951 and 1953,[112] she almost made it a third time in 1952 but lost out to Betty Foss by one point. That was the year she had an amazing win-loss record of 20–2 for a .909 percentage. In the Blue Sox's final game of the post-season championships, she pitched a 6–3 victory and hit two triples.[113]

Jean Faut was a versatile player throughout her career. In addition to pitching, she also played third base and outfield. In 1949 and 1952 she batted .291, and her lifetime average was a respectable .243. After her baseball days she continued her athletic career as a professional bowler.[114]

Betty (Weaver) Foss, 1952

The Weaver dynasty—Betty, Joanne, and Jean—from Metropolis, Illinois, joined the Fort Wayne Daisies in the 1950s and no doubt was a significant factor in the Daisies' pennants in 1952, 1953, and 1954. Betty (Weaver) Foss was the first of the sisters to try out, becoming a rookie in 1950. Her fourteen-year-old sister, Joanne, who had tagged along, won herself a place as a utility player. A year later Jean joined them.[115] Both Betty and Joanne became Players of the Year.

Betty Foss was already married when she tried out and had to convince both her husband and her parents that playing AAGBL ball was a good idea. Thank goodness she was persuasive, because she and her sister, Joanne, became outstanding stars. As one reporter stated, "They were fearsome—one or the other held the batting crown from 1950 through 1954.[116]

In her starting year Betty Foss was nominated Rookie of the Year, and in 1952 she was elected Player of the Year in a one-vote victory over Jean Faut, 25 to 24. She led the league in runs (79), hits (135), total bases (207), doubles (26), triples (17), and RBIs (74) and was second to her sister Joanne in batting with a .334 average.[117]

The World Champion All-American Program listed Betty Foss as 6 feet, 175 pounds and possessing tremendous hitting power. She was not only powerful but fast. "On many occasions she has hit infield rollers of average speed that are easy outs when other runners are involved, but she is across first base before the fielders can grab the ball.[118]

In 1951 she had the league's highest batting average of .368. While with the AAGBL she held positions of first and third base. In three of her five seasons of play she was elected to all Star teams. While she was with the

Daisies, they won four pennants. After the demise of the AAGBL she continued her career with Allington's All American World Champions.[119]

Joanne Weaver, 1954

Joanne Weaver was an outfielder with the Daisies from 1951 to 1954 and then continued her career with the Allington All Americans. She was the youngest of the four Weaver children.[120] The official program of the World Champions listed her as a powerful hitter like her sister. Her height was recorded as 6 feet and her weight 145 pounds.

In 1952, 1953, and 1954 she beat out her sister for the AAGBL batting crown with batting averages of .344, .346, and .429.[121] Her best year was 1954, when she was chosen Player of the Year. By mid-August of that year she led the league in five categories: batting average (.430), runs scored (98), base hits (125), total bases (214), and stolen bases (76).[122]

But the event that stands out most in her mind is the night she hit a grand slam home run in Fort Wayne and Babe Didrikson Zaharias was in the stands. After the game Babe came down to congratulate her and a photographer took their picture. Joanne said that she couldn't believe that Babe Didrikson, the most famous female athlete of the time, would actually come down to see her. She still cherishes that moment.[123]

These are only a few of the many outstanding players. The league had many exceptionally gifted players.

NOTES

1. Merrie Fidler, "The Development and Decline of the All-American Girls Baseball League, 1943–1954" (M.S. Thesis, University of Massachusetts, Amherst, 1976), 273.
2. *All-American Girls Baseball League 1949 Yearbook.*
3. AAGBL player file, NBHFL.
4. "The Daisy Chain," Fort Wayne *News Sentinel*, 19 May 1951 Roto Sec., AAGBL player file, NBHFL.
5. *All-American Girls Baseball League 1949 Yearbook.*
6. "Sox Complete Player Deal with Lassies," South Bend *Tribune*, 10 May 1951.
7. AAGBL player file, NBHFL.
8. Minutes of Meeting of Board of Directors, American Girls Baseball League, 14 Nov. 1951, Harold T. Dailey Records, 1943–1954, Pattee Library of the Pennsylvania State University.
9. Ibid.
10. Ibid.
11. David Young, "Season in The Sun," *Women's Sports*, Oct. 1982, 50.
12. Ibid.

13. AAGBL Cards 9 and 18, 1984; *The History of the All-American Girls Professional Baseball League, 1943–1946*, 2, AAGBL player file, NBHFL.

14. AAGBL Card 9, 1984.

15. Fidler, 312.

16. Young, 50.

17. Shirley Jameson, interview with author, AAGBL reunion, 26 Oct. 1991. Unless otherwise noted, information for this profile is from this interview.

18. AAGBL Card 1, 1984.

19. AAGBL Card 21, 1986.

20. Ibid.

21. Jack Moss, "Kalamazoo Lassies Left an Indelible Mark Here," *Kalamazoo Gazette*, 17 July 1988.

22. AAGBL Card 21, 1986.

23. Reyn Davis, "The Girls of Summer," *Winnipeg Free Press* (Canada), date unknown, NBHFL.

24. Moss.

25. AAGBL Card 20, 1984.

26. "Baseball: Babette Ruths," *Newsweek*, 29 July 1946, 69.

27. AAGBL Card 20, 1984.

28. Dottie Schroeder, letter to author, 29 July 1991.

29. AAGBL Card 12, 1984.

30. Larry LaRue, "Belles of the Ball," *Press-Telegram*, 17 May 1987, Sec. D.

31. Fidler, 348.

32. LaRue.

33. AAGBL Card 12, 1984.

34. LaRue.

35. Ibid.

36. Eric Zorn, "The Girls of Summer," *Chicago Tribune*, 12 July 1982.

37. LaRue.

38. AAGBL Card 28, 1986.

39. Ibid.

40. *All-American Girls Baseball 1948 Yearbook*, 5.

41. Ruth Richard, letter to author, 25 June 1991.

42. Ruth Richard, AAGBL contract.

43. Richard letter to author.

44. Ibid.

45. LaRue.

46. "Four Who Blazed the Trail," *Press-Telegram*, 17 May 1987 Sec. D.

47. Brenda Wilson and James Skipper, Jr., "Nicknames and Women Professional Baseball Players," *Names* 38 (Dec. 1990): 312.

48. Young, 72.

49. LaRue.

50. AAGBL Card 6, 1984.

51. Ibid.

52. AAGBL Card 16, 1984.

53. Jack Stenbuck, "Glamour Girls of Big League Ball." *Magazine Digest*, July 1946, 71.

54. "Baseball: Babette Ruths," 69.

55. Stenbuck.
56. *All-American Girls Baseball League 1946 Yearbook*, 160.
57. Stenbuck.
58. Fidler, 324.
59. AAGBL Card 38, 1986.
60. Ibid.
61. Fidler, 325.
62. AAGBL Card 38, 1986.
63. Ibid.
64. Fidler, 326.
65. "All-American Girls Baseball League All-Time Records 43–48," AAGBL file, NBHFL, 27–30.
66. Ron Coons, "Short-Pants Star? Sophie Wins the Trophy!" *Courier-Journal and Times*, Sept. 1976, NBHFL.
67. "Scorecard: Women of Steal," *Sports Illustrated*, 15 April 1991, 18.
68. Coons.
69. Ibid.
70. *1947 Racine Belles Yearbook*, 11.
71. AAGBL Card 14, 1984.
72. Fidler, 329.
73. *Major League Baseball 1949* (New York: Dell Pub., 1949), 23.
74. "Scorecard: Women of Steal," 18.
75. *1949 Racine Belles Yearbook*, 17.
76. AAGBL Card 14, 1984.
77. Coons.
78. AAGBL Card 14, 1984.
79. Coons.
80. Fidler, 327–328.
81. Coons.
82. AAGBL Card 19, 1984.
83. *Major League Baseball Yearbook 1948* (New York: Dell Pub., 1948).
84. AAGBL Card 19, 1984.
85. Fidler, 332.
86. Qtd. in W.G. Nicholson, "Women's Pro Baseball Packed the Stands...," *Women's Sports*, April 1976, 33.
87. Jack Marshall, "Outstanding Girl Athlete Got Start in Ringer Meet," *Knoxville News-Sentinel*, 1949, Doris Sams scrapbook.
88. "Still Going Strong—Doris Sams Adds Laurels to Pro Baseball Crown," *Knoxville News-Sentinel*, 1949, Doris Sams scrapbook.
89. "Doris Sams Nominated for Tennessee Hall of Fame," *Knoxville Journal*, 7 Aug. 1969.
90. AAGBL Card 19, 1984.
91. Doris Sams, letter to author, 23 Aug. 1991.
92. AAGBL Card 19, 1984.
93. Sams letter to author.
94. AAGBL Card 1, 1984.
95. *Major League Baseball 1949* (New York: Dell Pub., 1949), 23.
96. Fidler, 334.

97. AAGBL Card 1, 1984.

98. Fidler, 334.

99. Coons.

100. Qtd. in Fidler, 335.

101. Ibid., 334.

102. AAGBL Card 39, 1986.

103. Qtd. in Young, 51.

104. AAGBL Card 39, 1986.

105. Ibid.

106. AAGBL Card 8, 1984.

107. Young, 52.

108. Ibid.

109. Fidler, 341.

110. AAGBL Card 8, 1984.

111. Young, 52.

112. AAGBL Card 8, 1984.

113. Fidler, 341.

114. AAGBL Card 8, 1984.

115. Fidler, 343.

116. Young, 52.

117. Fidler, 343.

118. Ibid., 342.

119. *World Champion Official Program*, 1957, 7.

120. Ibid., 6.

121. Sharon Roepke, *Diamond Gals: The Story of the All American Girls Professional Baseball League* (Marcellus, Mich.: AAGBL Cards, 1986), 22.

122. Fidler, 345.

123. Joanne Weaver, telephone interview by author.

10

"Never Say Die": Allington's World Champion All Americans, 1954–1957

The All American Girls' Professional Baseball League may have officially disbanded in September 1954, but one man refused to let women's baseball die. Bill Allington, one of the most successful coach/managers in AAGBL history, believed that he could successfully put together a team that would challenge the best of men's semi-pro teams. So in September when the league folded, he assembled an eleven-woman team made up of players primarily from the Rockford Peaches and Fort Wayne Daisies, the two teams that he had coached. The team called Allington's All Americans played exhibition games against local men's teams in the tri-state area: Indiana, Michigan, and Illinois. Copying the program of black barnstorming teams, the women participated in pre-game attractions. At the opening game on Monday, September 6, Labor Day, a $50 prize was offered to any girl who could beat Jo Weaver, the "Ty Cobb of girl's league baseball," in a 50-yard dash. Jo was the unofficial batting champion of the AAGBL with a .429 batting average. She was also credited with leading the AAGBL in runs scored with 109, base hits with 143, total bases with 254, home runs with 29, and stolen bases with 79. The newspaper article announcing the game requested that managers of "good" men's teams reserve bookings.[1]

Billed as "the battle of the sexes," the idea proved so popular that the team was quickly booked through October. This post-season launched Allington's All Americans touring team, which barnstormed throughout the United States and Canada from 1955 to 1957.

The team played regulation baseball with the exception that the two teams exchanged batteries. In other words, the pitcher and catcher for the men's team played for the women's and vice versa. Male pitchers then

28. The World Champion All American Women's Baseball Club.

pitched against the men, and female pitchers against the women. Allington believed this would compensate for any physical differences in strength.

Switching batteries proved to be very successful. In fact, one men's team was so impressed with the female pitcher that they offered her a job. Noelle Leduc Alverson remembers that 1954 game with pride. She said, "It was my turn to pitch. I won the game for the men. The coach of the men's team asked me if I would pitch for his team the next year." Unfortunately, she didn't get to pitch for the men's team or Allington's because she had to return home to care for her mother.[2]

Start-up costs for the touring team were virtually non-existent. The old Fort Wayne Daisies' red, white, and blue uniforms with the name changed became the official All American uniforms. Since the women were former AAGBL players, they had their own equipment. Transportation was supplied by Allington's white station wagon, called the "White Dragon," and by a player's blue two-door Ford.

Mat Pascale of Omaha, Nebraska, was chosen as the booking agent for the team. It was his responsibility to advertise the team and to find challengers. He was also the agent for the Kansas City Monarchs; the Carolina Hoboes, formerly the Asheville Blues; the Detroit Stars; the Omaha Tigers; and games between the Indianapolis Clowns and the New York Black Yankees. Full-page ads, the first half of which were devoted to Allington's All Americans, ran in the *Sports Review*, a bimonthly sportsman's paper, which was published in Omaha, Nebraska. The ad also listed other attractions such as "Bobo Nickerson, 'Screwball of Baseball', Does Everything but Tear Down the Stadium, Formerly with the House of Davids; Emmet 'Red' Ormsby, Former Major League Umpire, Top-Flight After-Dinner Speaker; and Wayne Robinson, 11-Year-Old Boy Wonder, Performs Sensational Batting Exhibition." The ad boasted, "We Have the Best Attractions You Can Get to Raise Money for Any Worthy Cause."[3]

Although the ads indicated that the All Americans were available to play any men's teams, in reality it meant only white teams. The one time that they were scheduled to play against a black team in Jasper, Texas, the game was cancelled when it "almost caused a racial riot."[4]

Apparently the idea of an All Star women's baseball team playing against local men's teams was a big hit because Mat Pascale was able to book seventy-nine games from May to September in 1955.[5]

The 1955 season lasted from May 29 to September 18, a total of 113 days on the road. The team played in ten states (Indiana, Iowa, Kansas, Michigan, Minnesota, Missouri, Nebraska, Ohio, South Dakota, and Wisconsin) and Canada. According to Katie Horstman's log, the players traveled 13,626 miles. Of the seventy-nine scheduled games, seventy-four were actually played. One game was postponed and probably never played, and four games were rained out.

On the whole, the women played late afternoon or evening games. After the game they changed either at the ball park or in private homes that had been set up for that purpose. Then they hit the road for the next destination. If they were lucky, it was a short hop to the next game. Of course, distances between games varied. For example, on July 31, 1955, they played in Clarkson, Nebraska, and on August 1 in Fremont, Nebraska, just thirty-five miles away. The next night they played in Parkersburg, Iowa, 288 miles away, and then the next day in Hinkley, Minnesota, 306 miles away. One has to keep in mind that most of this travel was on rural roads. This usually meant that if they had an evening game, they traveled most of the night. They then stopped at a motel for a few hours of sleep before the next evening's game. It was a rough existence.

There were usually twelve players, the coach, and all the luggage and equipment in the cars. Joan Berger described traveling as "the pits." In order to cut expenses on the road, the women often slept four people to a room. Luckily, they were a close-knit group. Hotel or motel expenses averaged about $1.44 a night per person. Some nights they didn't have a motel room and were put up locally. In 1955 the estimated cost for motels was $143.26 per person. Food at $3.00 a day for 109 days was $327. Food and lodging then amounted to a total of $470.26. That figure, of course, doesn't include miscellaneous expenses such as laundry. For example, under expenses in July, Jean Geissinger lists $1.00 for movies, $5.00 for spikes, $15.00 for a jacket, and $1.25 and $2.85 for laundry. Of course, what every player feared was injury. The team needed and counted on every player being healthy, and doctors were expensive.

The women were all paid by the game. Usually they split equally a percentage of the game receipts. For example, the contract with the sponsoring team might read that the All Americans received a 60–40 split of the gate. Gas and mileage expenses were taken off the top, and then the rest was split evenly among Allington and the women. In most instances, the All Americans received a larger percentage of the gate than the home team. The booking fee to Pascal was the responsibility of the home team. In 1955 the amount paid per game ranged from $1 to $34. The $34 payment, the largest amount received for a single game, was in Fort Wayne, the hometown of the then-defunct AAGBL Daisies. Many of the women on the team were past Daisy stars, so the hometown fans really came out for the game. A more typical payment was when the women played back-to-back games, as in the June 27 and June 28 games in Port Arthur, Canada. Each person received $19 for the first night and $11 the second. Thus the average amount received per game was about $12.

The price of a ticket was usually $1.00 for adults and children under twelve were usually free, although sometimes they were charged 50 cents. The price of the tickets was left up to the sponsoring home team.

Adding up all receipts for games listed in Maxine Kline's diary indicates that she received $868.48 for the three-and-a-half-month season. This amounted to about $248 a month. Jean Geissinger, on the other hand, played three more games and grossed $889.48, or about $254 a month. But road expenses cut that amount dramatically. After subtracting for food and lodging expenses, Maxine Kline netted $471.46 for the season. Jean Geissinger's net after expenses was $419.22. So the average player probably netted somewhere between $420 and $470 for the three and a half months, or about $120 to $134 per month. For most of the players this was a significant decline in pay from their AAGBL days. For example, Ruth Richard, the catcher, had signed a contract with the Rockford Peaches in 1952 for $430 a month. So compared to the glory days of AAGBL ball, the pay wasn't very good. At least the women could still play professional baseball, though. There were no other opportunities at the time, but there was hope. After all, it was the first year of the tour, and things were expected to improve.

Looked at another way, the pay wasn't that bad. For 1955 the average gross yearly wage for a woman clerical worker was $2,597, or $216 a month. The average woman sales worker grossed $1,182, or $98.50 a month, while the average operative or factory worker grossed $2,048, or $170.67 a month.[6] Therefore, if the women on the Allington tour were making approximately $250 a month, their pay was still higher than that they would have been making as secretaries, sales clerks, or factory workers. Since the majority had only a high school education, their prospects for obtaining high-paying jobs were slim. Opportunities for women in the labor market in the 1950s, regardless of educational level, were very limited. And the women will tell you that it was the love of the game, and not the money, that kept them playing.

Just for comparison, let's look at the Yankees. That year they played a 154-game schedule. This included the seven-game World Series. They played from April 11 to October 4. The top major league salary that year was $135,000 and went to Ted Williams of the Boston Red Sox. The eleventh highest salary dropped precipitously to $36,000. By these standards, women's salaries weren't even in the ball park.

The 1955 Allington's All American team started out with twelve players: Betty Foss, Katie Horstman, Jean Geissinger, Maxine Kline, Dottie Schroeder, Joan Berger, Gertrude Dunn, Ruth Richard, Lois Youngen, Dolores Lee, Dolly Vanderlip, and Jeneane DesCombes. Betty Foss left the team in mid-season, so they were left with eleven.[7]

All the women were sensational players, but a few were billed as world wonders. Like the circus and other forms of traveling entertainment, most barnstorming teams put on a good show along with playing good baseball. Black teams had their clowns and trick antics on the field. Allington's All Americans had players who could perform superhuman feats. Joanne Weaver was billed as the fastest woman alive and once as a promotional stunt even raced against a horse. Dolores Lee was advertised as the pitcher who could throw two baseballs at the same time.

Local newspapers announcing the All Americans' games against men's teams often publicized the girls' pre-game infield warmup. "The girls go through the antics made famous by such celebrated baseball teams as the House of David and a host of clowning colored teams."[8]

An official program sold at the games gave pictures with brief biographic sketches of each of the players. The number of AAGBL records listed by players was impressive.

Betty Weaver Foss was twenty-five and had had an outstanding career in the AAGBL, where she had played first base for the Daisies from 1950 to 1954. In 1952 she had been voted AAGBL Player of the Year. Elected to the All Star team three times, she was a power hitter and held the AAGBL record for the highest batting average, .368. For the All Americans she usually played either first base or outfield.

Catherine "Katie" Horstman, a pitcher and catcher, was another ex-Daisy player. She was 5 feet 7 inches, from Minster, Ohio. At nineteen she was one of the youngest players on the Allington team, but she already had five years of experience playing AAGBL ball. In 1950 at age fourteen she was one of the youngest players to ever sign an AAGBL contract.

In 1957, when the All Americans wrapped up their last season of play, Katie had played eight years of professional ball and had a two-year medical librarian college degree. In 1960 she entered the novitiate of the Franciscan

Sisters of Sacred Heart in Mokena, Illinois, where she remained until 1965. While at the convent she began her coaching career and obtained a bachelor's degree from DePaul University. After various teaching jobs she came home to Minster, Ohio, to teach physical education and to coach. She has received almost every high school coaching honor.

Dottie Schroeder was from Sadorus, Illinois, and was 5 foot 7 inches. She played with the AAGBL all twelve years from 1943 to 1954 and ten of the twelve was chosen for the All Star team. She was also voted the most popular player when she played for the Kalamazoo, Michigan, Lassies. At twenty-seven she was the oldest and most experienced member of the team. She usually played in the infield. A news article in 1957 described her as "the greatest infielder that ever wore spikes" and said that Phil Wrigley, president of the Cubs, had said, "If Dottie was a male player she would be gobbled up by a major league club in a hurry."[9]

Joan Eisenberger, 5 feet 5 inches, who later shortened her maiden name to Berger, was from Garfield, New Jersey. She had played AAGBL ball for the Rockford Peaches from 1951 to 1954. She was a versatile player who played second and third base and was also a pitcher.

Gertie Dunn, 5 feet 2 inches, was from Sharon Hill, Pennsylvania. She had played AAGBL ball from 1951 until 1954 for the South Bend, Indiana, Blue Sox. During part of the 1951 season, however, she was loaned to the newly established Battle Creek team. When she joined the Allington All Americans, she was twenty-two. She was noted for being a consistent shortstop who, according to her teammates, "had the best wrists in the game."[10]

Ruth Richard, or "Ritchie," as she liked to be called, was from Sellersville, Pennsylvania. She was 5 feet 4 inches. Ritchie began her AAGBL career in 1947 with the Grand Rapids Chicks and then was traded to the Rockford Peaches, where she remained as an outstanding catcher from 1948 to 1954. For five years from 1949 to 1954 she was selected by the league sportswriters as the All Star catcher for the All Star team. She is credited with once having caught two back-to-back no-hit games in the playoffs.[11] According to the official 1957 program for the World Champion All Americans, "In true big-league fashion, she enjoys the off seasons by hunting and fishing."

Lois Youngen was from Leroy, Ohio. At 5 foot 3 inches, she was one of the smallest players. In 1951 after graduating salutatorian from Westfield High School in Leroy, she joined the Fort Wayne Daisies and played AAGBL ball until the league folded in 1954. She then played one year with Allington's All Americans.

Lois has an interesting connection to an earlier female baseball player from Ragersville, Ohio, Alta Weiss. Alta played baseball from 1907 to 1922. Lois's uncle, Edwin Youngen, was a pitcher with Alta Weiss for the

Ragersville, Ohio, ball club. So Lois was one of the few women players who was aware of the fact that women pioneers had gone before her.

In 1953 she was traded to the South Bend, Blue Sox, with whom she played through the beginning of the 1954 season. It was here that she had the biggest thrill of her AAGBL career when she caught a perfect game against the Kalamazoo Lassies in 1953. The second half of the 1954 season, she was traded back to Fort Wayne. She played with Fort Wayne the rest of 1954 and then joined Allington's All Americans.

She remembers the 1955 season with the Allington All Americans as being the most competitive season she played. According to her, the men were out to win and played their very hardest against the women. As she said, "Every man worth his salt, I suppose every competitive woman as well, wants to win. The men were not about to let a bunch of women beat them." Because of the high level of competition, the play was very strenuous, and she worried about injuries.

Even during her playing days, baseball was not her major focus. As Lois Youngen said, "This [baseball] was a nice little stop over for me." Getting an education was her primary goal. In fact she is one of the few women who played AAGBL but didn't play softball afterward. She was too busy getting her M.A. from Michigan State University and then her Ph.D. from Ohio State University and pursuing her career goals. She went on to become a college professor and administrator in physical education at the University of Oregon.

Twenty-one-year-old Jean Geissinger was from Philadelphia, Pennsylvania, and was 5 foot 6 inches. She played AAGBL ball for five years from 1950 to 1954. For three years she held the league home run record. For the All Americans she played outfield and second base. In the off-season she returned to her typing job.

Maxine Kline from North Adams, Michigan, was another veteran AAGBL player. She had played from 1948 to 1954. She was twenty-seven years old and was an outstanding pitcher. "Maxine is gifted with a very strong pitching arm, and has uncanny control." She also played in the outfield. In the winter she returned home to the farm, where she was one of ten children.[12]

Dolores "Pickles" Lee was from Jersey City, New Jersey, and had played for the Rockford Peaches from 1952 to 1954. One of "the junior members of the group in age and service,"[13] she pitched and played infield for the All Americans.

Dolores's outstanding pitching ability was recognized early. She used to play stick ball on the boys' team with the police officers who worked in the Bright Street Police and Fire Repair Shop.

One of the officers mentioned to her that there was a girls' baseball team in Garfield, New Jersey. The team was coached by the father of another future AAGBL and Allington player, Joanie Berger, and was sponsored by the mayor of Garfield. The girls played other men's teams, the Haydew girls, and the Amputees. Every year some of the girls went out to Rockford, Illinois, to try out for the Daisies. In 1952, when she told the police officers from her old neighborhood in Jersey City that she was going to the tryouts, they took up a collection and paid for her ticket and bought her a new glove.

After retiring from baseball in 1958, "Pickles" came home to become a police officer. She eventually became an undercover narcotics detective. Again she was in a nontraditional female role. But as she said, she was totally accepted. After all, she knew all the cops.[14]

Two other players were Dolly Vanderlip and Jeneane DesCombes. Vanderlip was from Charlotte, North Carolina, and had previously played for the Fort Wayne Daisies in 1952 and 1953. She was traded to the South Bend Blue Sox in 1954.[15] Jeneane DesCombes, 5 feet 5 1/2 inches, was from Lakeview, Ohio. She had played for the Grand Rapids Chicks in 1953 and 1954. Her baseball career had gotten its start while she was a student at Ohio Northern University in Ada when a friend of hers saw an ad in the newpaper for tryouts for the AAGBL. It sounded like a fun summer job that paid pretty well, so Jeneane tried out. Being a left-hander with a good pitching arm, she was selected to become the rookie relief pitcher for the Grand Rapids Chicks. She was one of the few left-handed pitchers in the league and soon had the nickname of "Lefty." By her second season, 1954, she had proven so valuable that she earned a starting position. Her pitching record was excellent that year with twelve wins and eight losses. Her batting average, however, was rather mediocre. As she frankly admitted in 1992, "My batting average was not good. In those days, they didn't expect pitchers to be hitters and they did not work with us at all."[16]

Just as she had secured her position on the team, the league folded. But then a guardian angel in the form of Bill Allington contacted her about joining his touring team. It was an ideal situation. While completing her college studies, she could play baseball and travel across the country. As a pitcher for the All Americans, she'd pitch every second or third night. After the team disbanded in 1957, Jeneane became an avid golfer. She played on the LPGA tour from 1964 to 1965. Today she is a real estate agent in Washington state and the mother of three sons.

Then, of course, there was the coach, Bill Allington. He had coached AAGBL ball for ten of the twelve years that the league existed—eight years (1944–1946 and 1948–1952) for the Rockford Peaches and two years (1953–1954) for the Fort Wayne Daisies. During that time the Peaches won the post-championship playoffs four times—1945, 1948, 1949, and 1950—and the Fort Wayne Daisies once, in 1953.[17]

His players described him as a hard-working professional coach who took his job seriously. Dottie Green, a player and chaperon, said that Bill

29. Dolores Lee, Bill Allington, and Katie Horstman. *From the Collection of the Northern Indiana Historical Society.*

expected his players to know everything about baseball. "We had to recite the rules. He'd say to you what is rule 44 section 8. You'd say the infield fly rule." Another player, Ruth Richard, said, "He was a strict disciplinarian, and excellent coach and almost like a father. The only players who didn't like him were the ones who played against him."

Allington continued to be a winning coach with the All Americans. A 1956 article in the *Sports Review* extolled the virtues of the All Americans. It stated that the" All-American girls team has become so popular in the short time of three months that they are drawing more fans to their games on tour than any other team on the road." And that the fans are astounded that "the girls can play such flashy and sensational ball." As of July the All Americans had already won twenty-three out of fifty-one games against male teams, many of them strong semi-pro teams.[18]

The article went on to praise the skills of the women players.

> The infield is really a million dollar infield. With "Bullet Arm" Joan Berger at first, reliable Gertie Dunn at second, Jean Geissinger, the Hal Chase of girl baseball, at first playing such a wonderful game and the flashy Dottie Schroeder playing shortstop. . . . Then with Ruth Richard who was the girls league best catcher, the girls have a real smooth working infield. . . . Lee . . . has the finest curve ball of any girl pitchers.[19]

Allington went one step further in describing Lee's throwing arm. He said, "Lee is a star at short, 3rd and on the mound. She has a better throwing arm than many of the men infielders. She has a rifle throw across the diamond to third.[20]

The pitchers—Katie Horstman, Jeneane DesCombes, Dolly Vanderlip, Maxine Kline, Lois Youngen, and Dolores Lee—alternated as outfielders.[21] According to Dottie Schroeder, they also had the job of selling picture postcards of the team to the fans in the stands. They did this while the other players took infield practice.[22]

The 1955 season had gone well and the prospects for 1956 looked even better. Rumors spread that the team might go on tour in Japan, and there was the possibility of other foreign junkets. A newspaper article proclaimed, "Baseball promoters in Japan attempted to induce the team to tour their country playing local competition, but satisfactory financial arrangements have not materialized.[23]

The prospect of touring abroad was not out of the question. In the off-season, Negro baseball players regularly had signed on to play in Latin American countries. In fact the AAGBL had held its 1947 spring training in Havana, Cuba. Then in the fall at the end of the AAGBL regular season, three touring teams returned to Cuba to play exhibition games.[24] In the winter of 1948 AAGBL players participated in exhibition games in Nicaragua, Costa Rica, Panama, and Venezuela. Two Allington All Americans,

Ruth Richard and Dottie Schroeder, had been part of that tour.[25] There were exciting prospects for Allington's All Americans to play games all over the United States, Canada, and even the world.

The team prepared for the 1956 season with ten days of spring training in Fort Wayne starting on May 10. They then played six or eight days of exhibition games in eastern Indiana and western Ohio before beginning their regular schedule.[26] An article in the April *Sports Review* gave their tentative season schedule. "Plans are to send the team through the Dakotas, Montana, Idaho, Oregon and Washington and then back to the middle west and wind up their season in the east."[27]

The 1956 team roster contained fourteen players from nine states. With the exception of Betty Foss, all the players from 1955 were returning. There were also three new players: Mamie Redman from Valders, Wisconsin; Jean Smith from Harbor Springs, Michigan; and Margaret Holland, hometown not mentioned.

The pre-season newspaper propaganda declared, "The girls have won thousands of fans with their sensational fielding, hitting, pitching and all around playing. And they play a headier game than many of the fast semi pro clubs of the country. . . . The girls have outdrawn most any other clubs that play on the road. They have played to capacity crowds at many of their games."[28]

But the 1956 financial picture was not as rosy as it had been in the first year. The team was scheduled to play sixty-nine games on an eighty-three-day tour from June 6 to August 28. They actually played sixty-five, since three games were rained out and one cancelled. In 1955 there were seventy-nine games scheduled but only seventy-four played. The number of games declined as well as the revenue per game. Thus in 1955 the average per game per player was $12, whereas in 1956 it was $7.70. The gross per player in 1956 was $500.57, or a decrease of somewhere between $370 to $390 from the previous year. And although they played fewer games, they clocked about the same mileage. This meant a dramatic decrease in a player's net income at the end of the 1956 season compared to 1955. In 1956 the net was about $152.78 compared to a 1955 net of somewhere between $471.46 and $419.22. In 1955 the tour covered ten states and Canada. In 1956 the tour covered fifteen states, mostly in the mid-west and west. With revenue declining, the call went out to Mat Pascale to schedule more games for the 1957 season. Somehow revenue had to be increased.

The name of the team was changed from the All Americans to the World Champions. Glossy six-page official programs with pictures of the team and stats were printed up. Spring training was moved from Fort Wayne, Indiana, to Harlingen, Texas. A new image seemed to bring the promise of a more successful season.

The pre-season promotion paid off because Pascal was able to schedule eighty-three games—seven exhibition games in Texas and seventy-six regular games in fifteen states. The schedule looked good. The team was playing more games and in new locales. But the distances between games were great. The team had some bad luck in that seven games were rained out and one had to be cancelled. This meant that they played only sixty-nine regular-season games.

In 1957 eight of the original members of the 1955 Allington All Americans were still with the team: Joan Eisenberger or Berger, Maxine Kline, Jean Geissinger, Ruth Richard, Dolores Lee, Dottie Schroeder, and Betty Weaver Foss. Together the eight had played a total of seventy-two years of AAGBL and All Americans baseball. The average number of years played was nine. Dottie Schroeder holds the record for having played all fifteen years that the two leagues existed. By the 1957 season she had played 1,500 games. This was now a highly experienced and extremely cohesive team. (See the table for a complete listing of all the players who ever played for Allington's All Americans.)

Record of Years Played

Players	AAGBL	All-Star Team[1]	All Americans
Joan Berger	51–54	54	55–57
Wilma Briggs	48–54	54	—
Hazel Brooks	—	—	57**
Jeneane DesCombes	53–54	—	55–56
Gertie Dunn	51–54	—	55–56
Betty Weaver Foss	50–54	54	57
Jean Geissinger	50–54	54	55–57
Jean Havlish	53–54	54	—
Margaret Holland	—	—	56*
Katie Horstman	50–54	54	55–57
Maxine Kline	48–54	54	55–57
Noelle LeDuc	51–54	54	—
Dolores Lee	52–54	54	55–57
Mamie Redman	—	—	56
Ruth Richard	47–54	54	55–57
Jean Smith	48–54	—	56–57
Dottie Schroeder	43–54	—	55–57
Dolly Vanderlip	52–54	—	55–56*
Jo Weaver	51–54	54	55
Mary Wilson	—	—	57**
Lois Youngen	51–54	—	55–56

[1]   1954 Allington All American All-Star Exhibition Tour.
*   On 1956 initial roster, but no record of playing during game.
** Newspaper announcement would play in 1957, but no record of playing during season.

In August the team broke its rule of playing only against men's teams and played a nostalgic game against some of the AAGBL ex–Blue Sox stars who had made their homes in South Bend after the league folded. Karl Winsch, manager of the Blue Sox until 1951, came out of retirement to coach his old team. Jane Stoll, Betty Wagoner, Lou Arnold, Barbara Hoffman, Jean Faut, Sue Kidd, Frances Janssen, and Lib Mahon, all former Blue Sox living in South Bend, plus Jetty Mooney, Mary Baumgarten, and Janet Rumsey, came back for the occasion. The game was sponsored by the South Bend Ushers Club, the organization that had been responsible for tickets and seating when the Blue Sox were part of the AAGBL. It was a marvelous game with the town coming out to support the girls in what was to be the last women's exhibition game ever to be played in South Bend.[29]

That year, 1957, marked the last season of play. Over the years the team had played in more than 150 cities in twenty-three states and Canada. However, the tour schedule no longer could generate enough revenue to cover expenses and still have a profit. What was insidious about the schedule was that the more the All Americans were in demand and the more states they covered, the higher the expenses and the lower the revenue. Travel expenses were devouring profits. Without home games the team was in trouble financially. Most professional baseball teams, in fact, play only about half of their games on the road.

In 1957 each player received approximately $560.50 for playing; after expenses that left a net profit of only $98.74. And this figure is high because it doesn't include miscellaneous items such as laundry. Less than $100 for five months of living out of a suitcase, traveling almost every day to play a game in a new locale, just wasn't worth it, no matter how much one loved baseball. So at the end of 1957, everyone called it quits and a baseball era came to an end. Fifteen years of women's baseball was over, largely to be forgotten.

But the women who played remember those days fondly. Jean Geissinger Harding said, "In our travels we crossed the wide Missouri, the Great Divide, thru the Badlands, Blackhills, Flats of Utah, and a lot of Iowa. Crossing paths with the Black Knights and 'Old Satch'—playing amidst rodeo's, circuses, and town socials. . . . a twin bill day, in neighboring towns—first game—11 innings, jumped in car, hit next town late, and played 11 more—hey terrific."[30] She also remembered the generosity of the fans and the players. "[People] let us change in their basement, fed us, and [were] always amazed at the quality of play." One opposing player in Iowa took pity on her when a throw from third ripped the webbing in her glove. He gave her his glove to finish the tour with. She said, "When I got home to Philley and working, I sent him the money to replace the glove I finished the tour with."[31]

As Dottie Schroeder said, "The years spent playing ball were the

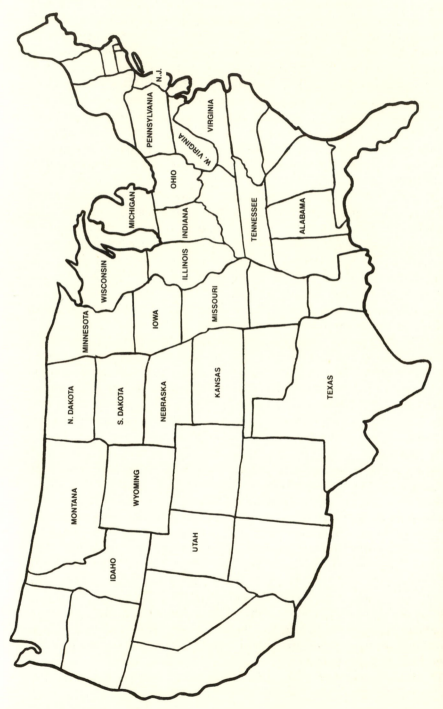

30. Allington All American tour schedule of twenty-three states and Canada, 1955–1957.

happiest ever—the people I met and was privileged to play with shall always remain close to my heart. We were born at the right time and we were truly pioneers."[32]

NOTES

1. "Allington Leads Girl Stars on Exhibition Tour," newspaper article circa 5 Sept. 1954, Jean Harding scrapbook.

2. Noelle Leduc Alverson, author's Allington All American questionnaire, Oct. 1991.

3. *Sports Review*, April 1956.

4. Katie Horstman, author's Allington All Americans questionnaire, 7 Oct. 1991.

5. This number is based on daily travel diaries of players Maxine Kline, Jean Geissinger, and Katie Horstman.

6. Bureau of the Census, *Historical Statistics of the United States: Colonial Times to 1970*, vol. 1 (Washington, D.C., GPO, 1975), 304.

7. Maxine Kline, personal travel diary, 1955–1957.

8. *Fairmont Daily Sentinel*, 26 July 1957.

9. "All-American Girls Team to Train in the South," *Sports Review*, 1 March 1957.

10. Qtd. from AAGBL Card 23, 1986.

11. AAGBL Cards, 1986.

12. *World Champion Official Program*, 1957.

13. Ibid.

14. Dolores Lee Dries, telephone interview by author, 14 Jan. 1992.

15. Jean Geissinger Harding, letter to author, 15 Jan. 1992.

16. Jeneane DesCombes Lesko, letter to author, 1 April 1992.

17. AAGBL Cards, 1984.

18. "All-American Girls Baseball Team Completes Very Successful Season," *Sports Review*, Sept. 1956.

19. Ibid.

20. Ibid.

21. "All-American Lassies Play to Top Gate; Are Top Attraction," *Sports Review*, July 1955.

22. Dottie Schroeder, Allington's All American questionnaire, 24 Oct. 1991.

23. "Bill Allington Sends All-American Girls to Spring Training," newspaper article probably from Fort Wayne paper from Maxine Kline's scrapbook, 1956.

24. Merrie Fidler, "The Development and Decline of the All-American Girls Baseball League, 1943–1954" (M.S. thesis, University of Massachusetts, Amherst, 1976), 162–163.

25. Ruth Richard, letter to author, June 25, 1991; Max Carey, letter to tour All-American Girls, 22 Dec. 1948.

26. "Bill Allington Sends All-American Girls to Spring Training."

27. *Sports Review*, April 1956.

28. "Bill Allington Sends All-American Girls to Spring Training."

29. "Ex–Blue Sox Stars Await Touring Foe," *South Bend Tribune*, 18 Aug. 1957; "Ex–Blue Sox Await Game: Former Girl Stars in Exhibition at Playland," *South Bend Tribune*, 28 Aug. 1957.

30. Jean Geissinger Harding, "Tour Thoughts by Ball Player," *All-American Girls Professional Baseball League 1943–1954 Souvenir Program*, Fort Wayne, Indiana, 1986.

31. Geissinger Harding letter to author.

32. Schroeder, Allington All American questionnaire.

Epilogue:

The Current Ambiguity about Women's Role in Baseball

Baseball today is conceived of as a male sport. That women have played baseball since 1866 is a fact few Americans know. The public has been socially conditioned to think of softball as the female equivalent. Prior to the unveiling of the women in baseball exhibit at Cooperstown in the spring of 1989 (see photo 31), few people realized that women had ever played organized ball. But the biggest impact on public awareness has come from the movie *A League of Their Own*, which was released in July 1992. The movie is a fictionalized account of the All American Girls' Professional Baseball League of World War II. Unfortunately, most people are aware *only* of the AAGBL. Its existence is equated with the manpower shortage of the war and is accepted as a fluke of history.

The idea that women could or would want to be major leaguers is not taken seriously. Most parents still encourage their daughters to play Little League softball rather than baseball, and by high school even girls who started out playing baseball are usually playing softball. This is the result of social conditioning and the opportunity structure. Most high schools and colleges have female softball but male baseball teams. Women are recruited for college athletic scholarships in softball, but not in baseball. Julie Croteau has the distinction of being the first and only woman to ever play NCAA baseball, and that was in the Division III level. Unless girls develop their baseball skills at early ages and pursue the sport the same way boys do, there is little hope of a girl ever acquiring the necessary skills to play major or minor league ball.

The issue of physical ability, however, is still hotly debated. A recent article in the Illinois *Daily Herald* quoted some of the top men in baseball as saying that women were physically unable to compete with men. According to Dr. Bob Brown, president of the American League, the reason

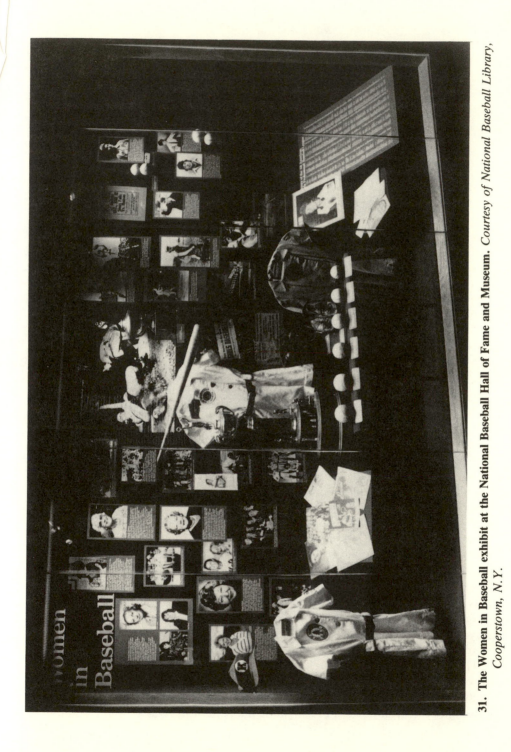

31. The Women in Baseball exhibit at the National Baseball Hall of Fame and Museum. *Courtesy of National Baseball Library, Cooperstown, N.Y.*

that women are not found in baseball is due not to prejudice but to physical differences. And he believes that women are always going to have a problem physically. Dr. Robert C. Cantu, president-elect of the American College of Sports Medicine, agrees: "Elite women will never be as strong, never be as fast as elite men. A woman is not bio-medically best designed to compete with men at that sport [baseball]."[1]

A dissenting voice is Bob Hope, vice president of marketing for the Atlanta Braves. He said, "In all my years I was with the Braves it didn't seem like there was any good reason athletically women couldn't play baseball." Hope recalled how Hank Aaron used to say that women could play baseball, if men just gave them the chance.[2] Maybe Hank Aaron was recalling how Toni Stone played baseball for the Indianapolis Clowns, the same Negro American League team for which he had played.

Former baseball Commissioner Fay Vincent believes that baseball is a perfect meritocracy and that if a woman had the skills to play major league ball, she would be allowed to play. But as to the question of whether or not women are physically capable of competing with men, he said, "We won't know until we see it done. I'm one of those who tends to think it can [be done]."[3]

There is much evidence to suggest that women would be able to successfully compete with men. In the last twenty years records in other sports indicate that women's performances have come within 10 percent of men's.[4] For example, in 1966 Joan Joyce set the record for the fastest pitch in softball. The pitch was clocked at 118 mph. The record for men set in 1962 is only 108 mph.[5]

Certainly in the past there were women such as Lizzie Murphy who could compete and did. She and others were considered novelties that attracted the crowds and improved the profit margin. They were not considered a threat to the male establishment. During World War II it was reported that Dottie Kamenshek was offered a minor league contract but rejected the offer to continue to play AAGBL ball. The offer was probably not a serious one. During the same time period Charlie Grimm of the Chicago Cubs was quoted as saying that another AAGBL player, Dottie Schroeder, "would be worth $50,000 if she were a man."[6] The obvious assumption here is that one had to be a man to play regardless of skill level.

In 1952 Eleanor Engle, a twenty-four-year-old stenographer, signed a contract to play shortstop for the Harrisburg Senators. Ford Frick, the baseball commissioner, immediately ruled women ineligible to play on the basis of sex. An AAGBL news release on June 27, 1952, stated that the Fort Wayne Daisies would be happy to have her try out for the team.[7] Apparently she did not take them up on the offer. In 1984 Bob Hope of the Braves tried to establish an all-female team in Daytona Beach, Florida, called the Florida Sun Sox. However, the team could not qualify for a franchise.[8] Ironically, the fact that women were now considered serious competitors with men caused prejudice and discrimination to rear their ugly heads.

Politically, most baseball executives know that the only way to bar women from baseball today, is on the grounds that they do not have the skills to compete. Legally, they cannot be excluded just because they are female. But that does not mean that their presence is welcome. A quote from Bob Apodaca, a former Mets player, probably expresses the view of many men in baseball. When asked about the possibility of women playing baseball in 1976 he said, "You mean, with the men? No, I don't think it will ever come to that. I don't think the 'lords of baseball' would allow it. . . . It might be the year A.D. 3000, but I don't see any in the foreseeable future. I don't see anything wrong with women starting their own professional baseball leagues. They have it in softball."[9]

In 1988 Darlene Mehrer, a forty-four-year-old freelance writer, lived out her baseball dreams when she started a newsletter, *Base Woman*, and a women's amateur baseball league, the American Women's Baseball Association (AWBA). Former AAGBL players attended the inaugural game on July 16, 1988. The idea was that the two-team league in Glenview, a suburb of Chicago, would eventually lead to a professional league reminiscent of the AAGBL. Women from ages seventeen to fifty-five from all occupational backgrounds came out to play. Unfortunately, Mehrer died at the end of the second season of play and her dreams for a professional league never materialized.[10]

A recent article in the *Denver Post* stated that John Horan was trying to establish a women's professional fast-pitch softball league similar to Wrigley's All American Girls' Professional Baseball League. If all goes as planned, the league will begin play in 1994 with two six-team leagues in California and the Midwest.[11] Whether or not the movie *A League of Their Own* will inspire the public to support a women's league remains to be seen. Unless women have a league of their own or girls begin to participate in large numbers in high school and college ball, the chances of a woman playing in the major leagues is remote. And if women do not become players, there is no real possibility of their gaining access to the coaching or managerial ranks.

The only opportunity structure that now exists for a woman to participate on the field is in the role of umpire. This path was established by Pam Postema, Teresa Cox, Christine Wren, and Bernice Gera. Even in this realm, however, women are not truly welcome. All the women met discrimination, and Pam Postema is currently suing the major leagues for sex discrimination. She claims that she was barred from becoming a major league umpire because of her sex. The case has not been settled, and the major leagues contend that her umpiring was not up to major league standards. Regardless of the outcome, because of Pam there is greater acceptance of the idea of a woman major league umpire. Although the

32. Pam Postema, umpire. *Courtesy of National Baseball Library, Cooperstown, N.Y.*

opportunity structure now exists, presently there are no women vying to be either minor or major league umpires.

Women have exercised some power and control in baseball through ownership. Money has always had its privileges. Most of the women inherited the ownership of teams from their fathers, husbands, or other male relatives. Helene Britton, for example, inherited the St. Louis Cardinals from her uncle in 1915. In 1922 Mrs. Dunn inherited the Cleveland Indians from her husband. Other owners in the 1920s were Florence Killilea, who inherited the Milwaukee club from her father; and the wife and daughter of Phil Ball, who inherited stock in the St. Louis Browns. In 1939 seven women owned controlling stock in four major league clubs. The New York Yankees were owned by three women. Colonel Jacob Ruppert bequeathed one-third interests to each of his nieces, Mrs. Joseph Holleran and Mrs. J. Basil Maguire. The final third went to his friend, former actress Helen Winthrope Weyant. The three, however, left the running of the club to Ed Barrow. Mrs. Charles Stoneham shared ownership of the New York Giants with her daughter and son after the death of her husband. Marie McKeever, daughter of the late Steve McKeever, owned a large portion of the Brooklyn Dodgers, and Mrs. Barney Dreyfuss with her daughter, Mrs. William Benswanger, owned most of the Pittsburgh Pirates. In 1941 Grace Comiskey, wife of Charles Comiskey, inherited the Chicago White Sox. She owned them until 1956.[12]

One owner who did not inherit that title was Joan Whitney Payson. In 1961 she bought an 80 percent interest in the Mets for $3 million just because she loved baseball. She had previously had a partial interest in the New York Giants. She was a regular at Mets games until her death in 1975.[13] Another late 1960s, early 1970s owner was Carol Smith Shannon, who owned 68 percent of the San Diego Padres with her father. But she was a silent partner.[14]

More recent owners of major league teams are Jean Yawkey, owner of the Boston Red Sox from 1976 to her death in 1992; Marge Schott, owner of the Cincinnati Reds from 1985; and Joan Kroc, owner of the San Diego Padres from 1976 with her husband, Ray Kroc, and then sole owner in 1984 at his death.

Jean Yawkey inherited the Boston Red Sox from her late husband, Tom Yawkey, who had been the sole owner of the team for forty-four years. She took an active interest in the management of the team.[15]

Marge Schott, like Joan Payson who had owned the Mets, acquired ownership of the Cincinnati Reds through her own investment rather than by inheritance. She had been a minority owner in the team beginning in 1981. In 1984 the owners grew tired of financial losses and wanted to sell the team. When no one from Cincinnati came forth to buy the team, Marge Schott did. As she said, "I just kept waiting . . . hoping a Cincinnati man would step up." Marge is not a silent owner, but a hands-on leader. As a former associate said, "[She] has one theory of power. She is the boss."[16]

Joan Kroc's husband, Ray, was the founder of McDonald's. In 1976 he purchased the San Diego Padres. When he died in 1984 Joan inherited the team. Dissatisfied with the male baseball establishment's acceptance of her leadership skills, she began trying to sell the team in 1987[17] and in 1990 sold to the Tom Werner group.

Today the amount of money that it takes to buy a major league team is so great that in most instances companies or syndicates rather than individuals are purchasing teams. For example, Turner Broadcasting owns the

Atlanta Braves, and Anheuser-Busch the St. Louis Cardinals. The price tag for purchasing one of the National League's two new expansion clubs was $95 million. But wealthy women will still acquire ownership either through their own capital or by inheritance, and many of these women will expect to have a say in their investment.

Although women will probably continue to be owners, other high-level administrative positions will remain closed to them. This is because of two factors. First, there are no women coming up through the ranks of baseball as players, managers, or coaches. Second, baseball is still a man's world, and the old boy network reigns supreme. Because of the unwelcome atmosphere, women with management, financial, and legal skills may be more prone to seek opportunities outside of baseball. In all likelihood women will continue to hold only minor administrative posts.

One ray of hope for changing the baseball establishment will be if little girls in large numbers decide that they want to play. Girls will no longer be silenced with the refrain that only boys can play. They now have role models in the AAGBL stars. One of these future Little Leaguers may become a major leaguer.

NOTES

1. "What's the Catch? Why Women Aren't Playing Major League Baseball," Arlington Heights, Ill. *Daily Herald*, 14 Aug. 1991, Sec. 2.

2. Ibid.

3. Ibid.

4. Yvonne Zipter, *Diamonds Are a Dyke's Best Friend* (Ithaca, N.Y.: Firebrand Books, 1988), 205.

5. Ibid., 46.

6. Ibid., 42.

7. Harold T. Dailey AAGBBL Records, 1943–1954, Microfilmed by Pattee Library of the Pennsylvania State University, Aug. 1976.

8. "Girls of Summer: An All-Female Lineup for the Sun Sox?" *Sporting News*, 1 Oct. 1984.

9. Kathyrn Parker, *We Won Today: My Season with the Mets* (Garden City, N.Y.: Doubleday, 1977), 169–170.

10. Steve Wulf, ed., "Scorecard: The Girls of Summer," *Sports Illustrated*, 1 Aug. 1988, 11; Bob Gordon, "Play Ball Women Hope New League Makes a Hit," Arlington Heights, Ill. *Daily Herald*, July 1988, Sec. 3, NBHFL.

11. Donna Carter, "Pitching a Women's Pro League," *Denver Post*, July 1992.

12. "It's Ladies' Day," *Phoenix Gazette*, 8 Feb. 1939; Arthur Susskind, Jr., "Lady Exec Primes Mets for Major Debut," *Sporting News*, 15 Nov. 1961.

13. Sidney Fields, "When Mrs. Payson's Mom Tossed an Egg at the Babe," New York *Daily News* 8 June 1968.

14. "All Woman Ball Club?" newspaper article, 24 Oct. 1973, NBHFL.

15. "Robert Thomas, Jr., "Red Sox and Patriots: Who'll Be in Charge?" *New York Times*, 22 Feb. 1992.

16. Francis Loewenheim, "Major League Woman: Marge Schott," *Harper's Bazaar*, Sept. 1985, 291.

17. Mark Kreidler, "A Woman's Prerogative," *Sporting News*, 8 June 1987.

Appendix:

Additional Sources for Information on Women and Baseball

Exhibit on Women and Baseball.

National Baseball Hall of Fame and Museum, Inc.
P.O. Box 590
Cooperstown, NY 13326

Newspaper clippings, magazine articles, books and photographs on women in baseball.

National Baseball Hall of Fame Library
P.O. Box 590
Cooperstown, NY 13326

Collection of memorabilia, scrapbooks, and photographs of the All American Girls' Professional Baseball League.

Northern Indiana Historical Society
808 W. Washington
South Bend, IN 46601

AAGBL Collection
Joyce Sports Research Collection
Hesburgh Library
University of Notre Dame
Notre Dame, IN 46556

Unpublished materials on the All American Girls' Professional Baseball League.

Harold T. Dailey AAGBBL Records, 1943–1954, microfilmed.
Pattee Library
The Pennsylvania State University Library
University Park, PA 16802

Information on Effa Manley and Toni Stone.

Negro Leagues Baseball Museum
1601 East 18th St.
Suite 260
Kansas City, MO 64106

Index

About the Author

GAI INGHAM BERLAGE is a Professor of Sociology, Iona College. She is the author of numerous articles on women in sports.